EXPLORING GOD'S GRACE

A Five Day a Week Devotional about a Good God

Jacob Hudgins

Exploring God's Grace

Cover designed by Damonza

Visit my website at www.jacobhudgins.com

Printed in the United States of America

ISBN-13 978-1-7352970-2-6

Also by Jacob Hudgins

The School of Christ: Learning Character from Jesus

Humility Practice: 27 Ways to Think Less of Yourself—and of Yourself Less

A Year with Jesus: A Five Day a Week Devotional through the Gospels

INTRODUCTION

The idea of God provokes different reactions in everyone. Some of us picture God as an implacable perfectionist with his glasses on the end of his nose, examining our behavior and attitudes to find something to condemn. Others see God as an indulgent grandpa who occasionally offers weak advice ("now you kids be careful!") but is basically just happy with us all the time. And there are gradations within these extremes, in which some of us feel a vague sense of insufficiency or others a groundless sense that everything is fine.

But this is not an issue that we can merely chalk up to human variation and ignore. *It matters how we view God.* A God who will not be pleased eventually frustrates and disillusions us. A God who never corrects us cannot be taken seriously. All our spiritual life springs from this core—from worship to gratitude to hope to discipline to a sense of God's presence.

But what if we were able to define God on the basis of his own words about himself? What if we could look deeply and extensively at how he has interacted with people? This is our goal in *Exploring God's Grace*.

Before I began this study, I would have gladly affirmed that the God of the Bible is a gracious God. But having spent a year reading about, detailing, thinking through, and explaining God's grace, I feel differently. My vision of God's grace has expanded tremendously. He lays claim to so many more blessings and gifts than I realized. He is good to us even when we do not acknowledge him. Frankly, I was shocked by how much of the Bible spoke about God giving gifts and showing kindness and mercy. People often characterize the Old Testament as emphasizing judgment and the New Testament mercy. As you will see, almost the entire first half of this book analyzes God's grace in the Old Testament, strongly refuting the contention. God didn't learn how to give gifts when he sent Jesus; he has *always been a gracious God.*

But does that mean that God is indulgent and freewheeling? No, the picture of God's grace is more complex than that. Can we build an image of God that is both serious about sin, yet gracious to forgive it? A God who is kind to the unthankful and evil, but still wants them to live by his will? A God who exposes our needs, then freely chooses to meet them? This is the God of the Bible. He is the one we will pursue through the course of this study.

I prepared this study as a part of the daily reading program for our local church (the Fairview Park Church of Christ in Little Rock, AR) in 2021. It is the first time we used a daily reading schedule that was not a study of a certain section of the Bible. I found these readings by searching for certain keywords (grace, mercy, giving, gift, etc) and then by working through the Bible from beginning to end. This book (with the exception of the first reading) will move straight through the Bible. This may leave you with the sensation that we are jumping around a bit. In the devotional readings I try to set the context carefully so that we never lose a sense of where we are.

Exploring God's grace contains five readings for each week—one for each weekday—and devotional comments to follow after the readings. I do not intend for my words to stand alone. I encourage you to read the biblical passage carefully prior to my comments. After the devotional comments, each day has "one thing to think about"—a thought question or two to guide us in what we might take from the reading—and "one thing to pray for"—a direction these thoughts can take in prayer and future application. The goal here is to do more than check a box. I would especially encourage setting aside time to reflect and meditate on the reading. Even a few moments of intentional thought, reflection, and prayer can change the course of our lives.

I am confident that if you take the time to consistently read and meditate on these passages, it will permanently change your view of God. My prayer is that these words will draw you closer to him.

WEEK 1—MONDAY

Reading: James 1:16-18

Exploring God's Grace

Having refuted the false belief that God tempts us with evil, James works to correct the thought. Sin and its fruits are not what God gives. "*Every good gift and every perfect gift is from above, coming down from the Father of lights*"(James 1:17). God is a giver. He lays claim to everything good and perfect that we experience in our world. He wants us to properly attribute these gifts to their giver so that we can realize his goodwill toward us. James also assures us that with this benevolent God "*there is no variation or shadow due to change*"(James 1:17). His willingness to shower good blessings on his creation is an enduring truth that we can count on. It stems from his unchangeably good nature.

These daily devotional readings will revolve around "Exploring God's Grace." We will look deeply into the ways and times God blesses his people throughout Scripture. Often Christians struggle with viewing the Old Testament as showing a harsh God while the New Testament shows him as gracious and loving. This study will correct that misconception. We will spend the first half of the year in the Old Testament, seeing clearly the nearly infinite patience and forgiveness of God. He gives gift after gift to his people, whether they respond positively to him or not. The New Testament will then show us how that giving nature reaches its height in the gift of God's own Son, offered for our forgiveness. We will emerge from this study with a deeper, more robust sense of God's goodwill toward us—and a desire to serve him from deep gratitude for undeserved blessings.

If "*every good gift and every perfect gift is from above*," then God has already flooded our lives with grace. It will help us to name these gifts, declare them as gifts (rather than our due), and bow in praise of his grace.

One Thing to Think About: What good gifts have I received from God?

One Thing to Pray For: Deeper appreciation for God's goodwill toward me

WEEK 1—TUESDAY

Reading: Genesis 1:26-31

The Grace of God's Image

At the apex of creation, God consults with himself. "*Let us make man in our image, after our likeness. And let them have dominion over the fish of the sea and over the birds of the heavens and over the livestock and over all the earth and over every creeping thing that creeps on the earth*"(Gen 1:26). Man will be fundamentally different from the previously created landforms, heavenly bodies, and animals. Although a part of creation, God wants him to "*have dominion*" over the other creatures. "*So God created man in his own image, in the image of God he created him; male and female he created them*"(Gen 1:27). The repetition seems to be for emphasis; man emphatically bears God's image.

There are more gifts here. "*And God blessed them*"(Gen 1:28), giving them not only his image but a work to accompany it. "*Be fruitful and multiply and fill the earth and subdue it, and have dominion*"(Gen 1:28). God also gives all the plants for food (Gen 1:29). At every turn God supplies the various needs for his creation, especially mankind who will have dominion over it.

Lots of ink has been spilled on the precise meaning of man being in the image of God. Like God, man has a spiritual dimension to his being. Like God (and definitely unlike other creatures), man has the ability to reason at high levels and communicate. Some see God giving man a role as his representative on earth, using his dominion to bless those beneath him. Though we will likely never exhaust the depth of the idea, it is a remarkable blessing. God has blessed man above other creatures. "*You are of more value than many sparrows*"(Matt 10:31). With this grace comes an expectation that we will live up to the image we bear.

One Thing to Think About: How does it change my view of others—and myself—to remember that all people are made in God's image?

One Thing to Pray For: A stronger connection to the God whose image I bear

WEEK 1—WEDNESDAY

Reading: Genesis 2:15-25

The Grace of Companionship

After creating man, Jehovah places him in the garden of Eden and commissions him to "*work it and keep it*"(Gen 2:15). As he works, Adam is free to eat from any of the trees save one—the tree of the knowledge of good and evil. Even in Eden, God gives man work to do and boundaries to limit him. Yet in all his good creation, God sees one thing that is not ideal: "*It is not good that the man should be alone; I will make a helper fit for him*"(Gen 2:18). Isolation is not man's proper state. It is not good. God decides to change it.

As Adam sorts through the animals and names them, "*there was not found a helper fit for him*"(Gen 2:20). None of the other creatures complements Adam in the ways he needs. It is not clear if Adam expresses this need or God simply meets it for him. When Jehovah makes woman from Adam's rib, he presents her to him and watches as Adam rejoices. "*This at last is bone of my bones and flesh of my flesh; she shall be called Woman, because she was taken out of Man*"(Gen 2:23). Adam is happy to name her! His "*at last*" implies that—whether he realized it or not previously—Adam has been waiting for just such a companion. Now he has a helper and a pattern for humanity is begun.

Jehovah wants good for his creatures—including people. If it is not good for man to be alone, then God provides a companion so that man is not alone. To be sure, man could *survive* without companionship; he still has food to eat. But God is concerned with the fact that it is not *good*—and acts out of a desire to make man's life good. God does not promise all people lifelong companions and marriage partners, but he does express his will that we be interconnected with other people. He knows that we need this—and wants us to have it as an act of grace.

One Thing to Think About: Who are my companions? How do I feel when I am alone for long periods of time?

One Thing to Pray For: Gratitude for the personal connections in my life

WEEK 1—THURSDAY

Reading: Genesis 6:5-22

The Grace of Election

Many years after the events of the Garden of Eden, man has multiplied. As the numbers expand, so does evil. "*The LORD saw that the wickedness of man was great in the earth, and that every intention of the thoughts of his heart was only evil continually. And the LORD regretted that he had made man on the earth, and it grieved him to his heart*"(-Gen 6:5-6). Out of this regret, Jehovah decides to destroy man and the animals he has created. There appears to be only one exception to God's frustration with man: "*But Noah found favor in the eyes of the LORD*"(Gen 6:8).

God tells Noah to build an ark, providing the details and dimensions that it will require to hold the large number of animals it will shelter. He warns him that "*everything that is on the earth shall die*"(Gen 6:17) but that "*I will establish my covenant with you*"(Gen 6:18). Jehovah wants to save Noah and his family because he sees in them a way to continue his creative work despite his regret. God *chooses* Noah.

The text is very complimentary of Noah. He "*found favor in the eyes of the LORD*" and "*was a righteous man, blameless in his generation*" and he "*walked with God*"(Gen 6:8, 9). Yet even with this report, Jehovah does not *have* to save Noah. God *chooses* Noah. It is a gift. He offers Noah a way of escape from his judgment. He gives Noah a task and a new promise and covenant (which will be fleshed out later). Election describes how God chooses people to bless and save. This election is not something that we *deserve* or *earn*, nor is it a result of being better than everyone else. It is always simply a gift from God.

One Thing to Think About: Do I ever feel unworthy to be chosen for salvation?

One Thing to Pray For: A passion to obey the God who has chosen me

Reading: Genesis 8:20-9:7

The Grace of Sustenance

As Noah, his family, and a host of animals exit the ark, there is an urgent piece of business to attend to. "*Then Noah built an altar to the LORD and took some of every clean animal and some of every clean bird and offered burnt offerings on the altar*"(Gen 8:20). God, pleased with this sacrifice, promises to never again bring such destruction because of man. "*While the earth remains, seedtime and harvest, cold and heat, summer and winter, day and night, shall not cease*"(Gen 8:22). He promises that the earth will remain orderly in a way that promotes—rather than destroys—life.

Jehovah then sends Noah and his sons to "*be fruitful and multiply and fill the earth*"(-Gen 9:1). "*Every moving thing that lives shall be food for you. And as I gave you the green plants, I give you everything. But you shall not eat flesh with its life, that is, its blood*"(Gen 9:3-4). God not only gives man dominion over his fellow-creatures, but he also gives them to him for food. Man's diet expands dramatically. Yet with this great gift comes the responsibility to not eat animals with the blood still in them. God also distinguishes between animal and man again, insisting that the shedding of human blood is a much graver offense, requiring a reckoning and the loss of one's own life (Gen 9:5-6).

"*And as I gave you the green plants, I give you everything.*" Sustenance is a gift from God. He is aware of the needs of his creatures and gives them what is required to survive and thrive. While he allows us to make choices in this area—and gives us some limits of what is unacceptable—we still benefit from his kindness to us.

One Thing to Think About: Why did God make us so that we regularly need food to survive?

One Thing to Pray For: Our daily bread

Reading: Genesis 9:8-17

The Grace of God's Promises

In the aftermath of the flood, God has instructed Noah and his family to be fruitful and multiply on the earth. But will God bring another flood and destroy all life again? "*Behold, I establish my covenant with you and your offspring after you…I establish my covenant with you, that never again shall all flesh be cut off by the waters of the flood, and never again shall there be a flood to destroy the earth*"(Gen 9:9, 11). God unilaterally makes a promise not to ever again destroy the earth by flood. This is grace.

God even gives people (and all animals) a sign of this covenant. "*I have set my bow in the lcoud, and it shall be a sign of the covenant between me and the earth*"(Gen 9:13). "*When the bow is in the clouds, I will see it and remember the everlasting covenant between God and every living creature of all flesh that is on the earth*"(Gen 9:16). With each rainstorm that comes, God puts a reminder (in the form of a rainbow) that he will restrict the destruction it causes. While rainbows can be explained as a natural phenomenon, God uses them to express his grace.

God often makes promises to man, willingly pledging himself to a certain behavior. Here his goal is reassuring and comforting his creation after a fearsome and devastating event. God's promises remind us of his goodwill and consistent love. He will always live to fulfill them and always be faithful to keep his word.

One Thing to Think About: What reassurances from God do I rely on?

One Thing to Pray For: Faithfulness to my promises—to God and others

WEEK 2—TUESDAY

Reading: Genesis 12:1-9

I Will Make of You a Great Nation

After a series of large-scale stories, the narrative of Genesis zooms in on Abram. He moves with his father's family from Ur of the Chaldeans to Haran and settles there. Yet Jehovah changes Abram's life forever by speaking to him: *"Now the LORD said to Abram, 'Go from your country and your kindred and your father's house to the land that I will show you'"* (Gen 12:1). This is the land which, upon his arrival, Jehovah will promise to his offspring (Gen 12:7) centuries in the future. *"And I will make of you a great nation, and I will bless you and make your name great, so that you will be a blessing"* (Gen 12:2). This small family will become a large one through Abram. The irony—and likely the part of the promise that strikes Abram most strangely—is that he currently has *no* children. He is not even on his way to having a great *family*, much less a great *nation*.

Jehovah will watch over Abram in the meantime. *"I will bless those who bless you, and him who dishonors you I will curse, and in you all the families of the earth shall be blessed"* (Gen 12:3). Enemies will not prevail over Abram, but those who show him kindness will be rewarded. God is with him. The promise of blessing to all families of the earth seems to enter the realm of the absurd for a mere childless nomad. This set of promises—and the series of events that God causes to occur to fulfill them—originate in the pure grace of God.

God longs to intervene in the life of his creatures to make them into what he wants them to be. He makes Abram a great nation, he makes Gideon a mighty man of valor, and he makes Peter into a rock. At first blush, each of these names is laughable, but nothing is impossible with God. Observing God's handiwork with these men leads us to wonder what he wants to do with *us*—and whether the project has already begun.

One Thing to Think About: What is God making me into?

One Thing to Pray For: The humility to accept God's transformation

WEEK 2—WEDNESDAY

Reading: Genesis 13:8-18

The Grace of Future Blessings

As Abram and his nephew Lot live in the land of Canaan, Jehovah blesses them with great flocks and herds. It soon becomes clear that the land will not support them living in close proximity. Despite his status as the elder of the two, Abram offers Lot the first choice of land: "*Is not the whole land before you? Separate yourself from me. If you take the left hand, then I will go to the right, or if you take the right hand, then I will go to the left*"(Gen 13:9). Lot sees the fertile Jordan Valley and settles near the land of Sodom. Abram goes in the opposite direction, living off the leftover land.

It is after this separation that Jehovah speaks to Abram again. "*Lift up your eyes and look from the place where you are, northward and southward and eastward and westward, for all the land that you see I will give to you and to your offspring forever*"(Gen 13:14-15). Even though Abram owns no part of the land at the moment, God reminds him that he will give it to him and his family forever. He even encourages Abram to investigate the land and see its goodness. "*Arise, walk through the length and the breadth of the land, for I will give it to you*"(Gen 13:17). Like a prospective buyer examining a potential home, Abram walks around land that will eventually belong to him.

Why does God choose this moment to repeat the land promise? I wonder if Abram is disheartened by Lot's naked ambition in grabbing the best land. It could be that despite the growth of his herds and flocks, Abram is worried that things aren't going well. Whatever the exact reason, God reminds him of future blessings to reassure him. Future blessings help make present hardships bearable. They remind us that things will not always be the way they are at the moment. They give us hope and peace in anticipation of even more goodness from God.

One Thing to Think About: What blessings am I looking forward to? How do they change me today?

One Thing to Pray For: A richer hope in the future grace of God

WEEK 2—THURSDAY

Reading: Genesis 15:1-6

Number the Stars

Years have passed since God called Abram to leave his country to travel to Canaan. With the exception of Abram becoming wealthy, there is little evidence of God's promises to him being fulfilled. He has no land, no nation, and not even any children. Here Jehovah appears to him: "*Fear not, Abram, I am your shield; your reward shall be very great*"(Gen 15:1). This time Abram voices his concern. "*But Abram said, 'O Lord GOD, what will you give me, for I continue childless, and the heir of my house is Eliezer of Damascus?*'"(Gen 15:2). Abram has believed God's promises, but he is confused and frustrated that he does not yet see them realized.

Jehovah speaks again. "*This man shall not be your heir; your very own son shall be your heir*"(Gen 15:4). God makes very clear that the promises will not come through Eliezer. Then God takes him outside to stare up at the night sky. "'*Look toward heaven, and number the stars, if you are able to number them.' Then he said to him, 'So shall your offspring be*'"(Gen 15:5). God engages Abram's imagination. Overwhelmed by the immense number of stars, Abram learns that his family will grow exponentially. "*And he believed the LORD, and he counted it to him as righteousness*"(Gen 15:6). Awed, Abram quiets his objection and trusts that Jehovah will somehow make this work.

God demonstrates his grace with Abram by not only giving unsolicited promises, but by clarifying and engaging his imagination. Numbering the stars gives Abram a sense of both the grandeur and goodwill of God. *God wants to bless him.* Part of the purpose of our imaginations is for us consider a world in which God creates a far better future. Like Abram, we learn that God can be trusted.

One Thing to Think About: Do I ever struggle to believe God's promises? Why?

One Thing to Pray For: Trust that God wants my good

WEEK 2—FRIDAY

Reading: Genesis 15:7-20

The Grace of Reassurance

Jehovah has just engaged Abram's imagination, telling him to number the stars and know that his descendants would be just as numerous (and come from his own body). God promises more. "*I am the LORD who brought you out from Ur of the Chaldeans to give you this land to possess*"(Gen 15:7). Emboldened, Abram now voices his doubt about the land promise as well. "*O Lord GOD, how am I to know that I shall possess it?*"(Gen 15:8). Because Abram trusts that Jehovah is good and wants to bless him, he is confident to voice his concerns.

What happens next is a bit baffling to modern readers. At God's request, Abram brings and slaughters certain animals. A "*deep sleep*" and a "*dreadful and great darkness*" come on Abram. "*Then the LORD said to Abram, 'Know for certain that your offspring will be sojourners in a land that is not theirs and will be servants there...And they shall come back here in the fourth generation*"(Gen 15:13, 16). In this unique state, God speaks directly to Abram's fears. Time will pass before the land is his. Abram himself will die. Yet God still wants him to "*know for certain*"(Gen 15:13) that his promises will come to pass. These animals and this vision are all part of a covenant ceremony (Gen 15:18) in which Jehovah pledges to give the land of Canaan to Abram's offspring.

I am intrigued by God's patience here. He could easily upbraid Abram for his lack of faith. He could show himself harsh and demanding. Instead, he gives Abram a gift on top of what he has already given: the gift of reassurance. He repeats the promises, spells out the specifics, and binds himself further by a covenant. God certainly does not always give us this reassurance, but when he does—through his word, through our brethren, or through our own experiences—it is an expression of his goodness and grace.

One Thing to Think About: How has God reassured me when I have doubted?

One Thing to Pray For: Confidence in God's fidelity to his word

WEEK 3—MONDAY

Reading: Genesis 18:1-15

The Grace of the Impossible

Jehovah appears to Abraham, somehow in the guise of a traveler. After receiving impressive hospitality from a tent-dweller who owns no land, God breaks big news to Abraham. "*The LORD said, 'I will surely return to you about this time next year, and Sarah your wife shall have a son*'"(Gen 15:10). The decades-long plan to bring about God's promises is finally coming to fruition! Yet, to understand Abraham and Sarah's reactions, we need more information. "*Now Abraham and Sarah were old, advanced in years. The way of women had ceased to be with Sarah*"(Gen 18:11). Sarah is biologically unable to have children and both of them are too old to expect anything of the sort. "*So Sarah laughed to herself, saying, 'After I am worn out, and my lord is old, shall I have pleasure?*'"(Gen 18:12). Sarah laughs not because she doubts God, but because some things seem too good to be true.

For his part, Jehovah calls attention to Sarah's laughter. "*Why did Sarah laugh and say, 'Shall I indeed bear a child, now that I am old?' Is anything too hard for the LORD? At the appointed time I will return to you, about this time next year, and Sarah will have a son*"(Gen 18:13-14). Nothing is too hard for God. Even the impossible is possible when he promises it. Hard as this may be to believe—hard as *all of God's promises* to Abraham have been to believe—Sarah will indeed "*have pleasure*" in her old age. When the baby is born, this involuntary response of incredulity will be a part of his name. Isaac means laughter.

As God, Jehovah certainly has the right to change the laws of nature as he sees fit. Yet we must realize that he does this for our *good*. God gives a good gift here that Abraham and Sarah could never have achieved on their own. Like Abraham and Sarah, scores of believers throughout time have been granted the seemingly impossible. The barren have conceived. Deadly diseases have been healed. The natural course of life has been radically changed. We do not always see such amazing things. They are not guarantees. Yet when we do, we praise. Is anything too hard for the LORD?

One Thing to Think About: What amazing things have I seen God do?

One Thing to Pray For: A childlike faith

WEEK 3—TUESDAY

Reading: Genesis 18:16-33

The Grace of Intercession

First, Jehovah shows Abraham grace by divulging his plans to him. "*Shall I hide from Abraham what I am about to do, seeing that Abraham shall surely become a great and mighty nation, and all the nations of the earth shall be blessed in him?*"(Gen 18:17-18). The ruler of the universe lowers himself to share with this lowly wanderer what his plans are. Perhaps he is also thinking about the fact that his current mission would directly affect Abraham because it would affect Lot, his nephew. Jehovah then reveals his purpose: following up on the great outcry caused by the behavior of the people of Sodom and Gomorrah.

This springs Abraham into action. As God turns to leave, "*Abraham drew near and said, 'Will you indeed sweep away the righteous with the wicked? Suppose there are fifty righteous within the city. Will you then sweep away the place and not spare it for the fifty righteous who are in it?*'"(Gen 18:23-24). This is audacity. Abraham knows exactly to whom he is speaking—he calls him "*the Judge of all the earth*"(Gen 18:25)—yet he urges him to reconsider. Abraham seems to know that God will find Sodom utterly corrupt, so he begs for God to spare the city. At each point, he presses further, coupling his audacious request with humility ("*I who am but dust and ashes*", Gen 18:27). So God allows himself to be bargained down, ultimately promising that he will not destroy the city if he finds ten righteous people there.

It is staggering that God is willing to tell Abraham his plans, then change those plans based on Abraham's request. Yet this is what intercession is. We approach the "Judge of all the earth" and ask him to alter his prescribed course of events to grant our small need—to heal our brother, to watch over our family, to forgive someone's sin. We leverage *our* relationship with God to benefit *others*—and God not only lets it happen, but often grants our requests and changes his will to include ours. What a gift!

One Thing to Think About: In what ways have I seen God grant my intercession for others?

One Thing to Pray For: A heart to care deeply for—and pray on behalf of—others

WEEK 3—WEDNESDAY

Reading: Genesis 19:15-29

Grace in the Midst of Judgment

After Abraham intercedes for his nephew Lot and the city of Sodom, the angels arrive in the city and find it completely worthy of judgment. Shortly Jehovah will rain sulfur and fire on Sodom and Gomorrah. Yet first the angels warn Lot. "'*Up! Take your wife and your two daughters who are here, lest you be swept away in the punishment of the city.' But he lingered. So the men seized him and his wife and two daughters by the hand, the LORD being merciful to him, and they brought him out and set him outside the city*"(Gen 19:15-16). When Lot delays after the initial caution, the angels literally seize him and his family and pull him out of the doomed city. The author describes this as "*the LORD being merciful to him.*" It is grace in the midst of judgment.

The angels instruct Lot to "*escape to the hills*"(Gen 19:17), but Lot balks at this as well. "'*Behold, this city is near enough to flee to, and it is a little one. Let me escape there—is it not a little one?—and my life will be saved!' He said to him, 'Behold, I grant you this favor also, that I will not overthrow the city of which you have spoken*'"(Gen 19:20-21). Now the angel again amends his plans for Lot. "*I grant you this favor also.*" Lot's wife ignores the angels' warnings about looking back and dies as a result. Yet our author does not want us to focus on this. He summarizes, "*So it was that, when God destroyed the cities of the valley, God remembered Abraham and sent Lot out of the midst of the overthrow when he overthrew the cities in which Lot had lived*"(Gen 19:29). God remembers Abraham and shows Lot grace.

When we read sections like these, it is tempting to think only of God's harshness and severity. Yet there is grace even here. Peter reminds us of God's differentiation between the men of Sodom and Lot and concludes that "*the Lord knows how to rescue the godly from trials, and to keep the unrighteous under punishment until the day of judgment*"(2 Pet 2:9). In hard times, when there is suffering as a result of sin, God still shows grace.

One Thing to Think About: If my family, nation, or church suffers, how can I still observe God's grace?

One Thing to Pray For: A tenacious faith that sees blessing even in judgment

WEEK 3—THURSDAY

Reading: Genesis 21:8-21

God Opened Her Eyes

After the birth of Isaac, the promised son, tensions grow in Abraham's household. Sarah sees Ishmael laughing mockingly at Isaac and insists that Abraham cast Hagar and Ishmael out of their home. "*And the thing was very displeasing to Abraham on account of his son*"(Gen 21:11). God reassures him that the boy will survive—and even thrive—because God will continue to be with him. "*And I will make a nation of the son of the slave woman also, because he is your offspring*"(Gen 21:13). Reluctantly, Abraham gives them provisions and sends them away.

The next scene is pitiful. Hagar and Ishmael run out of water and she puts the boy under a bush and retreats so that she doesn't have to watch and listen to him die. God hears his screams, though. He speaks to Hagar: "*Fear not, for God has heard the voice of the boy where he is. Up! Lift up the boy, and hold him fast with your hand, for I will make him into a great nation*"(Gen 21:17-18). In addition to reassurance, God grants her tangible help. "*Then God opened her eyes, and she saw a well of water. And she went and filled the skin with water and gave the boy a drink. And God was with the boy, and he grew up. He lived in the wilderness and became an expert with the bow*"(Gen 21:19-20). The text does not indicate that God made a new well, but that he opened her eyes to see a well (perhaps that she had missed previously). God supplies their needs and wilderness living becomes a part of the boy's strength as he grows.

God's goodness here probably belongs under the umbrella of his grace to Abraham. Because Ishmael is his son, he receives God's careful attention. Yet there is something else intriguing here. God does not work a miracle for Hagar. Instead, he merely opens her eyes to notice provision that is *already there*. Sometimes God's grace is shown not by sudden supernatural intervention, but by the gentle reminder and newfound awareness of blessings already present. God opens our eyes to the good he is already doing.

One Thing to Think About: What good is there in my life that I tend to take for granted?

One Thing to Pray For: God to provide for me and those connected to me

WEEK 3—FRIDAY

Reading: Genesis 26:12-16, 23-30

The Grace of Wealth

After Abraham's death, his son Isaac continues to live in the land promised to his father. Jehovah instructs him not to go to Egypt, but to "*sojourn in this land, and I will be with you and will bless you*"(Gen 26:3). This happens swiftly. "*And Isaac sowed in that land and reaped in the same year a hundredfold. The LORD blessed him, and the man became rich, and gained more and more until he became very wealthy. He had possessions of flocks and herds and many servants, so that the Philistines envied him*"(Gen 26:12-14). This is a tremendous yield. Isaac becomes extraordinarily wealthy. His prospering is a blessing from Jehovah.

However, we soon learn that it is a mixed blessing; while Isaac has more than he needs, his wealth causes conflict with his neighbors. The Philistines tell him to leave (Gen 26:16). As he travels, digging new wells, the herdsmen of that area come and fight with his servants over the use of the wells. When Abimelech approaches him, he is clearly frustrated: "*Why have you come to me, seeing that you hate me and have sent me away from you?*"(Gen 26:27). Yet Abimelech admits that "*we see plainly that the LORD has been with you*"(Gen 26:28). He realizes that with Jehovah's help, Isaac could defeat him. The Philistines only want to make peace with a man who so clearly has Jehovah's blessing.

If every good gift comes from above (James 1:17), then wealth is a gift from God too. Not everyone who is wealthy is stingy, unscrupulous, or vain. Isaac shows us that this is a form God's blessings sometimes take. Yet we are naïve to seek riches while being blind to the difficulties they can cause—for our relationships (like Isaac) and for our walk with God. The proper perspective is to thank God when we have financial excess, then to put our wealth to work in helping others (1 Tim 6:17-19).

One Thing to Think About: How has God sustained and blessed me financially?

One Thing to Pray For: A heart that is free and willing to share God's blessings with others

WEEK 4—MONDAY

Reading: Genesis 28:10-22

The Grace of God's Presence

Jacob is running for his life from his brother Esau, whose blessing he has stolen. Sleeping on a stone, he dreams of a ladder going up to heaven with angels moving up and down and Jehovah himself standing above it. God speaks: "*The land on which you lie I will give to you and your offspring…Behold, I am with you and will keep you wherever you go, and will bring you back to this land. For I will not leave you until I have done what I have promised you*"(Gen 28:13, 15). Not only does Jacob see an amazing sight, but he also receives incredible promises of land, family, and God's presence and protection. God will go with Jacob and bring him back to the land he has promised him.

Jacob is amazed and afraid. "'*Surely the LORD is in this place, and I did not know it.' And he was afraid and said, 'How awesome is this place! This is none other than the house of God, and this is the gate of heaven*'"(Gen 28:17). What before seemed like an ordinary land is now holy. Jacob anoints his stone pillow and renames it Bethel, or house of God. Having listened carefully to God's promises, he also makes his own: "*If God will be with me and will keep me in this way that I go, and will give me bread to eat and clothing to wear, so that I come again to my father's house in peace, then the LORD shall be my God*"(Gen 28:20-21). Jacob especially wants God to *be with* him as he goes on this risky journey to a foreign land.

The presence of others is often a comfort to us. We can handle grief, fear, and frustration better when we share it with others. We take courage from others—even if there is no actual change in our circumstances. God tells Jacob, "*I am with you*" and "*I will not leave you*". God could leave his people to face an uncertain life alone, but he chooses to go through life with us. He gives us the gift of his presence.

One Thing to Think About: How does God's presence give me comfort?

One Thing to Pray For: Reassurance that God will be with me through the ups and downs of life (Heb 13:5)

WEEK 4—TUESDAY

Reading: Genesis 32:1-12

I Will Surely Do You Good

Many years after he fled the land of Canaan out of fear of his brother Esau, Jacob is now returning home. Yet when he sends messengers and a present to Esau, Esau approaches him with 400 men. "*Then Jacob was greatly afraid and distressed. He divided the people who were with him, and the flocks and herds and camels, into two camps, thinking, 'If Esau comes to the one camp and attacks it, then the camp that is left will escape'*"(Gen 32:7-8). Unsure of Esau's intent, Jacob has the harrowing experience of dividing up his family so at least some of them will survive the coming battle.

That night Jacob cries out to God in his distress. "*O God of my father Abraham and God of my father Isaac, O LORD who said to me, 'Return to your country and to your kindred, that I may do you good,' I am not worthy of the least of all the deeds of steadfast love and all the faithfulness that you have shown to your servant, for with only my staff I crossed this Jordan, and now I have become two camps*"(Gen 32:9-10). Jacob reminds Jehovah that this trip home was *his* idea, coupled with the promise "*that I may do you good.*" He humbly recounts how God has blessed him so richly before he makes his request. "*Please deliver me from the hand of my brother, from the hand of Esau, for I fear him, that he may come and attack me, the mothers with the children. But you said, 'I will surely do you good, and make your offspring as the sand of the sea, which cannot be numbered for multitude*'"(Gen 32:11-12). Jacob asks God for help on the basis of his promise, "*I will surely do you good.*" After a long night of Jacob wrestling—literally and figuratively—with God, he is reconciled with his brother.

There are points in our lives when we begin to question God's goodwill. If you love me so much, then why is this happening? If you said you would provide for me, where will it come from? While we do not have Jacob's direct promises that God will do us good, the Bible provides ample evidence of his love and goodwill toward us. Jacob teaches us that God's grace can be trusted—even when we don't see *how* he will bless us.

One Thing to Think About: How has God done me good?

One Thing to Pray For: God to intervene in ways that both are good for me and bring him glory

WEEK 4—WEDNESDAY

Reading: Genesis 39:1-6, 19-23

The Grace of Favor in Others' Sight

Sold by his brothers into slavery in Egypt, Joseph finds himself in the home of Potiphar, the captain of the guard. Yet even in Egypt, "*the LORD was with Joseph, and he became a successful man, and he was in the house of his Egyptian master. His master saw that the LORD was with him and that the LORD caused all that he did to succeed in his hands. So Joseph found favor in his sight and attended him, and he made him overseer of his house and put him in charge of all that he had*"(Gen 39:2-4). Jehovah blesses Joseph and his master's house. Not surprisingly, Potiphar is extremely pleased with Joseph, entrusting him with the complete operation of the house so that he only worries about the menu (Gen 39:6).

When Joseph, though innocent, is thrown into prison, the story repeats. "*But the LORD was with Joseph and showed him steadfast love and gave him favor in the sight of the keeper of the prison. And the keeper of the prison put Joseph in charge of all the prisoners who were in the prison. Whatever was done there, he was the one who did it*"(Gen 39:21-22). Even in prison, Joseph shows himself so faithful and dependable that he quickly earns the trust of his master. Jehovah "*gave him favor in the sight of the keeper of the prison,*" which opens doors for Joseph that will ultimately lead to his release.

The temptation is to make a character study of Joseph, focusing on his dependability, hard work, and integrity. This is the wrong lesson. While Joseph certainly does his part, the author repeatedly makes it clear that *Joseph's success is due to Jehovah, not Joseph.* When others are favorably disposed toward us—when others notice and help us—when our good efforts are allowed to succeed—we can thank God that he has given us another gift.

One Thing to Think About: Has God ever given me favor in others' sight?

One Thing to Pray For: Opportunities to influence others for good—while not merely trying to please them

WEEK 4—THURSDAY

Reading: Genesis 41:37-45

The Grace of Promotion

Joseph has languished in prison for several years after being falsely accused by Potiphar's wife. He has faithfully discharged his duties over the other prisoners. The butler and baker, whose dreams he interpreted by God's power, have forgotten him. Potiphar and his wife have surely moved on. It is only when, years later, Pharaoh dreams, that this quietly spiritual man comes to mind. Rushed from the prison and brought before Pharaoh, Joseph refuses to seize his moment: "*It is not in me; God will give Pharaoh a favorable answer*"(Gen 41:16). Only after interpreting the dreams does Joseph suggest that Pharaoh "*select a discerning and wise man, and set him over the land of Egypt*"(Gen 41:33) to help in the coming famine. It is unclear whether Joseph is promoting himself or merely giving advice.

Pharaoh, though, has heard all he needs to. "*Can we find a man like this, in whom is the Spirit of God?*"(Gen 41:38). The combination of Joseph's humility, interpretive ability, wisdom, and good reputation makes him a no-brainer. "*Then Pharaoh said to Joseph, 'Since God has shown you all this, there is none so discerning and wise as you*'"(Gen 41:39). Pharaoh elevates Joseph over all his house and all the land of Egypt. He gets new clothes, a signet ring, royal honors, and a wife. It is truly a rags-to-riches moment. Yet Joseph acknowledges this as God's doing, naming his children Manasseh because "*God has made me forget all my hardship*" and Ephraim because "*God has made me fruitful in the land of my affliction*"(Gen 41:51, 52). Jehovah is still with him—and Joseph knows it.

Joseph reminds us that advancement in career and status is a gift from God. For many years he works hard and faithfully, yet is never respected for his talents. The point is not that if we work in obscurity long enough, someone will eventually recognize us. The point is that there is no direct correlation between our hard work and social or workplace promotion. When we are blessed with more responsibility, human honors, or fruitful families, we are not responsible. It is a gift of God.

One Thing to Think About: What advancements in my life do I need to praise God for?

One Thing to Pray For: The humility to give God the honor for my talents

WEEK 4—FRIDAY

Reading: Genesis 45:4-15

The Grace of Provision

Joseph has been a major leader in Egypt for some time now, helping the entire region navigate the famine Pharaoh's dream foretold. Now his brothers have come to Egypt, not recognizing him. Here Joseph, overcome by emotion and perhaps only beginning to grasp God's full plan, reveals himself to his brothers. *"And now do not be distressed or angry with yourselves because you sold me here, for God sent me before you to preserve life. For the famine has been in the land these two years, and there are yet five years in which there will be neither plowing nor harvest. And God sent me before you to preserve for you a remnant on earth, and to keep alive for you many survivors"*(Gen 45:5-7). Joseph has heard their bickering and knows that they still feel guilt over selling him into slavery. He wants them to know that this has actually become a blessing. "*God sent me before you to preserve life.*" Through their evil, God has given a gift: providing food for a desperate people.

We should note carefully how much of this Joseph attributes to God. "*So it was not you who sent me here, but God. He has made me a father to Pharaoh, and lord of all his house and ruler over all the land of Egypt*"(Gen 45:8). He wants his brothers to go tell Jacob that "*God has made me lord of all Egypt*"(Gen 45:9). And now he takes this gift as a unique opportunity to take care of his family. "*There I will provide for you*"(Gen 45:11). With Joseph's consent, God's plan to preserve Jacob's family—and by it the line of Abraham—will succeed.

There is so much to unpack here. God's good gift of provision comes in an evil wrapper. Sometimes what looks like an awful circumstance can be a blessing in disguise. God continues to provide, elaborately planning a way to fulfill his will. At each step he cares for all of his creatures, expressing his goodness. And sometimes God gives grace by enabling *us* to give grace to *others*—changing our hearts and creating a chain of blessing at the same time.

One Thing to Think About: How has God provided for me in ways I did not expect?

One Thing to Pray For: A willingness to be a channel for God's blessings to pass on to others

WEEK 5—MONDAY

Reading: Exodus 3:7-12

I Have Come Down

Many years after Joseph brings his family down to Egypt, Abraham's descendants have multiplied and become enslaved there. *"And God heard their groaning, and God remembered his covenant with Abraham, with Isaac, and with Jacob. God saw the people of Israel—and God knew"*(Ex 2:24-25). Aware of his people's deep need and the promises he has given to Abraham, Jehovah prepares to act. His plan for action begins by calling to the disgraced prince Moses on Mount Sinai out of an ever-burning bush.

God speaks of himself as having senses like people. *"I have surely seen the affliction of my people who are in Egypt and have heard their cry because of their taskmasters. I know their sufferings, and I have come down to deliver them out of the hand of the Egyptians and to bring them up out of that land to a good and broad land"*(Ex 3:7-8). God sees, hears, and knows. But *"I have come down"* emphasizes that Jehovah is so moved by what he has observed that he cannot stand aloof. When Moses resists this plan to lead the people out, God reassures him: *"But I will be with you, and this shall be the sign for you, that I have sent you: when you have brought the people out of Egypt, you shall serve God on this mountain"*(Ex 3:12). God graciously offers him a proof he will see in hindsight: he will know he has succeeded when the entire nation worships in the shadow of this same mountain.

Jehovah often uses the picture of descending from heaven to describe his awareness of our situation, his willingness to judge and help, and the gift of his presence among us. Ruler of the universe, God is perfectly capable of working through proxies and remaining where he is. Yet coming down to see and experience our pain helps us know he truly cares for us and wants our good. The ultimate expression of this is Jesus, who literally comes down from heaven to walk beside us, experience the joy and hardship of human life, and offer himself for us.

One Thing to Think About: Do I feel that God is aware of my everyday life?

One Thing to Pray For: Gratitude for God's mindfulness of people—especially his people

WEEK 5—TUESDAY

Reading: Exodus 13:17-22

Jehovah Went Before Them

As the liberated people leave Egypt, God guides them. "*When Pharaoh let the people go, God did not lead them by way of the land of the Philistines, although that was near. For God said, 'Lest the people change their minds when they see war and return to Egypt.' But God led the people around by the way of the wilderness toward the Red Sea*"(Ex 13:17-18). God's leading is counterintuitive; they do not take the direct route to the land of Canaan but out into the desert around the Red Sea. From one perspective, this looks like God does not know what he is doing. Yet God is aware of the salvation he plans to work at the Red Sea, the people's response if they see war, and the promise he made to Moses to bring the people out to Mt Sinai.

As they continue to march out of Egypt, God gives them a visible symbol of his leading. "*And the LORD went before them by day in a pillar of cloud to lead them along the way, and by night in a pillar of fire to give them light, that they might travel by day and by night. The pillar of cloud by day and the pillar of fire by night did not depart from before the people*"(Ex 13:21-22). These pillars have important roles: lighting up the night sky and pointing the way forward. Yet the author says that "*the LORD went before them,*" meaning that God gives them this gift to reassure them that he is still there, leading them in the right way.

Jehovah leads his people. He has a way he wants them to go and he walks it with them. In the course of our lives, we sometimes wonder why we take a roundabout route. Sometimes we even think we know better than our guide. This story reminds us that God has higher purposes in mind than simply getting somewhere fast. We may not see a pillar of fire or cloud, but we follow God's will confidently, knowing that he goes before us (Rom 8:14).

One Thing to Think About: How is God leading me? How has it been different than what I expected?

One Thing to Pray For: Guidance for the times of temptation and hardship I face

WEEK 5—WEDNESDAY

Reading: Exodus 14:15-31

The Grace of Salvation

Pinned between the Egyptian army and the Red Sea, Israel cries out to God for help. Jehovah springs into action. Notice all the things he does. "*And I will harden the hearts of the Egyptians*"(Ex 14:17). "*Then the angel of God who was going before the host of Israel moved and went behind them…coming between the host of Egypt and the host of Israel*"(Ex 14:19). "*The LORD drove the sea back by a strong east wind all night and made the sea dry land, and the waters were divided*"(Ex 14:21). "*The LORD in the pillar of fire and of cloud looked down on the Egyptian forces and threw the Egyptian forces into a panic, clogging their chariot wheels so that they drove heavily*"(Ex 14:24-25). Jehovah's intervention is so noticeable and terrifying that the Egyptians cry out that "*the LORD fights for them against the Egyptians*"(Ex 14:25).

As God acts, Moses does too. He stretches out his staff over the sea. The people must enter the somehow dry seabed. Even after Israel has passed through, God still will not act before Moses: "*Stretch out your hand over the sea, that the water may come back upon the Egyptians, upon their chariots, and upon their horsemen*"(Ex 14:26). Yet as he does, "*the LORD threw the Egyptians into the midst of the sea*"(Ex 14:27). Breathless at the wonder of what has just happened, the people rejoice, celebrate, and fear. "*Thus the LORD saved Israel that day from the hand of the Egyptians*"(Ex 14:30).

Sometimes we find ourselves in threatening circumstances far beyond our power. We need help. Our lives, our families, our finances, our hopes, our souls are at stake. We cry out. We may not be able to diagram exactly how God responds or in what ways he intervenes, but we see his hand. We still must act—obeying, working, moving forward. But when the crisis passes, when our sins are washed away, or when we begin to recover, we praise God. He has saved us—and it is an act of his grace.

One Thing to Think About: How have I experienced God's salvation?

One Thing to Pray For: Awareness of my helplessness

WEEK 5—THUSRDAY

Reading: Exodus 16:9-21

The Grace of Daily Bread

After the great deliverance at the Red Sea, the people of Israel continue on to the Sinai desert. In the harsh conditions, they begin to complain about the lack of food and water. Jehovah promises, "*I am about to rain bread from heaven for you*"(Ex 16:4). But with this grace will come a test "*whether they will walk in my law or not*"(Ex 16:4). God causes a dew to fall around the camp. "*And when the dew had gone up, there was on the face of the wilderness a fine, flake-like thing, fine as frost on the ground*"(Ex 16:14). Confused, the people call it "manna," meaning "what?". God has covered the ground with food.

There are two interesting wrinkles to the manna. First, the people are unable to gather more than what they need. "*They gathered, some more, some less. But when they measured it with an omer, whoever gathered much had nothing left over, and whoever gathered little had no lack. Each of them gathered as much as he could eat*"(Ex 16:17-18). Everyone has enough; no one has too much or too little. Second, the manna will not keep for a second day. "*Some left part of it till the morning, and it bred worms and stank… Morning by morning they gathered it, each as much as he could eat; but when the sun grew hot, it melted*"(Ex 16:20, 21). Only on Fridays does the manna last for two days so that the people do not have to gather on the Sabbath. God does not just provide bread; he provides *daily* bread.

Manna becomes a test: will the people trust that God will give them bread *tomorrow* just as he has *today*? Or will they insist on grabbing up as much as they can today, while they can? Jesus teaches his disciples to ask God for daily bread (Matt 6:11) and sends his disciples out to teach without money or food, trusting God to provide (Matt 10:9-10). God continues the daily grace of giving his people want they need *for each day*. Do we trust him to do it today—and tomorrow?

One Thing to Think About: Do I have what I need today?

One Thing to Pray For: Trust in God to provide for me—instead of feeling I need to grab up all I can today

WEEK 5—FRIDAY

Reading: Exodus 17:1-7

Grace for the Unbelieving

As Israel meanders toward Sinai through the desert, they encounter more trouble. "*There was no water for the people to drink. Therefore the people quarreled with Moses and said, 'Give us water to drink.' And Moses said to them, 'Why do you quarrel with me? Why do you test the LORD?*'"(Ex 17:1-2). The people quickly turn on Moses, blaming him for their trouble. Things get worse from there. "*Why did you bring us up out of Egypt, to kill us and our children and our livestock with thirst?*"(Ex 17:3). In their desperation, they grow more irrational and unfair. Also, there seems to be little consideration of Jehovah and his ability to provide, other than the taunting question, "*is the LORD among us or not?*"(Ex 17:7).

Moses takes the problem to God. "*So Moses cried to the LORD, 'What shall I do with this people? They are almost ready to stone me*'"(Ex 17:4). He receives a swift answer from God—one that is surprisingly indulgent of Moses' frustration and the people's challenge. "*Behold, I will stand before you there on the rock at Horeb, and you shall strike the rock, and water shall come out of it, and the people will drink*"(Ex 17:6). God graciously provides for these taunting, angry people. The time will come when God challenges the people for their obstinacy, but here he chooses to give a gift even to his unbelieving people.

To say that God has grace for the unbelieving does not mean that he provides eternal life to people who rebel against him. Instead, it means that God continues to give good gifts to his children, even when they are not what they should be. "*He is kind to the ungrateful and evil*"(Luke 6:35). He shows compassion on us in desperate situations (like extreme thirst) because "*he knows our frame, he remembers that we are dust*"(Psalm 103:14). God shows his goodness by continuing to bless even the evil.

One Thing to Think About: Do I have compassion on those who are unkind to me, like God?

One Thing to Pray For: The patience to do good to those who do not deserve it

WEEK 6—MONDAY

Reading: Exodus 23:20-33

The Grace of Gradual Progress

Jehovah is meeting with Israel on Mount Sinai. Here he gives them the plan on where they go from here. "*Behold, I send an angel before you to guard you on the way and to bring you to the place that I have prepared*" (Ex 23:20). There is so much grace in this verse: God sends an angel, promises to guard the people as they travel, commits to bringing them into the promised land, and assures them that he has prepared this particular place for them. His only expectation is that they obey the angel (Ex 23:21, 22).

Specifically, as they conquer the Canaanite peoples, "*you shall not bow down to their gods nor serve them, nor do as they do, but you shall utterly overthrow them and break their pillars in pieces*" (Ex 23:24). God also details the way this conquest will happen. "*I will not drive them out before you in one year, lest the land become desolate and the wild beasts multiply against you. Little by little I will drive them out from before you, until you have increased and possess the land*" (Ex 23:29-30). The land will turn to Israel gradually—"*little by little*"—as the people grow and slowly displace the inhabitants.

Sometimes God gives gifts through *gradual process* rather than instant fulfilment. Incremental blessing lightens the load of having to conquer all of the land at once. This would max out the troops and leave some territories undefended. It would also increase wild beasts and harm the land (Ex 33:29). But incremental blessing also holds a challenge—that we would begin to doubt that God's promises are coming true at all. Growth—both physical and spiritual—is gradual. Encouragement, character, and life-change often happen in degrees rather than in one fell swoop. A gift gradually given shows both God's goodness *and* his wisdom.

One Thing to Think About: What blessings have I received—or come to realize—gradually?

One Thing to Pray For: The patience to remain faithful to God while awaiting the slow development of his plan

WEEK 6—TUESDAY

Reading: Exodus 32:7-14

The Grace of Relenting

Jehovah's anger is understandable. As the people he has delivered and sustained all the way to Sinai sit around the mountain—as they beg for Moses to meet with him in their stead—as they chew on the command not to make graven images—they grow restless and hold an idolatrous festival. God declares that the people "*have corrupted themselves*" and "*turned aside quickly out of the way that I commanded them*"(Ex 32:7, 8). God also informs Moses as to his response: "*I have seen this people, and behold, it is a stiff-necked people. Now therefore let me alone, that my wrath may burn hot against them and I may consume them, in order that I may make a great nation of you*"(Ex 32:9-10). Jehovah has had enough of their stubbornness and is ready to kill them all.

In steps Moses. He reminds God that these are *his* people whom he has already delivered once (Ex 32:11). He speculates on what the Egyptians will say about Jehovah if his people die at Sinai (Ex 32:12). He encourages God to remember Abraham, Isaac, and Jacob and the promises he made to them (Ex 32:13). What happens to God's people reflects on the glory of God's name, which is a concern to both God and Moses. "*And the LORD relented from the disaster that he had spoken of bringing on his people*"(Ex 32:14).

God doesn't have to relent. He is just to be angry. Yet he graciously allows Moses to intercede for the people. He graciously lets Moses express the good that can come if he relents. He allows the people to see how close they have come to disaster. The power of this story is best seen when we place ourselves in the place of the Israelites. Each one of us has done things that deserve punishment from a just God, yet God has relented and given us opportunity to repent and seek his forgiveness. This is another dimension of his grace.

One Thing to Think About: Is it possible to take for granted God's patience with me?

One Thing to Pray For: A zeal for repentance when I see my sin

WEEK 6—WEDNESDAY

Reading: Exodus 33:12-23

Show Me Your Glory

In the aftermath of the golden calf incident, matters are still dicey between God and his people. Jehovah has relented from his initial desire to destroy the people. He sends a plague on them (Ex 32:35). He then tells Moses to lead the people to Canaan under the leadership of an angel, but with the ominous statement that "*I will not go up among you, lest I consume you on the way, for you are a stiff-necked people*"(Ex 33:3). Moses, concerned over the prospect of going without the presence of Jehovah, speaks to him. "*See, you say to me, 'Bring up this people,' but you have not let me know whom you will send with me...Now therefore, if I have found favor in your sight, please show me now your ways, that I may know you in order to find favor in your sight*"(Ex 32:12, 13). Moses wants God—as a sign of his favor and grace—to fill him in on who he is and how he is going to accomplish this. He is also asking God to reconsider and go with the people—a request he is willing to grant (Ex 32:14).

But there is something deeper here. Just as when Jehovah called him in the burning bush, Moses feels that his credibility in leading the people is contingent on his knowledge of God. "*Please show me your glory*"(Ex 32:18). God is surprisingly receptive to this—to a point. "*I will make all my goodness pass before you and will proclaim before you my name 'The LORD'...But...you cannot see my face, for man shall not see me and live*"(Ex 32:19, 20). God will show Moses *part* of his glory. Moses does not seem to realize that there is danger in his request; Jehovah's full glory is so great that man cannot see it and live. Yet God grants Moses a vision of him coming back to lead his people, places him in the cleft of a rock for his safety, covers him with his "hand," and lets him see his "back." All of this is framed as grace: "*I will be gracious to whom I will be gracious, and will show mercy on whom I will show mercy*"(Ex 33:19).

Revelation is a gift. Each time we reveal part of ourselves to another, we honor and bless them. We know nothing of God until he shows us who he is and what he wants (see 1 Cor 2:11). Yet God has revealed himself to us in nature, in Scripture, and often in the lessons of life. His greatest revelation of himself is Jesus. While God could easily remain aloof, he instead chooses to show us his glory.

One Thing to Think About: Do I appreciate that God has opened up to me?

One Thing to Pray For: God's help to understand and treasure his will

WEEK 6—THURSDAY

Reading: Exodus 34:1-9

A God Merciful and Gracious

God has agreed to show Moses his glory as part of his promise to travel with Israel up to Canaan. He instructs Moses to cut two new stone tablets, rise early in the morning, and ascend Mount Sinai alone. He swiftly obeys. "*The LORD descended in the cloud and stood with him there, and proclaimed the name of the LORD*"(Ex 34:5). Jehovah has agreed to show Moses *part* of his glory—his back and not his face—and also to "*proclaim before you my name*"(Ex 34:19). Jehovah will tell Moses his name—and what it reveals about his nature.

"*The LORD passed before him and proclaimed, 'The LORD, the LORD, a God merciful and gracious, slow to anger, and abounding in steadfast love and faithfulness, keeping steadfast love for thousands, forgiving iniquity and transgression and sin, but who will by no means clear the guilty, visiting the iniquity of the fathers on the children and the children's children, to the third and fourth generation*"(Ex 34:6-7). Jehovah describes himself. He is "*a God merciful and gracious,*" patient and longsuffering, full of loyal love, eager to forgive. Yet he is at the same time not a God to be trifled with, not an indulgent pushover. He "*will by no means clear the guilty*" and will punish rebellion. In response to this revelation, Moses bows and worships, begging Jehovah to continue to live among his people despite the fact that they are a "*stiff-necked people*"(Ex 34:9).

When we are asked to describe ourselves, the results are not always accurate. Sometimes we try too hard to impress others, or use terms that are how we *want* to be rather than how we are. Jehovah is not so. He knows himself and declares that the best way to understand him is as "*a God merciful and gracious.*" He has shown his mercy by patiently enduring the people's complaining, forgiving their golden calf rebellion, and continuing to uphold his promise of the land of Canaan. If we think of God as weak and all-accepting—or as angry and implacable—then we miss him.

One Thing to Think About: Do I think of God as gracious and good—or as hard and impossible to please?

One Thing to Pray For: A proper balance in my view of who God is

WEEK 6—FRIDAY

Reading: Numbers 21:4-9

The Grace of Healing

Israel is on its way to Canaan. The epic failure after the spies' report is in the rear-view mirror, yet as they approach the land, more obstacles arise. Edom has refused to let Israel pass through its land, so as they travel out of the way, "*the people became impatient on the way*"(Num 21:4). This prompts a breakdown: "*And the people spoke against God and against Moses, 'Why have you brought us up out of Egypt to die in the wilderness? For there is no food and no water, and we loathe this worthless food*'"(Num 21:5). After a long line of persistent complaints, Jehovah has had enough and sends poisonous snakes—"*fiery serpents*"—who bite the people and many of them die.

This may seem a strange entry in a study of grace, until we notice what happens next. The people approach Moses in repentance: "*We have sinned, for we have spoken against the LORD and against you. Pray to the LORD, that he take away the serpents from us*"(Num 21:7). Moses prays for the people, but instead of taking the snakes *away*, God instructs to make a bronze serpent that would bring life to the bitten. Instead of salvation, God provides healing. The people may have to learn to live with the snakes for a little while, but God graciously gives a remedy to their sting.

There is much to learn here. God is unafraid to allow his people to hurt—sometimes even *causing* the pain—to turn them back from evil, destructive behavior. God responds favorably to those who will acknowledge their sin and ask for mercy—not because he has to, but because it is the kind of God he is. Most powerfully, God does not always answer our prayers by simply taking away the problem we are facing, but by giving us healing and strength to deal with the problem. God would be right to ignore us and leave us to the fate we deserve, yet the bronze serpent stands as a visible symbol of God's amazing grace.

One Thing to Think About: Has God ever answered my prayers in a different way than I expected?

One Thing to Pray For: God's healing from the damage my sin has done to others—and myself

WEEK 7—MONDAY

Reading: Deuteronomy 6:1-15

The Dangers Grace Brings

Moses is preparing the Israelites for their imminent invasion of Canaan, stressing that God is *giving* them the land. He wants them to obey Jehovah's commands "*that it may go well with you, and that you may multiply greatly, as the LORD, the God of your fathers, has promised you, in a land flowing with milk and honey*"(Deut 6:3). He charges them to teach God's commands to their children at all times as they go about the domestic duties that will accompany having their own homes (Deut 6:7-9).

There is a concern behind all this instruction. "*And when the LORD your God brings you into the land that he swore to your fathers, to Abraham, to Isaac, and to Jacob, to give you—with great and good cities that you did not build, and houses full of all good things that you did not fill, and cisterns that you did not dig, and vineyards and olive trees that you did not plant—and when you eat and are full, then take care lest you forget the LORD, who brought you out of the house of slavery*"(Deut 6:10-12). The people are about to receive a land that they have not worked for at all. The cities, crops, and land are rich, but not due to their effort. They will benefit from others' work and from the free gift of God. Moses is wary that the people will "*forget the LORD, who brought you out of the house of slavery.*" When the battle dies down and the people grow fat and happy, they may forget where they have been, how richly they have been blessed, and who is truly responsible.

Grace brings dangers. Just as we fret over too many gifts spoiling our children, so God's rich blessings can spoil us. We happily receive his goodness and forget where it comes from. We rip off the wrapping paper and enjoy the toy, experience, relationship, wealth, or life, while neglecting the giver. For Christians, it is even possible that we retreat to the slavery God sent his Son to deliver us from, forgetting the source of our own forgiveness (2 Pet 1:9). The challenge is to receive God's blessings while remaining humble and thankful.

One Thing to Think About: In what ways have God's rich blessings spoiled me?

One Thing to Pray For: Gratitude for God's blessings—and for the people whose hard work has blessed me

Reading: Deuteronomy 6:16-25

Reciting Stories of Grace

Moses continues to speak to the people about their expected behavior after they enter the land of Canaan. "*You shall not put the LORD your God to the test*"(Deut 6:16) but "*diligently keep the commandments of the LORD your God*"(Deut 6:17) so that "*it may go well with you*"(Deut 6:18). It is definitely in their best interests to actually obey God. Their obedience won't *earn* them the land, but it will ensure that God continues to help and bless them by removing their enemies and fighting their battles. Obedience doesn't make grace not grace.

But Moses looks farther ahead. He envisions a Jewish child asking his father the meaning of all of Jehovah's rules. "*Then you shall say to your son, 'We were Pharaoh's slaves in Egypt. And the LORD brought us out of Egypt with a mighty hand. And the LORD showed signs and wonders, great and grievous, against Egypt and against Pharaoh and all his household, before our eyes. And he brought us out from there, that he might bring us in and give us the land that he swore to give to our fathers*'"(Deut 6:21-23). The LORD brought us out, showed signs, brought us here, kept his promise, and gave us this land. This retelling stresses how much God has done—and almost nothing about what Israel has done. In this context, obedience is natural: "*And the LORD commanded us to do all these statutes, to fear the LORD our God, for our good always, that he might preserve us alive, as we are this day*"(Deut 6:24). A God who so clearly wants our good can be trusted. His commands are "*for our good always.*"

It is important to recite stories of grace. We remind our families and friends—and ourselves—of how much God has done for us. We keep his works fresh. We reexamine his power and genius. We glorify him anew. Then, when challenged to obey him in a difficult or confusing command, we remember that he does things that are "*for our good always.*" God is so good that we can *always* trust him to be good and do good.

One Thing to Think About: What stories of grace can I tell?

One Thing to Pray For: Opportunities to speak—especially with those close to me—about the good God has done me

WEEK 7—WEDNESDAY

Reading: Deuteronomy 8:1-10

The Grace of Discipline

Moses urges the people of Israel to learn the lessons of the forty years they have wandered in the wilderness. "*And you shall remember the whole way that the LORD your God has led you these forty years in the wilderness, that he might humble you, testing you to know what was in your heart, whether you would keep his commandments or not*"(Deut 8:2). The hardship of the desert—the continual scarcity of water, the frustrations of the menu, the difficulty of always moving—is recast as a way God has tested his people to determine their willingness to obey.

But with the hardship, Jehovah also has still continually provided for his people. "*And he humbled you and let you hunger and fed you with manna, which you did not know, nor did your fathers know, that he might make you know that man does not live by bread alone, but man lives by every word that comes from the mouth of the LORD. Your clothing did not wear out on you and your foot did not swell these forty years. Know then in your heart that, as a man disciplines his son, the LORD your God disciplines you*"(Deut 8:3-5). God uses their hardship to humble them. He shows them their need—their hunger and their need for clothes—and then meets their need. Part of the lesson is learning that "*man does not live by bread alone*"—combining their physical need with the essentiality of spiritual instruction. It all comes from God. He wants them to "*know... in your heart*" that God has used this experience to train them like an engaged father working with his son. When they enter a land where they will have abundance rather than lack, it is essential that they remember the desert lessons—and the God who loves them like a son.

We discipline our children because we love them. They need to learn. Sometimes the process is painful—for both child and parent—because hardship and pain are excellent teachers. Yet discipline is a gift we give our kids. God gives us the same gift by working with us, allowing us to need and struggle, while always driving us toward what is good (Heb 12:3-11). The challenge is to see a good God while in circumstances that are not good.

One Thing to Think About: What have I learned from hard times?

One Thing to Pray For: God to continue to work on me, molding me into the person he wants me to be

WEEK 7—THURSDAY

Reading: Deuteronomy 9:1-8

Grace Is Not About Us

As Moses speaks about the battles that will soon face Israel as they enter Canaan, he stresses their disadvantage. "*Hear, O Israel: you are to cross over the Jordan today, to go in to dispossess nations greater and mightier than you, cities great and fortified up to heaven, a people great and tall, the sons of the Anakim, whom you know, and of whom you have heard it said, 'Who can stand before the sons of Anak?'*"(Deut 9:1-2). The battle between this giant, well-established people and a ragtag band of desert nomads is an epic mismatch. Jehovah is the difference. "*He will destroy them and subdue them before you. So you shall drive them out and make them perish quickly, as the LORD has promised you*"(Deut 9:3).

But Moses is not just encouraging the people; he is wary of a specific kind of revisionist history after the battle is won. "*Do not say in your heart, after the LORD your God has thrust them out before you, 'It is because of my righteousness that the LORD has brought me in to possess this land,' whereas it is because of the wickedness of these nations that the LORD is driving them out before you. Not because of your righteousness or the uprightness of your heart are you going in to possess their land*"(Deut 9:4-5). After the battle, Israel will assume this outcome was inevitable. They will attribute the victory to their own goodness. Moses sharply rejects this. Their victory is due to God's intervention, the Canaanites' wickedness, God's patience with Israel, and his commitment to fulfill his promises. In fact, Moses reminds them that they are a stubborn people (Deut 9:6-8), unworthy of this great victory. When they win the day, it will be *in spite* of their "righteousness," not because of it.

Grace is not about us. This passage identifies an all-too-human tendency to look back on our successes and blessings as deserved. God gives us blessings because we *deserve* them, we reason. Israel might think they are *better* than Canaan. These are dangerous thoughts for Christians as well. We assume our salvation, our financial blessings, our families, and our healthy relationships are the just rewards for our own righteousness. This, of course, means that they are not gifts from God, but what we deserve. Grace leaves us praising God (not ourselves) because grace is not about us.

One Thing to Think About: Do I think I am better than others? Who? Why?

One Thing to Pray For: The clarity to see my own unworthiness

WEEK 7—FRIDAY

Reading: Joshua 1:1-9

I Will Not Leave You or Forsake You

This section is saturated with grace. Joshua is the newly installed leader of Israel and has a daunting task before him: leading the people to conquer the land of Canaan. Jehovah graciously reassures him. He insists that this is "*the land that I am giving to them*" and that "*every place that the sole of your foot will tread upon I have given to you*"(-Josh 1:2, 3). The land is God's (not the Canaanites') and he *gives* it to Israel.

Jehovah also takes pains to encourage Joshua personally. "*No man shall be able to stand before you all the days of your life. Just as I was with Moses, so I will be with you. I will not leave you or forsake you*"(Josh 1:5). Moses possessed a legendary relationship with God; God insists that he will be with Joshua in the same way. "*I will not leave you or forsake you*" stresses both the presence and the help of God. He will not leave Joshua on his own to accomplish this work. Because of this, he repeatedly charges Joshua to "*be strong and courageous*"(Josh 1:6, 7, 9). Certainty about God's presence translates into boldness and bravery. He also expects Joshua to be a spiritual leader who is "*careful to do according to all the law that Moses my servant commanded you*" and "*meditate on it day and night*"(Josh 1:7, 8). God's presence and help is not a one-way street. He is seeking a relationship with someone who will hear him, trust him, and obey his will.

God's presence does not mean that everything goes smoothly for Joshua. There will be difficulty and poor judgment in the days ahead. But God offers *himself* to Joshua—an indescribable gift. Christians share in this promise. The Hebrew writer tells us to "*keep your life free from love of money, and be content with what you have, for he has said, 'I will never leave you nor forsake you*'"(Heb 13:5). When God is with us, our path is not rose-strewn, but we have a deeper gift than ease. We walk with our God.

One Thing to Think About: How has God been with me through the hardships of life?

One Thing to Pray For: The contentment of knowing God is with me

WEEK 8—MONDAY

Reading: Joshua 2:8-14, 22-24

Jehovah Has Given You the Land

When the Israelite spies enter the land of Canaan, they find a sympathetic helper in Rahab. She redirects the soldiers seeking the spies (by lying to them), then confesses to the spies: *"I know that the LORD has given you the land, and that the fear of you has fallen upon us, and that all the inhabitants of the land melt away before you"* (Josh 2:9). She invokes the name of the Hebrew God, Jehovah (Yahweh), confident that he has already granted Israel the city of Jericho. If God has given the land, there is no resisting his will.

Rahab explains that she and her fellow Canaanites have heard of Jehovah's extraordinary deliverance of Israel—the Red Sea and the victories on the other side of the Jordan. *"And as soon as we heard it, our hearts melted, and there was no spirit left in any man because of you, for the LORD your God, he is God in the heavens above and on the earth beneath"* (Josh 2:11). Seeing the writing on the wall, she convinces the spies to save her and her family when the inevitable victory comes. Their encounter with Rahab leads the spies to report back to Joshua: *"Truly the LORD has given all the land into our hands. And also, all the inhabitants of the land melt away because of us"* (Josh 2:24). They are assured that Jehovah really will give them the land.

This repeated emphasis on God *giving* the land to Israel reminds us that all things are God's to give. It ensures proper perspective for Israel and other observers, reminding them that all the battles and tactics and bravery of the soldiers are not the crux of this victory. But most of all, it stresses the *certainty* that Israel can operate with. When God gives something, no one can stop him.

One Thing to Think About: How does God's goodness give me confidence about the future?

One Thing to Pray For: The faith of Rahab—to see what is coming and prepare accordingly

WEEK 8—TUESDAY

Reading: Joshua 21:43-45

The Grace of Rest

We have moved forward to the latter stages of Joshua's conquest of Canaan. After describing the lands and cities that have been conquered, the narrator concludes, "*Thus the LORD gave to Israel all the land that he swore to give to their fathers. And they took possession of it, and they settled there*"(Josh 21:43). This does not mean that Israel has completely conquered the land; there is still quite a bit of work left to be done (Josh 13:1-6, Judges 1:19-36). The point here is that any failures in conquering the land belong to the people. Jehovah has kept his promise.

But Jehovah not only gives them the land; he also gives rest. "*And the LORD gave them rest on every side just as he had sworn to their fathers. Not one of all their enemies had withstood them, for the LORD had given all their enemies into their hands*"(Josh 21:44). Rest here means peace and the removal of enemies and war. Jehovah has given gifts—the land, rest, and victory over their enemies—and any residual difficulty belongs to the people. After years of wandering and instability—after years of looking forward—the people finally achieve some level of rest. All of this serves to prove the faithfulness of God. "*Not one word of all the promises that the LORD had made to the house of Israel had failed; all came to pass*"(Josh 21:45).

God gives rest. He establishes the priority of rest in the Sabbath, then promises rest in the land of Canaan (Ex 33:14). Jesus promises that with his yoke we will "*find rest for your souls*"(Matt 11:29). Yet the Hebrew writer stresses that the rest described in Joshua is a mere foreshadowing, an incomplete version of the rest that awaits the people of God (Heb 4:8-9). The point is that just as Israel sought rest from their physical travails, so we await a rest for our spirits and bodies in the life-giving presence of our God. We yearn for this great gift because we have learned that Jehovah keeps his word.

One Thing to Think About: In what ways does rest sound appealing to me?

One Thing to Pray For: A home with God, a place in his courts to rest

WEEK 8—WEDNESDAY

Reading: Judges 2:11-23

Jehovah Was Moved by Pity

Now established in the land, Israel promptly stops serving Jehovah. "*And they abandoned the LORD, the God of their fathers, who had brought them out of the land of Egypt. They went after other gods, from among the gods of the peoples who were around them, and bowed down to them. And they provoked the LORD to anger*"(Judg 2:12). After all of Moses' warnings about remembering God and not serving the gods of the Canaanites, the people still leave Jehovah behind to serve the Baals. This makes God angry and "*he gave them over to plunderers, who plundered them. And he sold them into the hand of their surrounding enemies, so that they could no longer withstand their enemies*"(-Judg 2:14). Israel has lost its only advantage.

Where we might be tempted to wash our hands of such people, God does not give up. "*Then the LORD raised up judges, who saved them out of the hand of those who plundered them*"(Judg 2:16). Great men and women become charismatic leaders of the people, helping rally the people and (with God's help) overthrow their enemies. But why does God give judges? "*For the LORD was moved to pity by their groaning because of those who afflicted and oppressed them*"(Judg 2:18). Hearing Israel's groaning, Jehovah feels compassion. He sees their hardship and need. In pity, he is willing to overlook their rebellion as they turn to him for help. The problem is that this positive development is short-lived; soon the people turn away from God again. Yet each time the people cry out, Jehovah continues to care—and show grace.

God's pity is a part of his grace. He doesn't *have* to pity us. I struggle to feel compassion for people who have chosen their condition, convinced that they have no one to blame but themselves. God goes beyond this, feeling pity for us *even when* we are at fault for our troubles. Jesus died for us "*while we were still sinners*"(Rom 5:8). In pity, he even helps rescue us from problems of our own making.

One Thing to Think About: What prevents me from feeling pity for others?

One Thing to Pray For: A willingness to admit how I have contributed to my state

Reading: Judges 7:2-15

The People Are Too Many

During the time of the judges, God will often allow Israel to be captured or dominated by another nation. In this time, the Midianites are the oppressors and Jehovah has raised up Gideon to deliver Israel from them. But there is a problem. "*The LORD said to Gideon, 'The people with you are too many for me to give the Midianites into their hand, lest Israel boast over me, saying, 'My own hand has saved me'*"(Judges 7:2). Israel's army is big enough that—after the battle is won—they may decide that they have done it all themselves. Jehovah takes this personally—"*lest Israel boast over me*"—because the glory should be his.

After 22,000 of the people return (because they are scared of the battle), Jehovah is still not ready. "*And the LORD said to Gideon, 'The people are still too many. Take them down to the water, and I will test them for you there*'"(Judges 7:4) Gideon watches the men drink water, dismissing those who kneel down to drink and only choosing those who cup water in their hands and lap it. Now he is down to 300 men—and Jehovah declares the army ready for the battle. "*With the 300 men who lapped I will save you and give the Midianites into your hand*"(Judg 7:7). For Gideon (who seems to always be a bit skittish), God also allows him to overhear a Midianite's dream that convinces him that God has given him Midian (Judg 7:14, 15).

This scene reveals God's deep insight into human nature—and how it can obstruct our spiritual lives. We want to think of ourselves as better than we are and revel in our great accomplishments. If we win a great victory, we want to boast in what we have done. Even when we have asked for God's help, we often leave out his part and focus on our own. Yet here we see that God regularly chooses to save, help, and bless in ways that *cannot possibly be misconstrued as our greatness*. 300 men—even 300 great ones—are not enough to win a battle like this. 12 apostles—even wise and powerful ones—are not enough to change the world on their own. We are left mystified at God's genius and in awe of his power.

One Thing to Think About: How do I try to take credit for things God has done?

One Thing to Pray For: Fresh awe at God's brilliance and strength

WEEK 8—FRIDAY

Reading: Judges 16:23-31

Please Remember Me

Samson is a larger-than-life character. As he acts on his intense passions—lust, anger, irritation—God uses him to deliver his people and strike a blow against the Philistines. Now he has been tricked by Delilah, captured by the Philistines, blinded, and humiliated. "*Now the lords of the Philistines gathered to offer a great sacrifice to Dagon their god and to rejoice, and they said, 'Our god has given Samson our enemy into our hand*'"(Judg 16:23). They interpret Samson's downfall as Dagon's victory over Jehovah. Yet Samson realizes that the gathering of so many influential enemies is an opportunity.

So he prays. "*Then Samson called to the LORD and said, 'O Lord GOD, please remember me and please strengthen me only this once, O God, that I may be avenged on the Philistines for my two eyes*'"(Judg 16:28). He asks for Jehovah to "*remember me*," calling his attention to the degradation and plight of Samson, who has been fighting for Jehovah's cause. He also acknowledges that he needs Jehovah's strength ("*strengthen me only this once*") to accomplish this great feat. God answers. Samson pulls down the two central pillars of the temple, collapsing the structure on himself and killing the Philistines with him. "*So the dead whom he killed at his death were more than those whom he had killed during his life*"(Judg 16:30).

This story is challenging both to interpret and apply. Suicide does not seem to be the issue here; Samson is thinking as a warrior willing to sacrifice himself to kill more of the enemy. Instead, we should see that for the first time, Samson is truly reaching out to God in faith for help and strength. God does not have to remember him or help him, but he has grace. While there is much to correct in Samson's behavior, God is eager to answer those who call out to him (instead of resisting or ignoring him). Since God has been seeking an opportunity to move against the Philistines (Judg 14:4), he appears more likely to give gracious gifts when they align with his will.

One Thing to Think About: Do my mistakes ever make me hesitate to cry out to God?

One Thing to Pray For: My will to become God's will

WEEK 9—MONDAY

Reading: Ruth 4:11-22

A Restorer of Life

The book of Ruth tells the story of some surprisingly ordinary people. Naomi flees a famine in Israel with her husband and two sons, sojourning in Moab. Her husband and sons all die, leaving her alone with her two widowed daughters-in-law. Returning home to Israel with only her daughter-in-law Ruth, Naomi declares, "*I went away full, and the LORD has brought me back empty*"(Ruth 1:21). Yet through Ruth's hard work and the intervention of Boaz, God provides for her.

In our text, we learn that Boaz and Ruth marry. "*And the LORD gave her conception, and she bore a son*"(Ruth 4:13). This grandchild revives Naomi. "*Then the women said to Naomi, 'Blessed be the LORD, who has not left you this day without a redeemer, and may his name be renowned in Israel! He shall be to you a restorer of life and a nourisher of your old age*'"(Ruth 4:14-15). They praise God for the promise this child holds. This little baby "*shall be to you a restorer of life and a nourisher of your old age.*" Suddenly the years of heartache and disappointment melt away as she looks into the face of this precious new life. Before he says a word, little Obed restores and blesses his grandmother. The women even declare that, "*a son has been born to Naomi*"(Ruth 4:17), emphasizing her even over Ruth, the boy's mother.

God gives Naomi a gift here—a grandchild who is "*a restorer of life*" for her. After her bitterness and suffering, she is given fresh joy in old age. God's gifts do not remove the pain of the past, but they can help heal old wounds and make us vibrant and positive again. Children are a gift from God—one way (but certainly not the only way) he restores life and makes it bearable for us.

One Thing to Think About: How do present joys give me perspective on past sufferings?

One Thing to Pray For: Thanks for the little things of life that restore and reenergize me

WEEK 9—TUESDAY

Reading: 1 Samuel 1:1-2, 9-20

Look on My Affliction

Hannah has a problem. One of two wives, she is unable to conceive while her fellow-wife ("*her rival*", 1 Sam 1:6) has several. Her rival then adds insult to injury, "*(provoking) her grievously to irritate her, because the LORD had closed her womb*"(1 Sam 1:6). Overwhelmed by her disappointment, helplessness, and frustration during a visit to the tabernacle, Hannah is "*deeply distressed and prayed to the LORD and wept bitterly*"(1 Sam 1:10). In her prayer, she promises Jehovah that "*if you will indeed look on the affliction of your servant and remember me and not forget your servant, but will give to your servant a son, then I will give him to the LORD all the days of his life, and no razor shall touch his head*"(1 Sam 1:11). In exchange for God's grace, Hannah promises a gift of her own—to give this child back to Jehovah.

Eli, the high priest, spots Hannah praying and misinterprets it as drunkenness. Unashamed, Hannah explains that she is speaking to God "*out of my great anxiety and vexation*" and "*pouring out my soul before the LORD*"(1 Sam 1:16, 15). Eli blesses her: "*Go in peace, and the God of Israel grant your petition that you have made to him*"(1 Sam 1:17). Upon returning home, "*the LORD remembered her*"(1 Sam 1:19). God answers her prayer and gives her a son.

Jehovah hears the impassioned, desperate prayer of the afflicted. Hannah shows us that God wants us to take these concerns and anxieties to *him*. Her commitment to give the child back to God is less about bargaining than about expressing the deepest desire of her heart. She would rather have a child she does not see than have no child. This text does not promise that God will always answer requests for children—or that he wants us to make vows—or that God always gives the afflicted what they ask for. It is instead a celebration of God's grace toward overlooked people like us.

One Thing to Think About: When did I last call on God out of my affliction?

One Thing to Pray For: Relief from the "anxiety and vexation" that plague me

WEEK 9—WEDNESDAY

Reading: 1 Samuel 7:3-14

The Grace of Help

For a great deal of time preceding our text, Israel has been estranged from God. Twenty years earlier, in a fit of desperation, they took the ark of the covenant into battle against the Philistines only to see it captured and Israel dominated. Now the people are ready for revival. "*And Samuel said to all the house of Israel, 'If you are returning to the LORD with all your heart, then put away the foreign gods and the Ashtaroth from among you and direct your heart to the LORD and serve him only, and he will deliver you out of the hand of the Philistines*'"(1 Sam 7:3). They gather together, put away their idols, and fast together.

The Philistines interpret the gathering as an attempt at rebellion and prepare to fight. The people are terrified, begging Samuel to keep praying for them. "*And Samuel cried out to the LORD for Israel, and the LORD answered him*"(1 Sam 7:9). The Philistines attempt to attack while Samuel is offering a sacrifice, but "*the LORD thundered with a mighty sound that day against the Philistines and threw them into confusion, and they were defeated before Israel*"(1 Sam 7:10). After this great victory, Samuel sets up a stone called Ebenezer because "*till now the LORD has helped us*"(1 Sam 7:12). The irony here is that Ebenezer, formerly infamous as the place of Israel's great defeat (1 Sam 4:1), now becomes a legendary symbol of Israel's great victory. God hears the penitent cries of his people—and "*the LORD has helped us.*"

God helps his people in a myriad of ways; he seems to revel in the variety. Sometimes he helps through great leaders; sometimes through weak (or no) leaders. Sometimes he fights with Israel's armies; sometimes they don't fight at all. The constant is that God graciously chooses to help his people even when they are rebellious, scared, or proud. It reassures us that we can ask for God's help in the difficulties we face—especially when we are trying to do God's will—confident that "*till now the LORD has helped us.*"

One Thing to Think About: How has God helped me in the last couple of days?

One Thing to Pray For: God to redeem my failures, to his glory

Reading: 1 Samuel 17:31-54

The Grace of Victory

King Saul and the Israelite army are camped opposite the Philistines, yet they are afraid of the massive, bellowing warrior Goliath. The giant keeps insisting on a winner-take-all battle that is too risky for Israel's liking. Into this stalemate comes David, who is too young to have a realistic chance at winning—and also too young to know better. He convinces Saul to let him fight by appealing to Jehovah's help: "*The LORD who delivered me from the paw of the lion and from the paw of the bear will deliver me from the hand of this Philistine*"(1 Sam 17:37).

At every stage, David lacks the proper preparation for the battle. His armor doesn't fit. He has no military experience. He has no weapon, settling for five smooth stones and a sling (1 Sam 17:40). Goliath chuckles at him—"*Am I a dog, that you come to me with sticks?*"(1 Sam 17:43)—before promising to feed him to the vultures. But David speaks too: "*This day the LORD will deliver you into my hand, and I will strike you down and cut off your head*"(1 Sam 17:46). This victory will be "*that all this assembly may know that the LORD saves not with sword and spear. For the battle is the LORD's, and he will give you into our hand*"(1 Sam 17:47). What comes next is legendary: a well-placed stone topples the giant and David cuts off Goliath's head with his own sword. It has happened just as David asserted it would. Jehovah has given Goliath into David's hand.

Just as with Gideon having too many men, so God seems here to highlight the weakness and insignificance of David to demonstrate his power. This is a victory *God gives.* At times we face seemingly insurmountable problems—in our families, in our jobs, in our own hearts. Yet when we receive victory over those problems—when we see a shift in others, when we grow past our old flaws, when we gain new hope—it is God's gift. Especially, the victory Jesus has achieved over sin and death is a rich blessing that is none of our doing (1 Cor 15:57). Rather than applauding ourselves, David teaches us to give credit back to the LORD.

One Thing to Think About: How have I experienced victory?

One Thing to Pray For: God's help to overcome obstacles too big for me

WEEK 9—FRIDAY

Reading: 1 Samuel 24:1-22

David Shows Grace

Saul and David's relationship has deteriorated since the great victory over Goliath. Driven mad with suspicion, Saul has hunted David and tried to kill him. But now David is hiding in the cave where Saul goes to relieve himself. His men insist that this is an act of grace from God: *"Here is the day of which the LORD said to you, 'Behold, I will give your enemy into your hand, and you shall do to him as it shall seem good to you'"*(1 Sam 24:4). Is this to be another great victory for David, like the battle with Goliath? He sneaks up to Saul and cuts off a corner of his robe.

Yet even this mild gesture bothers David. His "*heart struck him*"(1 Sam 24:5), a way of describing a guilty conscience. David's reasoning is that Saul is Jehovah's anointed king, so any removal of Saul should be done by Jehovah himself (not David) (1 Sam 24:6). David lets Saul go, then reveals that he has stayed his hand when he had the opportunity to harm him. Saul is convicted. *"And Saul lifted up his voice and wept. He said to David, 'You are more righteous than I, for you have repaid me good, whereas I have repaid you evil'"*(1 Sam 24:16-17). Saul acknowledges that David has shown him undeserved kindness—what we call grace. "*So may the LORD reward you with good for what you have done to me this day*"(1 Sam 24:19). Saul stops seeking after David (for the moment) and the tense situation is defused by an act of grace.

When we focus solely on what others have done, we will notice that they are undeserving of goodwill and kindness. Yet David has been a beneficiary of God's rich grace and now becomes a giver of grace. He will show similar mercy to Nabal (1 Sam 25:25-35) and Saul again (1 Sam 26:8-12). We learn from David that showing grace does not diminish our standing. We learn that grace does not mean others "get away" with their bad behavior; rather, they are shamed because we do not act the way they do. David shows us that grace is a higher, more honorable path.

One Thing to Think About: Am I eager to receive gifts from God—yet reluctant to give grace to others?

One Thing to Pray For: The courage to show mercy

WEEK 10—MONDAY

Reading: 2 Samuel 7:4-17

I Took You from the Pasture

Now well-established as king, David has proposed building a house for Jehovah just as he has built a palace for himself. God speaks to him through Nathan, reminding David that God has never requested this: "*In all places where I have moved with all the people of Israel, did I speak a word with any of the judges of Israel, whom I commanded to shepherd my people Israel, saying, 'Why have you not built me a house of cedar?*'"(2 Sam 7:7). While God acknowledges David's desire to honor him, God does not *require* any such thing and is willing to wait for Solomon to do the building (2 Sam 7:12-13).

But God has a deeper message for David. "*I took you from the pasture, from following the sheep, that you should be prince over my people Israel*"(2 Sam 7:8). David's is a rags-to-riches story that emphasizes God's blessing. "*And I have been with you wherever you went and have cut off all your enemies from before you. And I will make for you a great name, like the name of the great ones on the earth*"(2 Sam 7:9). God has been continually present with David—through all the intrigue with Saul and the long wait to be king—and has given him victory. But God especially wants David to know that *if anyone is building anyone a house, it will be God!* "*Moreover, the LORD declares to you that the LORD will make you a house*"(2 Sam 7:11). God will give David a dynasty that will continually govern and bless Israel, perpetuating the blessings that began back in the pasture.

God's words to David invite us to see God's grace toward us on a larger scale. He encourages David to look back to his beginnings and then see how far he has come. As Christians, we can do the same. God has, by sheer grace, taken us from the pasture, the pigsty, and slavery to become a people who wear his name. He has been with us wherever we have gone. This awareness of God's goodness leaves us humbled, like David: "*Who am I, O LORD God...that you have brought me thus far?*"(2 Sam 7:18).

One Thing to Think About: How has God changed my life?

One Thing to Pray For: God to be with me wherever I go

WEEK 10—TUESDAY

Reading: 2 Samuel 9:1-13

I Will Show You Kindness

In the ancient world, royal transitions were often bloody. Usually the new king would eliminate potential rivals by murdering members of the former king's family. This context makes our story all the more remarkable. It begins with David wondering to his counselors, "*Is there still anyone left of the house of Saul, that I may show him kindness for Jonathan's sake?*"(2 Sam 9:1). Perhaps David is reminiscing about his close relationship with Jonathan and remembers his promise to show kindness to his children (1 Sam 20:15-17). Shockingly, David appears unaware if there are any potential threats to him among Saul's family.

When Mephibosheth, Jonathan's son is discovered, he is terrified that he is about to be killed. He "*fell on his face and paid homage*"(2 Sam 9:6). Yet David soothes him: "*Do not fear, for I will show you kindness for the sake of your father Jonathan, and I will restore to you all the land of Saul your father, and you shall eat at my table always*"(2 Sam 9:7). Mephibosheth is suddenly hugely wealthy, of a much higher social status, and close to the king. He responds in the way appropriate for such displays of grace: "*What is your servant, that you should show regard for a dead dog such as I?*"(2 Sam 9:8). Despite his physical handicap (not looked on favorably in the ancient world) and his tie to the previous king, Mephibosheth enjoys undeserved blessings.

David's grace here illustrates something important about God's grace: it is based on faithfulness to promises rather than the worthiness of the recipient. Because David promised, he now acts to show kindness. Because God has promised, he acts to bring his Son into the world and offer salvation through faith in him. He does not choose us because we are worthy, but because he is trustworthy and committed to kindness. We do not leave this scene praising Mephibosheth, but David—and we do not leave our own lives praising ourselves, but God.

One Thing to Think About: How am I like Mephibosheth?

One Thing to Pray For: Opportunities to show kindness to others today

WEEK 10—WEDNESDAY

Reading: 2 Samuel 19:16-30

Refusing to Settle Scores

This reading describes the aftermath of Absalom's attempt at a revolution. Not long before, Absalom had seized power and appeared to be the future of the kingdom while David slinked out of Jerusalem. Now David returns triumphant—and there are scores to be settled. First is Shimei, one of Saul's descendants, who had cursed David and his party. Shimei begs for mercy: "*Let not my lord hold me guilty or remember how your servant did wrong on the day my lord the king left Jerusalem. Do not let the king take it to heart. For your servant knows that I have sinned*"(2 Sam 19:19-20). Abishai (Joab's brother) asks whether Shimei should be killed for his insolence. David balks. "*Shall anyone be put to death in Israel this day? For do I not know that I am this day king over Israel?*"(2 Sam 19:22). David is sick of the killing that has already happened. He thinks that attacking Shimei would be an act of insecurity: don't I already know that I am king?

Then comes Mephibosheth, the recipient of David's generosity, who remained in the city instead of fleeing with David (making his allegiances clear). David interrogates him, "*Why did you not go with me, Mephibosheth?*"(2 Sam 19:25). He claims that his servant Ziba deceived him and then badmouthed him to the king. Instead of sorting through who is lying, David simply extends mercy: "*Why speak any more of your affairs? I have decided: you and Ziba shall divide the land*"(2 Sam 19:29). Overjoyed and relieved, Mephibosheth urges Ziba to take it all.

No one in the ancient world would blame David if he took this opportunity to settle scores and quiet the dissent that has troubled his kingdom. But he refuses. I wonder if this is not related to David receiving mercy from Jehovah for his affair with Bathsheba and killing of Uriah ("*the LORD has put away your sin; you shall not die*", 2 Sam 12:13). David knows what it is to deserve punishment and death and to be pardoned—and now extends it to others. Part of grace is having the power to harm others in revenge and intentionally staying our hand.

One Thing to Think About: When do I most want revenge? How do I most often try to get it?

One Thing to Pray For: The power to leave vengeance to God

WEEK 10—THURSDAY

Reading: 1 Kings 3:1-14

The Invitation to Grace

Not long into the reign of Solomon, he travels to Gibeon to make a massive sacrifice. Not only do we learn that "*Solomon loved the LORD*"(1 Kings 3:3), but also that he "*used to offer a thousand burnt offerings on that altar*"(1 Kings 3:4). After one of these offerings, Jehovah appears to him and makes an incredible invitation: "*Ask what I shall give you*"(1 Kings 3:5). The treasure-room of heaven is open to Solomon, his for the asking. God is ready to bless him in whatever way he requests. Solomon responds by describing Jehovah's great care for his father David and the honor of making him king in his place "*although I am but a little child. I do not know how to go out or come in*"(1 Kings 3:7). Overwhelmed by the immensity of his task and his own insufficiency, Solomon asks for "*an understanding mind to govern your people, that I may discern between good and evil*"(1 Kings 3:9).

Jehovah is happy with this request—not only because it shows Solomon's hunger for wisdom, but because of what he *does not* ask for. "*Behold, I give you a wise and discerning mind...I give you also what you have not asked, both riches and honor, so that no other king shall compare with you, all your days*"(1 Kings 3:12, 13). As amazing as the initial offer is, God heaps grace upon grace as a sign of his pleasure.

God invites Solomon to choose his gift: "*Ask what I shall give you.*" He invites us as well: "*Ask, and it will be given to you*"(Matt 7:7). He opens up his treasure-room to us. What will we ask for? God's grace is not only a blessing; it is also a test of our character. Will we only seek his favors so that we can enjoy an easy and comfortable life? Or will we ask for gifts that will help us to serve others, accomplish God's will, and fulfill our purpose?

One Thing to Think About: What do my prayer requests reveal about my heart?

One Thing to Pray For: An understanding mind to discern between good and evil

WEEK 10—FRIDAY

Reading: 1 Kings 8:27-53

Future Mercies

Solomon oversees the dedication of the temple—the same temple that God did not allow David to build—with an epic prayer on behalf of Israel. He envisions crises in which the people of Israel will cry out to him in desperation, hunger, distress, and sin. "*And listen to the plea of your servant and of your people Israel, when they pray toward this place. And listen in heaven your dwelling place, and when you hear, forgive*" (1 Kings 8:30). Solomon seeks assurance of God's awareness of the temple and the people who use it as a place where they can find him.

A number of specific future situations follow: when a man is accused of sinning against his neighbor and swears his innocence, Solomon asks that Jehovah will act and judge (1 Kings 8:31). When in defeat in battle the people turn back to Jehovah, he asks that God will hear, forgive, and restore (1 Kings 8:33). In times of drought (1 Kings 8:35), famine (1 Kings 8:37), war (1 Kings 8:44), and exile (1 Kings 8:46), he asks for God to be receptive to their prayers. He even foresees foreigners coming to worship in the temple and asks for Jehovah to bless them (1 Kings 8:41). For his part, *Jehovah agrees*! He promises that "*my eyes and my heart will be there for all time*" (1 Kings 9:3). This is a present mercy that promises future mercies.

Solomon's prayer is powerful because he anticipates God's people being in deep need, usually of their own doing. He asks for God to bless a clearly undeserving people *even before they get in the pickles they will be in*. Solomon is not trying to justify sin; he is being honest about the reality of what will likely happen, given that all men sin (1 Kings 8:46). God's well of grace is so bottomless that he does not hesitate to pledge even future mercies to the repentant seeker.

One Thing to Think About: Do I expect that I will need grace in the future?

One Thing to Pray For: Praise to God for his willingness to accept me when I repent

WEEK 11—MONDAY

Reading: 1 Kings 9:1-9

Jehovah Appears a Second Time

Solomon has built a house for Jehovah, offered him a tremendous number of sacrifices, and made a lengthy prayer. He has asked for God to continually watch over, bless, and forgive his people. In response to his efforts and requests, "*the LORD appeared to Solomon a second time, as he had appeared to him at Gibeon*"(1 Kings 9:2). This time, instead of offering Solomon whatever he asks, God reassures him: "*I have heard your prayer and your plea, which you have made before me. I have consecrated this house that you have built, by putting my name there forever. My eyes and my heart will be there for all time*"(1 Kings 9:3). Jehovah finds the temple acceptable. He will receive worship there. It will be the focus of the attention of his "eyes" and his "heart."

God also addresses Solomon personally. "*And as for you, if you will walk before me, as David your father walked...then I will establish your throne over Israel forever, as I promised David your father*"(1 Kings 9:4, 5). While this blessing might seem inevitable in retrospect, God certainly doesn't *have* to establish David's throne. Yet he is able to juggle faithfulness to his promise and his expectations of Solomon. "*But if you turn aside from following me, you or your children...then I will cut off Israel from the land that I have given them, and the house that I have consecrated for my name I will cast out of my sight*"(1 Kings 9:6, 7). All this work Solomon has done—all this intense prayer he has offered—will come to nothing if it is not coupled with an obedient life.

This second appearance—and the promises and warnings that accompany it—is an act of God's grace. God is well within his rights to leave Solomon wondering about whether his temple is acceptable. And it is not as if Solomon does not know the importance of obedience. Each warning and each reassurance, each Bible passage and each word of encouragement, express God's intense desire for fellowship with us. They are signs of his grace.

One Thing to Think About: Do God's reassurances and warnings ever lose their intensity for me?

One Thing to Pray For: A renewed sense of the seriousness of my relationship with God

WEEK 11—TUESDAY

Reading: 1 Kings 17:8-16

The Grace of Just Enough

Elijah has caused a drought in the land of Israel, so Jehovah has sent him out of the country to widow in Zarephath. "*Behold, I have commanded a widow there to feed you*"(1 Kings 17:9), which must certainly sound strange to her because she has almost nothing to eat herself! Every part of this story implies extreme poverty: Elijah asks for "*a little water*"(1 Kings 17:10) and "*a morsel of bread*"(1 Kings 17:11), yet she protests that she has "*only a handful of flour in a jar and a little oil in a jug*"(1 Kings 17:12). Her intention is to make something for her son "*that we may eat it and then die*"(1 Kings 17:12). The situation is dire.

Elijah calms her: "*Do not fear; go and do as you have said*"(1 Kings 17:13), although skipping the dying part. He wants her to make him a little cake, then trust that by Jehovah's word, "*The jar of flour shall not be spent, and the jug of oil shall not be empty, until the day that the LORD sends rain upon the earth*"(1 Kings 17:14). So she does. Eljiah, the widow, and her son survive the famine by Jehovah's provision.

There is a similar story from Elisha's life in which a widow pours oil into all the vessels she can borrow, then sells the oil, pays her debts, and has plenty to live on. Yet this story is far different. Elijah's widow doesn't have excess. She has *just enough*—enough flour and oil to eat. She does not get rich. God gives her enough to live by. Grace is easy to see when it leads to remarkable wealth; it is harder to see when we have just enough. Yet sometimes "just enough" helps us to see our weakness, not grow attached to things, and learn to trust God.

One Thing to Think About: Do I have enough?

One Thing to Pray For: Eyes to see God's grace in everyday things

WEEK 11—WEDNESDAY

Reading: 1 Kings 17:17-24

Jehovah Listened to the Voice of Elijah

Elijah is still waiting out the drought he caused in Israel (and the resulting famine) by living in an upstairs room with a widow in the land of Sidon. Jehovah has been providing for them with a miraculous jar of flour and jug of oil that never empty out. Now tragedy strikes. "*After this the son of the woman, the mistress of the house, became ill. And his illness was so severe that there was no breath left in him*"(1 Kings 17:17). After the death of her husband, the famine, and now her work in taking care of Elijah, her son's death is too much. She is angry with Elijah: "*What have you against me, O man of God? You have come to me to bring my sin to remembrance and to cause the death of my son!*"(1 Kings 17:18). Overwhelmed by emotion—and a stranger to the religion of Jehovah—she blames Elijah.

For his part, Elijah is troubled by the events as well: "*And he cried to the LORD, 'O LORD my God, have you brought calamity even upon the widow with whom I sojourn, by killing her son?*'"(1 Kings 17:20). He sees this disaster as too much, yet he carries the young man up to his room, stretches out on him, and "*cried to the LORD*"(1 Kings 17:21). This in itself is amazing; Elijah is confident that God *can* raise the boy from the dead and asks for this favor. The response is even greater: "*And the LORD listened to the voice of Elijah. And the life of the child came into him again, and he revived*"(1 Kings 17:22). The widow, thrilled and relieved, is now certain that Jehovah is a true God—and that Elijah is truly his prophet.

This is an extreme prayer. Elijah's story here does not give us assurance that God will always give us what we ask for—particularly in amazing ways like this. But Elijah is confident that God is gracious. He wants this woman to experience a part of God's grace. He wants this boy to live again. He wants there to be limits to the calamity that everyone is experiencing. And he is so confident that God wants this too that he asks for an amazing miracle. We may not be prophets of Jehovah, but when we are confident in the power and goodness of God, our prayers hold tremendous potential (James 5:16-18).

One Thing to Think About: Do I believe that Jehovah listens to my voice?

One Thing to Pray For: The courage to pray for God to do great things for others

WEEK 11—THURSDAY

Reading: 1 Kings 19:9-18

The Grace of a Low Whisper

Elijah is in a low moment. He has confronted Ahab, called down fire from heaven, and led the people to revival after the drought ends. Yet his years of work surely seem pointless when Queen Jezebel immediately threatens his life (1 Kings 19:2). So Elijah runs for his life all the way to Mt Sinai. Jehovah asks him, "*What are you doing here, Elijah?*", and his response gives a sense of his mindset. "*I have been very jealous for the LORD, the God of hosts. For the people of Israel have forsaken your covenant, thrown down your altars, and killed your prophets with the sword, and I, even I only, am left, and they seek my life, to take it away*"(1 Kings 19:10). Elijah is beyond discouraged; he is so depressed that he prays for God to kill him (1 Kings 19:4).

Jehovah is patient with him. As Elijah stands where Moses once stood, Jehovah passes by. He observes a number of amazing weather phenomena. "*And behold, the LORD passed by, and a great and strong wind tore the mountains and broke in pieces the rocks before the LORD, but the LORD was not in the wind. And after the wind an earthquake, but the LORD was not in the earthquake. And after the earthquake a fire, but the LORD was not in the fire. And after the fire the sound of a low whisper*"(1 Kings 19:11-12). Each time, the author stresses that Jehovah is not in the terrifying whirlwind or earthquake or fire. Jehovah is in "*the sound of a low whisper*"—reasoning with Elijah and calling him back to service. God speaks again, giving Elijah work to do and reassuring him that he is not alone. After the low whisper, Elijah picks himself up and returns to Israel.

When we are discouraged, we usually don't need to be yelled at. In his grace, God chooses not to overwhelm Elijah—or to ignore him—or to threaten him. He comes to him in a low whisper, gently and warmly comforting him and encouraging him. God knows just how to approach us at different times in our lives—confronting us when we need it and consoling us when we need it. Whether we are left in awe, convicted of guilt, or restored to service, we have experienced God's grace.

One Thing to Think About: Are there times when I need to be challenged—and times when I need to be comforted?

One Thing to Pray For: Higher respect for God's approach in dealing with man—including me

WEEK 11—FRIDAY

Reading: 1 Kings 21:17-29

God Even Loves Ahab

King Ahab has committed a terrible evil. He has grown so consumed with desire for Naboth's vineyard that he has allowed his wife to kill him. He then seizes the land, probably assuming that this is the king's prerogative. Jehovah sends Elijah to confront Ahab: "*Thus says the LORD, 'Have you killed and also taken possession?' And you shall say to him, 'Thus says the LORD: "In the place where dogs licked up the blood of Naboth shall dogs lick your own blood*"'"(1 Kings 21:19). God promises a gruesome death for Ahab and vows to completely eliminate his family. Instead of a dynasty, Ahab's line will be a byword (1 Kings 21:21-24). Even the author joins in, explaining that "*there was none who sold himself to do what was evil in the sight of the LORD like Ahab, whom Jezebel his wife incited*"(1 Kings 21:25). God will act and avenge!

Yet this is what makes the next part so surprising. "*And when Ahab heard these words, he tore his clothes and put sackcloth on his flesh and fasted and lay in sackcloth and went about dejectedly*"(1 Kings 21:27). Shockingly, hard-hearted Ahab takes this message very seriously! He is upset to hear about his own demise and the destruction of his family. "*And the word of the LORD came to Elijah the Tishbite, saying, 'Have you seen how Ahab has humbled himself before me? Because he has humbled himself before me, I will not bring the disaster in his days; but in his son's days I will bring the disaster upon his house*"(1 Kings 21:28-29). Jehovah defends Ahab to Elijah! He is proud of Ahab's repentance, excited that he has finally gotten through to him, and willing to postpone the judgment as an act of grace. God even loves Ahab.

We are often tempted to view people as irredeemable. When someone does something as wicked as Ahab's murder and theft, we struggle to feel compassion, show patience, or care at all. *God is not so.* He has grace for Ahab. He does not excuse his sin, but he continues to try to reach him. He also seems to brag about his repentance much like he brags about Job ("*have you seen how Ahab*" and "*have you considered my servant Job*"). God perfectly balances justice for evil with compassion and love—even for Ahab. When I make horrible mistakes, I can rest assured that God will love even me.

One Thing to Think About: Do I struggle to feel compassion for those who commit horrible sins? Why might that be?

One Thing to Pray For: A heart humble before God—especially when I am wrong

WEEK 12—MONDAY

Reading: 2 Kings 5:9-19

The Grace of Doable Commands

Naaman, the commander of the Syrian army, is a leper who has come to Israel to seek healing from the prophet Elisha. He arrives in grand style, with an impressive entourage. "*So Naaman came with his horses and chariots and stood at the door of Elisha's house*"(2 Kings 5:9). Yet Elisha doesn't even come outside to talk with him! "*And Elisha sent a messenger to him, saying, 'Go and wash in the Jordan seven times, and your flesh shall be restored, and you shall be clean'*"(2 Kings 5:10). On top of the disrespect, Elisha's command seems to have nothing to do with Elisha at all. And why would seven times washing have some special healing power? All of this is decidedly odd.

Naaman is angry. "*Behold, I thought that he would surely come out to me and stand and call upon the name of the LORD his God, and wave his hand over the place and cure the leper. Are not Abana and Pharpar, the rivers of Damascus, better than all the waters of Israel? Could I not wash in them and be clean?*"(2 Kings 5:11-12). His servants work to convince him to wash in the Jordan anyway; what could it hurt? They ask him, "*My father, had* the prophet *told you* to *do some great thing, would* you not *have done* it? *How much more then, when* he *says* to you, 'Wash, and be clean'?"(2 Kings 5:13, NASB). The fact that the command is easy shouldn't discourage him! So Naaman obeys and is cleansed. He is so overjoyed that he praises Jehovah and makes plans to honor him in the future.

Naaman comes to Israel prepared to do whatever it takes to be clean, yet he is angry when the command seems so simple. Often we approach God's commands in a similar way. Whether we are discussing baptism, praying to relieve our anxiety, or the power of sacrifice in a marriage, we sometimes seek a more elaborate solution and disdain what is obvious. Naaman shows us that God gives us commands we can do—and attaches his healing power to them—as a gift to us. "*For this is the love of God, that we keep his commandments. And his commandments are not burdensome*"(1 John 5:3).

One Thing to Think About: When am I skeptical of God's simple solutions?

One Thing to Pray For: A passion to obey God—even when it seems simple

Reading: 2 Kings 17:7-23

The Grace of Warnings

The author is explaining why Jehovah has allowed the northern tribes of Israel to be carried into Assyrian captivity. *"And this occurred because the people of Israel had sinned against the LORD their God"*(2 Kings 17:7). Many of the sins are enumerated: fearing other gods, mimicking the Canaanite nations, doing secret evil, building pillars and Asherim. *"And they served idols, of which the LORD had said to them, 'You shall not do this'"*(2 Kings 17:12). No one can plead ignorance; this is simply rebellion.

This would be enough to justify God's drastic action, but there is more. *"Yet the LORD warned Israel and Judah by every prophet and every seer, saying, 'Turn from your evil ways and keep my commandments and my statutes'"*(2 Kings 17:13). He has already dramatically appeared to Israel, proven himself by miracles, saved them from slavery, and brought them into the promised land. He has explained his law clearly. Yet here he gives more grace, sending prophets and seers to remind the people about his message. *"But they would not listen, but were stubborn, as their fathers had been, who did not believe in the LORD their God"*(2 Kings 17:14). Instead, sadly, the warnings seem to only make their disobedience worse, leading even to human sacrifice to false gods. They followed Jeroboam's idolatry *"until the LORD removed Israel out of his sight, as he had spoken by all his servants the prophets"*(2 Kings 17:23). Though God was willing to pardon, there comes a point when the warnings must prove true and judgment must come.

Warning is a grace. A policeman could cite us, but instead warns us. A parent cautions a child that a continued behavior will bring consequences. Attempts at caution show a desire to help instead of punishing. When God warns, we may feel that he sounds threatening or intimidating, but in reality he is trying to pull us back from disaster. When we ignore his will—whether expressed through Scripture or people who repeat its warnings—we reject his grace.

One Thing to Think About: Why do I sometimes ignore warnings? Why do I sometimes think I know better?

One Thing to Pray For: A willingness to consider the possibility that I am wrong

WEEK 12—WEDNESDAY

Reading: 2 Kings 19:8-19, 32-36

Incline Your Ear

Assyria has taken Israel captive and is now threatening to destroy Jerusalem. It is a pivotal moment for the nation. The Rabshakeh, a high level Assyrian official, sends a message to Hezekiah: "*Do not let your God in whom you trust deceive you by promising that Jerusalem will not be given into the hand of the king of Assyria...Have the gods of the nations delivered them, the nations that my fathers destroyed, Gozan, Haran, Rezeph, and the people of Eden who were in Telassar?*"(2 Kings 19:10, 12). The message is intended to inspire fear in Hezekiah, reciting a list of the nations and gods Assyria has already defeated. It is an insult to God and his people.

King Hezekiah immediately takes the letter up to the temple, spreading the scroll out for God to read. Then he prays: "*Incline your ear, O LORD, and hear; open your eyes, O LORD, and see; and hear the words of Sennacherib, which he has sent to mock the living God*"(2 Kings 19:16). He wants God to take notice of the situation. Assyria is a truly terrifying power and they have destroyed other nations and false gods. "*So now, O LORD our God, save us, please, from his hand, that all the kingdoms of the earth may know that you, O LORD, are God alone*"(2 Kings 19:19). Hezekiah foresees the glory that will come to Jehovah if Judah resists the Assyrian invasion. Everyone will notice. God answers directly to Sennacherib: "*I will defend this city to save it, for my own sake and for the sake of my servant David*"(2 Kings 19:34). Hezekiah's courageous prayer saves his people.

Hezekiah asks God to "*incline your ear.*" The word means to lean over and listen closely. When our circumstances overwhelm us, we need to know that God is paying attention. We want him to lean in and hear the insults. We want him to open his eyes and see the unfairness. God shows grace here by paying attention to the plight of his people—and then rescuing them from it.

One Thing to Think About: Do I believe God sees and understands my hardships?

One Thing to Pray For: God to notice my needs

WEEK 12—THURSDAY

Reading: 2 Kings 20:1-11

I Have Seen Your Tears

King Hezekiah is already "*sick*" and "*at the point of death*"(2 Kings 20:1) when he gets bad news direct from God: "*Thus says the LORD, 'Set your house in order, for you shall die: you shall not recover*'"(2 Kings 20:1). He is devastated. Surely he thinks that Jehovah repelling the Assyrian army is merely the beginning of a much longer reign. "*Then Hezekiah turned his face to the wall and prayed to the LORD, saying, 'Now, O LORD, please remember how I have walked before you in faithfulness and with a whole heart, and have done what was good in your sight.' And Hezekiah wept bitterly*"(2 Kings 20:2-3). This is a tender scene: a true believer taking his broken heart to God. He asks for God to help and heal on the basis of his sincere attempts to do right. Why wouldn't God allow a faithful king to reign as long as possible?

Amazingly, God immediately changes his mind. Before the prophet Isaiah can leave the palace, Jehovah sends him back to reverse his pronouncement. "*I have heard your prayer; I have seen your tears. Behold, I will heal you...I will add fifteen years to your life. I will deliver you and this city out of the hand of the king of Assyria, and I will defend this city for my own sake and for my servant David's sake*"(2 Kings 20:5, 6). God listens to Hezekiah's prayer and sees his tears. Instead of allowing him to die, he will prolong his life and continue to bless him. God emphasizes his own role ("I have heard," "I have seen," "I will heal," "I will add," "I will deliver," "I will defend"). By granting this favor, God ensures that Hezekiah will always remember who is responsible for the time and blessings he enjoys.

"*I have heard your prayer; I have seen your tears.*" Our emotions, words, and concerns matter to God. He is touched by what touches us. He does not always answer our prayers by granting what we ask, but when he does, we can celebrate it as an amazing gift and give him the glory.

One Thing to Think About: How often has God given me what I asked for?

One Thing to Pray For: Gratitude for God's concern for me

Reading: 2 Kings 22:11-20

Grace for the Penitent Heart

As a young king, Josiah sets about the ambitious project of repairing the temple after decades of neglect and abuse. As the workmen fix the structures of the temple, the high priest discovers a book. The book is brought to Josiah and read aloud to him. "*When the king heard the words of the Book of the Law, he tore his clothes*"(2 Kings 22:11). He sends for the high priest to inquire of Jehovah about the matter "*for great is the wrath of the LORD that is kindled against us, because our fathers have not obeyed the words of this book, to do according to all that is written concerning us*"(2 Kings 22:13). Josiah is genuinely troubled and afraid. The years of neglect that have preceded him may be pointing the kingdom toward disaster.

When God is consulted, he confirms the threats in the book: "*Behold, I will bring disaster upon this place and upon its inhabitants, all the words of the book that the king of Judah has read*"(2 Kings 22:16). He will punish the evil and disobedience of the people. But that is not all. He singles out Josiah and his reaction to hearing this news: "*Regarding the words that you have heard, because your heart was penitent, and you humbled yourself before the LORD, when you heard how I spoke against this place and against its inhabitants, that they should become a desolation and a curse, and you have torn your clothes and wept before me, I also have heard you, declares the LORD*"(2 Kings 22:18-19). Jehovah promises not to bring the disaster in Josiah's lifetime as a mercy to him.

Josiah could have had many reactions to hearing the book of the Law. He might have viewed it as ancient history, irrelevant to his time. He might have dismissed it as unrealistic, since God does not always clearly and directly punish sin. He might have assumed that God would accept his efforts because his heart was right. Instead, Josiah is deeply upset by this violation of God's will and acknowledges his own part in it. He is sorry and ready to change, seeking God's forgiveness and hopeful that he will have mercy. When we take God's words seriously—and our sin seriously—and the plight of the world seriously—God seems more disposed to offer grace and mercy.

One Thing to Think About: Do I ever struggle to take God's word seriously?

One Thing to Pray For: An appropriate grief for the evil in the world—including myself

WEEK 13—MONDAY

Reading: 1 Chronicles 4:9-10

The Grace of Financial Help

This is a strange little aside in the midst of a list of the sons of Judah. Jabez is an otherwise unimportant man who is singled out for acclaim. We are told that "*Jabez was more honorable than his brothers*" (1 Chron 4:9), yet we are not told why. Instead, the author highlights that Jabez "*called upon the God of Israel*" (1 Chron 4:10) rather than resting on his own honor. He offers a spectacular prayer.

He asks that God "*would bless me and enlarge my border.*" These appear to be physical blessings. Jabez is asking for God to give him more territory and give him more material wealth. He also asks "*that your hand might be with me,*" acknowledging that such successes are only possible through the presence and intervention of God. Long ago, Joseph's master "*saw that the LORD was with him and that the LORD caused all that he did to succeed in his hands*" (Gen 39:3). Jabez asks for the same favor. Jabez then requests "*that you would keep me from harm so that it might not bring me pain!*" The word "harm" here is the word for "evil"; he is asking for God to help him do right so that he does not suffer from his own missteps. Perhaps he is thinking of his less honorable brothers, whom he sees struggling with the consequences of their own behavior. The next words are grace words: "*And God granted what he asked*" (1 Chron 4:10). Blessing, enlargement, God's hand, keeping him from harm—God approves every request.

It is tempting to take Jabez' story as a guarantee of God's desire to always give us financial blessings—and some have mistakenly done so. There are no guarantees here; it is all grace. It is a mistake to assume that following Jesus will enrich us. The first disciples and the early church dispel any such notion. Yet when we are in financial need, we *should* seek God. When we have success, we *should* glorify him and attribute it to him. When we live peaceful, joyful lives because we have learned from him the best way to live, we *should* thank him. God sustains us with financial help, along with every good and perfect gift, from the rich stores of his grace.

One Thing to Think About: How has God helped me survive financially up to this point?

One Thing to Pray For: The proper balance to acknowledge God's good gifts without assuming them

WEEK 13—TUESDAY

Reading: 2 Chronicles 14:9-15

We Rely on You

King Asa of Judah has a large army—about 580,000 total (2 Chron 14:8)—but it is a fraction of what the Ethiopians bring against him. "*Zerah the Ethiopian came out against them with an army of a million men and 300 chariots*"(2 Chron 14:9). It seems that when the two armies line up against each other, the disparity overwhelms Asa. "*And Asa went out to meet him, and they drew up their lines of battle in the Valley of Zephathah at Mareshah*"(2 Chron 14:10). It is one thing to hear about a difference in numbers; it is quite another to see 400,000 extra men ready to attack you.

In such a desperate circumstance, Asa reaches out to Jehovah. "*And Asa cried to the LORD his God, 'O LORD, there is none like you to help, between the mighty and the weak. Help us, O LORD our God, for we rely on you, and in your name we have come against this multitude. O LORD, you are our God; let not man prevail against you*'"(2 Chron 14:11). Asa looks to Jehovah as a source of grace. Jehovah is a helper ("*there is none like you to help*"). He defends the weak and is their only hope. But especially is Jehovah disposed to help those who rely on him rather than themselves or their human allies. It is no surprise, then, that Jehovah does help, routing the Ethiopians and giving victory to Asa.

Asa teaches us to think of God as a helper of the weak. Rather than relying on own strength and wisdom to solve problems, help others, or overcome personal flaws, he wants us to rely on him. He clearly looks favorably on those who acknowledge their dependence and seek his help. There is grace for the overlooked, the outnumbered, the overmatched, the incompetent, and the insecure.

One Thing to Think About: In what areas of my life do I hesitate to rely on God?

One Thing to Pray For: A consistent willingness to come to God with the pressing problems I experience

WEEK 13—WEDNESDAY

Reading: 2 Chronicles 20:1-12, 20-23

We Are Powerless

Much like his father Asa, Jehoshaphat faces an enormous enemy. Three nations are banded together to attack Judah. "*Then Jehoshaphat was afraid and set his face to seek the LORD, and proclaimed a fast throughout all Judah. And Judah assembled to seek help from the LORD; from all the cities of Judah they came to seek the LORD*"(2 Chron 20:3-4). Jehoshaphat is afraid (that is natural), yet he determines to seek Jehovah in his fear. He also declares a fast and leads the people to devote themselves to plead with God for blessing in these dire straits.

Then King Jehoshaphat stands before the people in the temple and prays: "*You rule over all the kingdoms of the nations. In your hand are power and might, so that none is able to withstand you*"(2 Chron 20:6). He praises God's greatness and recounts how God has given his people this land that he had promised. God has even blessed this temple in which Jehoshaphat stands, promising to hear prayers offered here (2 Chron 20:9). Now there is an unjust threat from evil men. "*O our God, will you not execute judgment on them? For we are powerless against this great horde that is coming against us. We do not know what to do, but our eyes are on you*"(2 Chron 20:12). Jehoshaphat utters words that would surely get him voted out of office in modern America: we are powerless and we do not know what to do. Yet in reaching out to God, he finds a greater power and wisdom. Jehovah turns the enemy nations against one another and the threat comes to nothing.

Jehoshaphat gives us a tremendous example here. He takes his fear to God in prayer and fasting. He shows us a brilliant model for prayer: telling God why he should help. This is not about Jehoshaphat wanting favors for his own enjoyment. Instead, it is about God's faithfulness to his promises, evil people attacking good people, and God helping the powerless. God shows grace to advance his cause.

One Thing to Think About: Why might it be important to tell God why he should help me?

One Thing to Pray For: Acceptance of my weakness and powerlessness

WEEK 13—THURSDAY

Reading: 2 Chronicles 30:1-9

Yield Yourselves to Jehovah

Upon becoming king, Hezekiah begins to undo the evil of his father Ahaz. He rallies the Levites to cleanse the temple and rid it of idols. He brings proper sacrifices to the temple. He determines that they should keep the Passover, even though it is the wrong month, in an effort to harness this newfound zeal for worship of Jehovah. Surprisingly, he even includes the northern tribes—which have mostly been taken into Assyrian exile—in the invitation to come keep the feast. "*So they decreed to make a proclamation throughout all Israel, from Beersheba to Dan, that the people should come and keep the Passover to the LORD, the God of Israel, at Jerusalem, for they had not kept it as often as prescribed*"(2 Chron 30:5). He specifically invites Israel to return to God, "*that he may turn again to the remnant of you who have escaped from the hand of the kings of Assyria*"(2 Chron 30:6). They have seen firsthand the damage caused by abandoning Jehovah.

Especially does Hezekiah urge them to have a different spirit than previous generations, whose intransigence led to their captivity. "*Do not now be stiff-necked as your fathers were, but yield yourselves to the LORD and come to his sanctuary, which he has consecrated forever, and serve the LORD your God, that his fierce anger may turn away from you*"(2 Chron 30:8). He holds out hope that Jehovah will suspend his anger if they will stop stubbornly fighting him. Why? "*For if you return to the LORD, your brothers and your children will find compassion with their captors and return to this land. For the LORD your God is gracious and merciful and will not turn away his face from you, if you return to him*"(2 Chron 30:9). Notice that he insists that God "*will not turn away his face from you, if you return to him.*" Hezekiah is counting on God's grace

When bad things happen to us—like the northern tribes who have suffered through a violent invasion—we usually either draw closer to God or run further from him. Hezekiah invites Israel to come closer, abandoning their stubborn willfulness and submitting to God's good will. No matter how far we have strayed, how long we have stayed away, or how hard the journey back, God has always been gracious to those who yield themselves to him.

One Thing to Think About: Why do we sometimes think God will not have us back after we wander from him?

One Thing to Pray For: A heart that yields to God's will

Reading: 2 Chronicles 30:13-22

Jehovah Healed the People

Hezekiah is renewing the people's devotion to Jehovah by removing idols and restoring proper worship. He has invited some of the remnants of the northern tribes of Israel to join Judah in a special observance of the Passover "*for they had not kept it as often as prescribed*"(2 Chron 30:5). Some of them come. There are several problems with this observance. It occurs in the second month instead of the first (2 Chron 30:13, Ex 12:18). There are altars and places for incense to idols throughout Jerusalem which must be removed (2 Chron 30:14). Some of the priests and Levites appear unprepared for the observance: "*And the priests and the Levites were ashamed, so that they consecrated themselves and brought burnt offerings into the house of the LORD*"(2 Chron 30:15). Embarrassed at the zeal of their countrymen, they resume their rightful place.

But the presence of Jews from the northern tribes adds another complication: "*For a majority of the people, many of them from Ephraim, Manasseh, Issachar, and Zebulun, had not cleansed themselves, yet they ate the Passover otherwise than as prescribed*"(2 Chron 30:18). The Passover law stresses purity (Num 9:10-14), but these men are unclean. The priests and Levites step in to kill the lamb for them (2 Chron 30:17) and Hezekiah prays for them. "*May the good LORD pardon everyone who sets his heart to seek God, the LORD, the God of his fathers, even though not according to the sanctuary's rules of cleanness*"(2 Chron 30:18-19). Hezekiah trusts that a good God will see the righteous intent and overlook the violation. "*And the LORD heard Hezekiah and healed the people*"(2 Chron 30:20). God gives grace.

Hezekiah's prayer—and Jehovah's response of healing—echoes God's answer to Solomon: "*If my people who are called by my name humble themselves, and pray and seek my face and turn from their wicked ways, then I will hear from heaven and will forgive their sin and heal their land*"(2 Chron 7:14). God heals those who seek him. Here Hezekiah is fanning the flame of revival and reunion. Things aren't perfect—not from deliberate oversight, but because the people are just now attempting to seek him. Yet God is gracious. The lesson here is not that God is fine with us ignoring his law, but that he is gracious when we turn to him in sincerity and repentance.

One Thing to Think About: Am I truly seeking God?

One Thing to Pray For: God's healing for times when my service is imperfect

WEEK 14—MONDAY

Reading: Ezra 1:1-11

The Grace of a Stirred Spirit

Judah has been in Babylonian captivity for 70 years (2 Chron 36:21), but now the kingdom has fallen into Persian hands. Immediately the new Persian king changes the fate of the Jews. "*In the first year of Cyrus king of Persia, that the word of the LORD by the mouth of Jeremiah might be fulfilled, the LORD stirred up the spirit of Cyrus king of Persia, so that he made a proclamation throughout all his kingdom and also put it in writing*"(Ezra 1:1). The author makes clear that *Jehovah* stirs up Cyrus' spirit to do this. Cyrus declares that Jehovah has "*charged me to build him a house at Jerusalem*" and invites all the willing Jews to go with his blessing to join the project (Ezra 1:2, 3-4). The stirring of Cyrus' spirit is good news for God's people.

Many of the people respond. "*Then rose up the heads of the fathers' houses of Judah and Benjamin, and the priests and Levites, everyone whose spirit God had stirred to go up to rebuild the house of the LORD that is in Jerusalem*"(Ezra 1:5). Now God stirs the *people's* spirits, filling them with the desire to travel back home and start the restoration of the land and temple. They will need this zeal for the difficult days ahead of them.

It is intriguing that Jehovah stirs up Cyrus' spirit and the Jews' spirit so that his will is accomplished. This does not necessarily mean that God plants this idea in people's heads (although I would not rule that out). It could be that Cyrus feels that it is a better policy to court the favor of lots of different gods—or that his kingdom has far too many displaced foreigners. Yet God can move in such considerations to fulfill his promises and bless his people. Meanwhile, when his people hear the good news of freedom, they surely see God at work. When God gives us passion for a new project or new direction, it is a gift—and it may even be a way he accomplishes his grander purposes.

One Thing to Think About: Has God ever stirred my spirit? What might that mean for me?

One Thing to Pray For: Motivation—a stirred spirit—to do the good work God has given me

WEEK 14—TUESDAY

Reading: Ezra 6:13-22

Jehovah Made Them Joyful

As the Jewish exiles return to their homeland under orders to rebuild the temple, they are quickly discouraged by the people living in the land. These adversaries oppose their building, bribe people to interrupt it, and send letters to the king to get them in trouble. Yet all these efforts backfire. Haggai and Zechariah prophesy, encouraging the Jews that God is with them in their building. The letter to Darius is answered with vigorous support of the project, to the shame of their enemies. The work prospers, but not because of the Jews. "*They finished their building by decree of the God of Israel and by decree of Cyrus and Darius and Artaxerxes king of Persia*" (Ezra 6:14).

Once complete, the people "*celebrated the dedication of this house of God with joy*" (Ezra 6:16). They observe the Passover again at the proper time and in Jehovah's temple. "*And they kept the Feast of Unleavened Bread seven days with joy, for the LORD had made them joyful and had turned the heart of the king of Assyria to them, so that he aided them in the work of the house of God, the God of Israel*" (Ezra 6:22). The people have joy again. They are back home and things are set aright again. Yet Jehovah is responsible for this, though his hand is unseen. He has given them favor in sight of the king and helped them complete the temple. The people rejoice, but their joy is *his* doing.

Joy is a gift from God. Paul says that God satisfies us "*with food and gladness*" (Acts 14:17). The little things that delight us, the felicitous turn of circumstances, and the accomplishment of major goals are all gifts from him. When we enjoy our joy, we have someone to thank.

One Thing to Think About: What kinds of joy has God put into my life?

One Thing to Pray For: A heart to celebrate the joys God has given me

WEEK 14—WEDNESDAY

Reading: Nehemiah 2:1-8

The Good Hand of My God Was Upon Me

Nehemiah is cupbearer to the Persian king, an influential position akin to a cabinet post. He has recently received a report that conditions back in Israel have deteriorated since the rebuilding of the temple. Through intense prayer, he has decided that he will attempt to use his position to help his countrymen. As he takes the wine to the king, Artaxerxes notices that he is sad and asks him why. "*I said to the king, 'Let the king live forever! Why should not my face be sad, when the city, the place of my fathers' graves, lies in ruins, and its gates have been destroyed by fire?*'"(Neh 2:3). Nehemiah lets his anguish come out, expressing his dismay that Jerusalem is an undefended wreck. This leads the king to ask the fateful question, "*What are you requesting?*"(Neh 2:4).

Before answering directly, Nehemiah prays again (Neh 2:4), then makes his pitch. "*If it pleases the king, and if your servant has found favor in your sight, that you send me to Judah, the city of my fathers' graves, that I may rebuild it*"(Neh 2:5). Nehemiah is himself volunteering for the job. The king asks for specifics of the timing of the plan and anticipated costs. Nehemiah has done his homework and has ready answers. "*And the king granted me what I asked, for the good hand of my God was upon me*"(Neh 2:8). This interview goes extremely well—Nehemiah receives all he requests—and the reason is that "*the good hand of my God was upon me.*"

Nehemiah is convinced that God is at work in his conversation with the king. He prays before and during the meeting. He does his own work—planning the trip, doing his job well before now—but in the moment of truth, he seeks God's help. God shows his grace by being active in ordinary conversations, everyday plans, and our regular work. Looking back when the task is accomplished, Nehemiah can only conclude that *his* part is far less than *God's*. All of this is possible because God's good hand is on him.

One Thing to Think About: What kinds of conversations, projects, and relationships is God working through in my life right now?

One Thing to Pray For: God to direct my plans and steps toward his purposes

WEEK 14—THURSDAY

Reading: Nehemiah 6:1-16

With the Help of Our God

Nehemiah has leveraged his position as cupbearer to convince the king to finance his trip to Jerusalem to rebuild the walls. What might sound like a simple construction project proves anything but. He must rally the dispirited people and resist armed enemies. Here the leaders of the opposition in the land invite him to a secret meeting. "*But they intended to do me harm*"(Neh 6:2). So Nehemiah refuses, but the opponents threaten to falsely accuse him to the king. "*For they all wanted to frighten us, thinking, 'Their hands will drop from the work, and it will not be done.' But now, O God, strengthen my hands*"(Neh 6:9). The battle here is to continue to trust in God's provision and refuse to act out of fear.

After another threat to Nehemiah's life, the walls are finally complete. "*So the wall was finished on the twenty-fifth day of the month Elul, in fifty-two days. And when all our enemies heard of it, all the nations around us were afraid and fell greatly in their own esteem, for they perceived that this work had been accomplished with the help of our God*"(Neh 6:15-16). Completing the project in 52 days—about 7 weeks—is amazing, particularly when considering the atmosphere in Jerusalem. It is far beyond the power of any one man, no matter how charismatic. Even the godless people around them understand that something special has happened—"*they perceived that this work had been accomplished with the help of our God.*"

God can help us in ways that are not miraculous. He changes people's opinions, brings plots to nothing, defuses enemy efforts, grants wisdom to his people, and answers prayers for strength. In some ways this work is dependent on the people's commitment and work, but they cannot honestly say that they did it all. Even their enemies understand that this happened "*with the help of our God.*"

One Thing to Think About: How has God blessed me in non-miraculous ways? What have I been able to accomplish with the help of my God?

One Thing to Pray For: "But now, O God, strengthen my hands"

WEEK 14—FRIDAY

Reading: Job 42:10-17

The Grace of Restored Fortunes

At the behest of Satan, Job has endured tremendous, unspeakable loss. His children are killed, his possessions stolen, his health ruined, and his wife is turned against him. Much of the book speaks to Job and his friends wrestling with whether God is punishing Job for his sins. Finally, after Jehovah appears in the whirlwind, Job repents of his desire to settle accounts with God (Job 42:1-6). Job prays for God to pardon his friends and "*the LORD accepted Job's prayer*" (Job 42:9).

Now comes the staggering grace: "*And the LORD restored the fortunes of Job, when he had prayed for his friends. And the LORD gave Job twice as much as he had before*" (Job 42:10). Some of this is literal—Job has twice as many sheep, camels, oxen, donkeys as before the disasters (Job 42:12, 1:2). Now his "*brothers and sisters*" come to eat with him—where he was left alone before (Job 42:11). He also has seven more sons and three more daughters, just as before (Job 42:13) Job is allowed to see his kids to the fourth generation before his own death.

Job's story is sad and challenging, but that may not be the primary message of the book. James has a different take: "*You have heard of the steadfastness of Job, and you have seen the purpose of the Lord, how the Lord is compassionate and merciful*" (James 5:11). James sees grace in Job's story. God engages with Job, speaking to him then directly blessing him. Children cannot be replaced. Tragedy cannot be undone. Scars do not heal over. Yet God has grace on Job, determining the limits of his suffering. Hardship is not the end of blessing. There is room for more blessing even after we suffer—and often blessing *through* suffering. Whatever our suffering and trouble, we can take confidence in the fact that "*the Lord is compassionate and merciful.*"

One Thing to Think About: How has God helped me even through my suffering?

One Thing to Pray For: Eyes to see God's grace when I am hurting

Reading: Psalm 8:1-9

The Grace of God's Mindfulness

This psalm is the fruit of David going outside to observe the night sky. It leaves him praising God. "*O LORD, our Lord, how majestic is your name in all the earth! You have set your glory above the heavens*"(Psalm 8:1). Jehovah's greatness is seen in the heavens and the earth—creation itself. But the majesty he sees there produces a burning question in David: "*When I look at your heavens, the work of your fingers, the moon and the stars, which you have set in place, what is man that you are mindful of him, and the son of man that you care for him?*"(Psalm 8:3-4). In the face of the heavenly bodies and the marvels of nature, man is weak, small, and rebellious. How could it be that God cares so much for man?

Yet the story of man on earth is the story of undeserved glory—grace. "*Yet you have made him a little lower than the heavenly beings and crowned him with glory and honor. You have given him dominion over the works of your hands; you have put all things under his feet, all sheep and oxen, and also the beasts of the field*"(Psalm 8:5-7). Despite our smallness, Jehovah has given mankind dominion over the animal world. He has made us "*a little lower than the heavenly beings*"—either angels or God, depending on translation—and given glory and honor. Man's status is not deserved, but God-given. He has *made us* a little lower, he has *crowned us*, he has *given us* dominion, he has *put all things* under our feet. Shaking his head, David returns to praise: "*O LORD, our Lord, how majestic is your name in all the earth!*"(Psalm 8:9).

The vastness of space reveals the insignificance of man, yet for David it does more. It boggles his mind to think that God would be mindful of such an unimportant and undeserving creature. "*What is man that you are mindful of him, and the son of man that you care for him?*" It is grace that God is willing to interact with us, provide for us, and give us glory, honor, and dominion. It is grace that makes us the conscious, self-aware, curious, needy, frustrating, loving, hopeful and powerful people we are.

One Thing to Think About: How might this psalm lead me toward humility?

One Thing to Pray For: Wisdom to be a better steward of what God has put under my feet

WEEK 15—TUESDAY

Reading: Psalm 16:1-11

The Grace of Security

Although this psalm begins with a cry for help, it quickly shifts into a praise for the goodness David has experienced from God. "*Preserve me, O God, for in you I take refuge. I say to the LORD, 'You are my Lord; I have no good apart from you'*"(Psalm 16:1-2). All the positives in his life he readily attributes to Jehovah ("*I have no good apart from you*"). Some of this has to do with physical blessings. "*The LORD is my chosen portion and my cup; you hold my lot. The lines have fallen for me in pleasant places; indeed, I have a beautiful inheritance*"(Psalm 16:5-6). This speaks of the tribal lands divided to Israel; David sees his family and its possessions as a gift from God.

There is more. "*I bless the LORD who gives me counsel; in the night also my heart instructs me*"(Psalm 16:7). Jehovah is the source of wisdom and advice. He is "*at my right hand*" and "*always before me*"(Psalm 16:8). The recipient of all these blessings cannot help but feel secure. "*Therefore my heart is glad, and my whole being rejoices; my flesh also dwells secure. For you will not abandon my soul to Sheol, or let your holy one see corruption*"(Psalm 16:9-10). David is confident that Jehovah will continue to bless him and not let his enemies win. Even in this statement of faith, there is far more than even David knows, since the resurrection of Jesus is involved in this divine protection (Acts 2:25-32). David remains certain that "*in your presence there is fullness of joy; at your right hand are pleasures forevermore*"(Psalm 16:11). It is good to follow God.

David's words well summarize the notion of a "relationship" with God. He sees God as responsible for all his good, including his own physical blessings. God grants wisdom. God gives joy and pleasure. So when danger comes, it is natural that David is confident that "*my flesh also dwells secure.*" This is not an invitation to expose ourselves to danger; rather, David knows that God can be trusted to watch over his people until the end he has decided for them. God—not enemies—will have the last word. We can rest secure in his will.

One Thing to Think About: Is my relationship with God like David's? Why or why not?

One Thing to Pray For: Security in the will of God

WEEK 15—WEDNESDAY

Reading: Psalm 19:1-11

The Grace of Law

David combines evidence from two vastly different arenas to praise Jehovah. First (as in Psalm 8), there is an extensive poetic description of the heavenly bodies. "*The heavens declare the glory of God, and the sky above proclaims his handiwork*"(Psalm 19:1). David pictures the sun, moon, and stars as speaking aloud all over the earth (Psalm 19:2-4), praising Jehovah and teaching about his power. Then the sun rises, speaking the same words with greater intensity through its heat (Psalm 19:5-6).

At this point, David switches topics completely. "*The law of the LORD is perfect, reviving the soul; the testimony of the LORD is sure, making wise the simple; the precepts of the LORD are right, rejoicing the heart; the commandment of the LORD is pure, enlightening the eyes; the fear of the LORD is clean, enduring forever; the rules of the LORD are true, and righteous altogether*"(Psalm 19:7-9). From nature we turn to Jehovah's law. David stresses the tremendous benefits of God revealing his will in law. It revives the soul, makes foolish people wise, causes hearts to rejoice, and teaches us truth and righteousness. Without law, we grope in the dark, wondering what is true and good. When God says that certain things are off-limits, he gives order to our lives and thinking. When he praises certain things, he gives direction for our desire to do right. Law is a gift.

It is easy for Christians to allow our thinking about law to be colored by the debates over the Law of Moses and grace in the New Testament. Broadly speaking, we need law and thrive under it. Knowledge of God's ways is essential to understanding our world and ourselves. God does not have to reveal right and wrong to us; he could judge us despite our ignorance. Law is a sign that God cares enough to teach and help us. While we are not saved by perfect obedience to a law, it does not change the fact that even law is a gift from God.

One Thing to Think About: Do I think of the Bible—even the parts about law—as a gift from God?

One Thing to Pray For: Willingness to listen to God's voice—in both nature and his word

WEEK 15—THURSDAY

Reading: Psalm 23:1-6

Jehovah Is My Shepherd

David meditates on his relationship with Jehovah by comparing it to his extensive experience as a shepherd. "*The LORD is my shepherd; I shall not want*"(Psalm 23:1). Jehovah is the shepherd while David is the sheep. David sees the relationship as almost purely one-sided; God does all the giving. "*He makes me lie down in green pastures. He leads me beside still waters. He restores my soul. He leads me in paths of righteousness for his name's sake*"(Psalm 23:2-3). Green pastures are full of fresh grass, not dried out or picked over. Still waters are safe for drinking without fear. Jehovah's leading provides all of David's needs and speaks to a tenderness and care that reassures him.

A shepherd does not just give food and water. "*Even though I walk through the valley of the shadow of death, I will fear no evil, for you are with me; your rod and your staff, they comfort me*"(Psalm 23:4). Shepherds are also protectors because sheep have no defensive attributes or instincts. Yet David is secure because Jehovah's "*rod*" and "*staff*" are signs that he will defend his people, even in the presence of the shadow of death itself. Breaking with the shepherd/sheep image, he also praises Jehovah for honoring him over his enemies (Psalm 23:5). "*Surely goodness and mercy shall follow me all the days of my life, and I shall dwell in the house of the LORD forever*"(Psalm 23:6). Why? Jehovah is my shepherd.

This psalm is one of the best-known and most influential poems in history. It shifts the picture from a sovereign God commanding obedience to a humble shepherd watching over his sheep. The metaphor highlights God's grace—giving us spiritual and physical sustenance, leading us toward good things, protecting us from dangers, vindicating our cause, and giving us confidence to face hardship. God does not stand aloof from us, but is in the pasture, walking alongside us to lead us toward good.

One Thing to Think About: Why do I sometimes hesitate to follow God? How does this picture help me overcome that?

One Thing to Pray For: "I will fear no evil, for you are with me"

WEEK 15—FRIDAY

Reading: Psalm 25:1-12

Teach Me Your Paths

David is in distress. "*To you, O LORD, I lift up my soul. O my God, in you I trust; let me not be put to shame; let not my enemies exult over me*"(Psalm 25:1-2). Yet what sounds like a common psalm crying out for God's help takes an interesting turn. In his turmoil, David wants to *learn*. "*Make me to know your ways, O LORD; teach me your paths. Lead me in your truth and teach me, for you are the God of my salvation; for you I wait all the day long*"(Psalm 25:4-5). David doesn't just want to win over his enemies; he wants to be on God's team. This will require instruction in God's truth and will. David recommits his life to seeking God's will. He needs more than help in this crisis. He needs to know—and walk in—God's ways.

He asks for Jehovah to not remember the sins of his past (Psalm 25:7) and is confident that he will instead remember his mercy (Psalm 25:6). "*Good and upright is the LORD; therefore he instructs sinners in the way. He leads the humble in what is right, and teaches the humble his way. All the paths of the LORD are steadfast love and faithfulness, for those who keep his covenant and his testimonies*"(Psalm 25:8-10). Out of God's goodness comes his instruction. Jehovah's way blesses his people now and also promises future blessings (such as salvation from distress). Yet learning from him requires a submissive posture: "*he leads the humble in what is right, and teaches the humble his way.*" He is willing to teach, but we must be willing to learn.

We often relegate learning to childhood. Adults are (usually) no longer in school. We are no longer preparing for life, but living it. Yet David advocates a different spirit: the eager learner of God's ways. He wants to know God's will because he knows and trusts God, because God's ways are good, and because he wants to do his part in their relationship. He is not a novice, but he continues to be a learner. There is never a time when we cannot pray "*teach me your paths.*"

One Thing to Think About: What do I still need to learn?

One Thing to Pray For: "Teach me your paths"

WEEK 16—MONDAY

Reading: Psalm 30:1-12

Mourning into Dancing

This psalm is the relieved smile of the desperate man who has been saved at the last moment. "*O LORD my God, I cried to you for help, and you have healed me. O LORD, you have brought up my soul from Sheol; you restored me to life from among those who go down to the pit*"(Psalm 30:2-3). We don't know the specifics of David's distress—there are certainly many candidates for such a setting throughout his life—but Jehovah has saved him. He praises God "*for his anger is but for a moment, and his favor is for a lifetime. Weeping may tarry for the night, but joy comes with the morning*"(Psalm 30:5). Just like the sun rising, David's dark cloud of anxiety and despair has lifted. Looking back, he sees how most of his life is full of the rich blessings of God's favor, while times of distress are "*for a moment.*"

David then retells his mental state through the crisis. "*As for me, I said in my prosperity, 'I shall never be moved'*"(Psalm 30:6). This confidence was misplaced. When Jehovah hid his face, "*I was dismayed*"(Psalm 30:7). So he cries out to God, pleading with him to save him from death (Psalm 30:8-10). "*You have turned for me my mourning into dancing; you have loosed my sackcloth and clothed me with gladness, that my glory may sing your praise and not be silent. O LORD my God, I will give thanks to you forever!*"(Psalm 30:11-12). David no longer mourns his life. He takes off his "sackcloth." He is saved.

There are tragedies in life. We are never assured that God will spare us from such things; that's a promise he hasn't made. Yet it is a common experience for us to fear the worst, to despair, and to brace for catastrophe—and then be spared from it. Without assuming this is our right, it is important for God's people to acknowledge that it is *God* who has turned our mourning into dancing. He has saved, reversed the course of the situation, answered our cries, and in some way acted for our good. When we dance, we must also praise!

One Thing to Think About: How has God turned my mourning into dancing?

One Thing to Pray For: Help for me not to trust in my prosperity

WEEK 16—TUESDAY

Reading: Psalm 32:1-11

The Grace of Forgiveness

David is happy. He is singing the sweet song of relief from a long-held burden. "*Blessed is the one whose transgression is forgiven, whose sin is covered. Blessed is the man against whom the LORD does not count iniquity, and in whose spirit there is no deceit*"(Psalm 32:1-2). David has lived with his sin for some time and now expresses joy at having it forgiven, covered, uncounted. He also implies that carrying the weight of guilt has affected him deeply. Sin causes us to lie to ourselves and others about how we really are, but the forgiven man is one "*in whose spirit there is no deceit.*"

As he thinks back over the torment sin has brought him, he uses physical terms. "*For when I kept silent, my bones wasted away through my groaning all day long. For day and night your hand was heavy upon me; my strength was dried up as by the heat of summer*"(Psalm 32:3-4). Trying to move forward carrying guilt brought intense pain; only when he relents and confesses is David set free. He confesses and God forgives (Psalm 32:5). When we are in denial about sin, we are stubborn. We justify ourselves, minimize the problem, and attack others. God speaks: "*Be not like a horse or a mule, without understanding, which must be curbed with bit and bridle, or it will not stay near you*"(Psalm 32:9). From David's experience, God wants his people to learn not to be stubborn, but to trust God's good will—even if it means confessing and seeking his forgiveness.

Christians sing with David the song of the forgiven. We know how heavy the burden of sin can be, but we have come, weary and heavy-laden, to Jesus. We have laid bare our hearts, weaknesses, and pasts to him (and to our brothers and sisters). We have found the humiliation of confession easier and more liberating than the pride of secrecy. Now we praise the God who has graciously forgiven us: "*Blessed is the one whose transgression is forgiven, whose sin is covered.*"

One Thing to Think About: What do I need forgiveness for?

One Thing to Pray For: Courage to confess my sin to God and others

WEEK 16—WEDNESDAY

Reading: Psalm 34:1-22

Taste and See that Jehovah is Good

The heading of this psalm tells us that David writes it after having to pretend insanity in the court of Abimelech, while on the run from Saul. This is a desperate, confusing moment, yet David sees his survival as an act of Jehovah. This song is the giddy aftermath of the narrow escape. "*I will bless the LORD at all times; his praise shall continually be in my mouth*"(Psalm 34:1). Though David's quick thinking helped, he wants to thank God for *his* help. "*I sought the LORD, and he answered me and delivered me from all my fears... This poor man cried, and the LORD heard him and saved him out of all his troubles*"(Psalm 34:4, 6). David's "*troubles*" and "*fears*"—though serious and real—are no match for Jehovah.

But David does more than celebrate. He is an evangelist for Jehovah now, urging those who hear him to trust God too. "*Oh, taste and see that the LORD is good! Blessed is the man who takes refuge in him! Oh, fear the LORD, you his saints, for those who fear him have no lack! The young lions suffer want and hunger; but those who seek the LORD lack no good thing*"(Psalm 34:8-10). "*Taste and see*" is an invitation to others to try God out. Like an excited diner wanting to share food with a friend, David encourages others to trust him and see what happens. This confidence rests in God's grace—that he is "*good*" and that his servants "*lack no good thing*." David proceeds to teach his hearers to honor God's law (Psalm 34:12-17) so that they can experience God's goodness when in need, as he has.

David's words stress the movement from a clinical book-knowledge of God to a real-life heart-knowledge of him. There is a difference in knowing a lot about God and trusting him when our lives are on the line. Yet when our trust is rewarded and we receive blessings from God, our spiritual life is often rejuvenated. We know the goodness of the Lord—and we invite others to know it too.

One Thing to Think About: How have I experienced the goodness of God?

One Thing to Pray For: A deeper, more vibrant, more sincere trust in God

WEEK 16—THURSDAY

Reading: Psalm 40:1-11

The Grace of a New Song

Unlike the clear reference in the heading of Psalm 34, it is not clear what crisis David is singing about here. What is clear is that he is on the happy side of God's salvation. "*I waited patiently for the LORD; he inclined to me and heard my cry. He drew me up from the pit of destruction, out of the miry bog, and set my feet upon a rock, making my steps secure*"(Psalm 40:1-2). He likens his desperate circumstances to sinking in muddy water, yet rejoices that God has lifted him out. "*He put a new song in my mouth, a song of praise to our God. Many will see and fear, and put their trust in the LORD*"(Psalm 40:3). Instead of the song of lament and need, David has a new song to sing. His relationship with God has a new verse—one that praises God for his grace in overwhelming situations.

Having received God's grace in this way, David is determined not to be quiet about it. "*You have multiplied, O LORD my God, your wondrous deeds and your thoughts toward us; none can compare with you! I will proclaim and tell of them, yet they are more than can be told*"(Psalm 40:5). Or again, "*I have told the glad news of deliverance in the great congregation; behold, I have not restrained my lips, as you know, O LORD. I have not hidden your deliverance within my heart; I have spoken of your faithfulness and your salvation; I have not concealed your steadfast love and your faithfulness from the great congregation*"(Psalm 40:9-10). When God blesses, David feels the personal burden to *tell others* what God has done. This is not a new song for David alone; it will lead others to praise—and perhaps trust God themselves.

"*He put a new song in my mouth.*" God keeps writing new songs in our lives. These experiences do not rival Scripture; they *confirm* Scripture. They help us see the reality of God in everyday life. They give us a fresh remembrance of his goodness. They encourage us as we walk in his ways. They drive us to trust. They help us to encourage others.

One Thing to Think About: What new songs has God given me lately?

One Thing to Pray For: Willingness to tell others what God is doing for me

Reading: Psalm 51:1-10

The Grace of a Clean Heart

David has committed adultery with Bathsheba, then attempted to cover up his sin by framing and then murdering her husband. After a chilling rebuke from the prophet Nathan, David now sees himself rightly and mourns his sin. This psalm is the fruit of his sorrow. He pleads with God to forgive him. "*Have mercy on me, O God, according to your steadfast love; according to your abundant mercy blot out my transgressions*"(Psalm 51:1). There is no reference to David's goodness, only God's mercy and steadfast love. David has acted shamefully, hurt others, shown a horrible example, and brought reproach on God's name. He is in need.

The predominant image in this section is cleanness. "*Wash me thoroughly from my iniquity, and cleanse me from my sin!*"(Psalm 51:2). David feels dirty. He needs washing, but washing the body won't help with his problem. He needs God's cleansing. "*Purge me with hyssop, and I shall be clean; wash me, and I shall be whiter than snow*"(Psalm 51:7). Jews are familiar with the ceremonial washings for ritual cleanness. David knows what it is to be defiled. Yet David instinctively sees these measures as insufficient to remove what he has done. "*Create in me a clean heart, O God, and renew a right spirit within me*"(Psalm 51:10). David seeks inner cleansing—a completely new creation within him. David asks to be remade, pure and whole.

When we sin, we seek cleansing. We take baths, but they don't wash away our guilt. We change our clothes or appearance, but we can't change our hearts. We leave town, but we can't leave behind the awareness of what we've done (Psalm 51:3). The good news is that God is willing to create in us clean hearts. God loves us enough to wash us clean, make us new, and give us a fresh start. As Christians, we experience this blessing in a special way because of the work of Jesus and the Spirit. Yet none of this is because we deserve it—like David, we are sinners, not righteous. Clean hearts are a gift of grace.

One Thing to Think About: How have I tried to cope with my sin without involving God? How successful was I?

One Thing to Pray For: "Create in me a clean heart, O God"

WEEK 17—MONDAY

Reading: Psalm 51:11-19

Jehovah Accepts Broken Spirits

David continues his prayer for forgiveness after his affair with Bathsheba. He laments that he feels distant from God, as if he has forfeited the privileges of his relationship. "*Cast me not away from your presence, and take not your Holy Spirit from me. Restore to me the joy of your salvation, and uphold me with a willing spirit*"(Psalm 51:11-12). As David wakes up from his stupor, he looks around and discovers how far he has fallen. If God pardons, he pledges to honor God. He will "*teach transgressors your ways*" and "*sing aloud of your righteousness*" and "*declare your praise*"(Psalm 51:13, 14, 15). David's story will serve as an encouragement to all kinds of sinners and seekers.

Finally David comes to the crux of his prayer: he knows that his sacrifices won't remove the guilt of this sin. "*For you will not delight in sacrifice, or I would give it; you will not be pleased with a burnt offering. The sacrifices of God are a broken spirit; a broken and contrite heart, O God, you will not despise*"(Psalm 51:16-17). Jehovah does not simply want more animals to die. Sacrifices don't address the real problem: the rebellious heart. What God wants is a heart truly humbled and ready to turn to him. "*The sacrifices of God are a broken spirit; a broken and contrite heart, O God, you will not despise.*" God responds to worship offered from a spirit overwhelmed by its sin, seeking help and forgiveness and cleansing. We cannot expect God to accept worship that springs from a haughty, complacent heart. Jehovah accepts broken spirits. This is our sacrifice.

David feels the helplessness of having nothing to offer God. What can I do to say I'm sorry? The only thing I have to offer is my own brokenness. The good news—the news of great grace—is that Jehovah accepts broken spirits. He welcomes the "*poor in spirit*"(Matt 5:3). He invites the "*heavy laden*"(Matt 11:28). When we are devastated by our sin, convinced of our own inadequacy, and emptied of our stubbornness, we are ready to come to God. This is our sacrifice—and Jehovah accepts it.

One Thing to Think About: Do I worship God out of a sense of pride or brokenness?

One Thing to Pray For: "Restore to me the joy of your salvation"

WEEK 17—TUESDAY

Reading: Psalm 65:1-13

You Visit the Earth

This psalm doubles as a hymn of praise to God and a request for his continued blessing—specifically rain to water the land. David sings to God as "*you who hear prayer*"(Psalm 65:2). "*When iniquities prevail against me, you atone for our transgressions*"(Psalm 65:3). God shows mercy by regularly removing the sin of the people and enabling them to remain in fellowship with him. He extends the blessing of choosing people and bringing them near to his temple (Psalm 65:4). When his people pray, "*by awesome deeds you answer us with righteousness, O God of our salvation, the hope of all the ends of the earth and of the farthest seas*"(Psalm 65:5). God is good to his world.

Now David moves forward to the land itself. "*You visit the earth and water it, you greatly enrich it; the river of God is full of water; you provide their grain, for so you have prepared it. You water its furrows abundantly, settling its ridges, softening it with showers, and blessing its growth*"(Psalm 65:9-10). God visits the earth, but not for punishment (as the biblical writers often picture God's "visitation"). He visits it to enrich it, soften it, and make it grow. He drives his wagon over the earth, leaving abundance in his wake (Psalm 65:12). He clothes the ground: "*the meadows clothe themselves with flocks, the valleys deck themselves with grain, they shout and sing together for joy*"(Psalm 65:13). Even the land is happy when God visits.

Ancient Israel depended completely on the cycle of rain and weather. God bringing rain was often the difference between life and death for them. These cycles are constant reminders that we are not in control; instead, a good God is. When we see the fruitful cycles of the earth, the rich gifts of food, or just the green vibrancy of life, we see God's grace.

One Thing to Think About: What do I learn about God from observing nature?

One Thing to Pray For: God to continue to visit the earth for our good

WEEK 17—WEDNESDAY

Reading: Psalm 84:1-12

No Good Thing Does He Withhold

This psalm stresses the yearning an ordinary Jew feels for the temple. "*How lovely is your dwelling place, O LORD of hosts! My soul longs, yes, faints for the courts of the LORD; my heart and flesh sing for joy to the living God*"(Psalm 84:1-2). The psalmist seems to be distant from the temple but beginning his trek toward Jerusalem, excitedly singing about what awaits him there. He considers that even the birds seek and find a place of rest in the temple—and sing his praise as well (Psalm 84:3-4)! Because Jehovah's presence is there, it is the place to be.

Even those who are unable to physically travel to the temple, the important part is that they see the greatness of God's place. As for those "*in whose heart are the highways to Zion,*" though not there in person, "*each one appears before God in Zion*"(Psalm 84:5, 7). God sees the devotion of their hearts. "*For a day in your courts is better than a thousand elsewhere. I would rather be a doorkeeper in the house of my God than dwell in the tents of wickedness*"(Psalm 84:10). Even the lowliest task in the temple is superior to great blessing among the wicked. Why all this praise of God's house? "*For the LORD God is a sun and shield; the LORD bestows favor and honor. No good thing does he withhold from those who walk uprightly*"(Psalm 84:11). God can be counted on to be gracious to us. The upright lack nothing. "*No good thing does he withhold.*"

If Jehovah is our sun and shield—if he is the source of all favor and honor—if he gives every good thing, then it is natural to seek to be near him. We are completely dependent on him for good things; Jesus tells us that "*apart from me you can do nothing*"(John 15:5). The fact that we have so much good in our lives means that we already have received from his bounty. While we do not worship in a physical temple today, we have ample grounds to praise and seek his presence.

One Thing to Think About: Do my "heart and flesh sing for joy" to God? Why—or why not?

One Thing to Pray For: A hunger to be near my God

WEEK 17—THURSDAY

Reading: Psalm 85:1-13

The Grace of Revival

This psalm begins with a look to God's past acts of grace. "*LORD, you were favorable to your land; you restored the fortunes of Jacob. You forgave the iniquity of your people; you covered all their sin*"(Psalm 85:2). God has proven himself faithful to Israel for many years—giving them the land, blessing them with productive crops, and helping them be at peace with their neighbors. Yet now, things have changed. It is not clear what has happened, but God is angry. "*Restore us again, O God of our salvation, and put away your indignation toward us! Will you be angry with us forever? Will you prolong your anger to all generations?*"(Psalm 85:4-5). The psalmist cries for Jehovah to forgive and show favor—the way he used to.

There is a word to describe the blessing he seeks: revival. "*Will you not revive us again, that your people may rejoice in you?*"(Psalm 85:6). Revival is the stimulation of new life and energy. It triggers hope in the people. A new spirit abounds as circumstances shift. The psalmist yearns for Jehovah to "*speak peace to his people*"(Psalm 85:8). He wants God's attributes to thrive again: "*Steadfast love and faithfulness meet; righteousness and peace kiss each other. Faithfulness springs up from the ground, and righteousness looks down from the sky*"(Psalm 85:10-11). These are not abstract values; the psalmist is praying that *God's people* will once again be loving, faithful, peaceful, and righteous. He is confident that "*the LORD will give what is good, and our land will yield its increase*"(Psalm 85:12). Revival like this is the work of Jehovah God.

Just like nature, people go through cycles of staleness and freshness. We lose energy and interest. We get frustrated and depressed. Things that use to excite or motivate us lose their punch. We seek God's gift of revival. It is God who renews our hearts, helping us to feel and seek and yearn and love and rejoice again.

One Thing to Think About: In what areas of my life have things gotten stale?

One Thing to Pray For: "Will you not revive us again, that your people may rejoice in you?"

WEEK 17—FRIDAY

Reading: Psalm 86:1-17

Show Me a Sign of Your Favor

David is in dire straits and he knows it. "*In the day of my trouble I call upon you, for you answer me*"(Psalm 86:7). His trouble seems to involve physical enemies who are threatening him. "*O God, insolent men have risen up against me; a band of ruthless men seeks my life, and they do not set you before them*"(Psalm 86:14). These men are seeking to hurt him, yet David is especially troubled that "*they do not set you before them*" while he trusts in God (Psalm 86:2). It is a classic story of the righteous crying for help against the aggressively wicked.

Humility runs through David's prayer. He asks God to hear him in this moment "*for I am poor and needy*"(Psalm 86:1). He seeks God's grace: "*be gracious to me*"(Psalm 86:3), "*listen to my plea for grace*"(Psalm 86:6), "*you, O Lord, are a God merciful and gracious*"(Psalm 86:15), "*turn to me and be gracious to me*"(Psalm 86:16). David only approaches as a supplicant needing a gift he has no right to. Yet he knows that what is a huge gift to him—physical salvation from enemies—is a small thing to God. "*Turn to me and be gracious to me; give your strength to your servant, and save the son of your maidservant. Show me a sign of your favor*"(Psalm 86:16-17). Just a bit of strength—just a sign of goodwill—this is all David seeks. The request for a sign here is not about testing God, but is borne of his desperate need. David needs help and knows that the smallest sign of God's approval will resolve his crisis.

When we face "*the day of my trouble,*" we naturally turn to our own wisdom and resources. We try to handle our problems ourselves, using our skills, money, and wits to resolve issues. David shows us a different model. He recognizes the limits of his own abilities and turns to a gracious God. Jehovah is full of power and brilliance and longs to help his people. When we seek him, we merely seek signs of his favor—everyday help that both springs from and confirms the deep relationship we have with him.

One Thing to Think About: What is my natural response to crises in my life?

One Thing to Pray For: God to graciously help me deal with the evil people in my life

WEEK 18—MONDAY

Reading: Psalm 103:1-14

Forget Not All His Benefits

David rouses himself to praise: "*Bless the LORD, O my soul, and all that is within me, bless his holy name! Bless the LORD, O my soul, and forget not all his benefits*"(Psalm 103:1-2). What follows is a recounting of all the good God has done and continues to do for David—an ancient form of "Count Your Blessings." Jehovah is the one who "*forgives all your iniquity, who heals all your diseases, who redeems your life from the pit*"(Psalm 103:3-4). When David has been in need—trapped in sin, physically sick, or in grave danger—it is Jehovah who has helped him, time and again, to survive. Not only that, he now "*satisfies you with good so that your youth is renewed like the eagle's*"(Psalm 103:5). David is not only surviving, but thriving. God is responsible. He tells his soul to bless Jehovah for this.

As his list continues, a few items stand out. "*He does not deal with us according to our sins, nor repay us according to our iniquities. For as high as the heavens are above the earth, so great is his steadfast love toward those who fear him; as far as the east is from the west, so far does he remove our transgressions from us. As a father shows compassion to his children, so the LORD shows compassion to those who fear him*"(Psalm 103:10-13). Three vivid pictures describe God's goodness. His covenant faithfulness is as great as the heavens are higher than the earth. He takes our sins away as far as the east is from the west. He has as much compassion as a father with his kids. The difference between what we deserve and how God actually treats us is as large as can be imagined.

We tend to take things for granted. Until we take the time to notice all the things our spouses do for us, we overlook them. Until we intentionally observe how good our lives are, we focus on the one or two things that are not perfect and complain about them. David presses us—and himself—to praise God by paying careful attention to all the daily blessings we receive. We look around—and look behind—and look forward—and see only the goodness of our God.

One Thing to Think About: What benefits have I enjoyed from God just in the last 24 hours?

One Thing to Pray For: A deeper compassion for others—to be more like God

WEEK 18—TUESDAY

Reading: Psalm 104:10-30

The Grace of Wine, Oil, and Bread

Everywhere the psalmist looks in the world, he sees God's hand. "*You make springs gush forth in the valleys*" (Psalm 104:10). "*From your lofty abode you water the mountains; the earth is satisfied with the fruit of your work*" (Psalm 104:13). "*O LORD, how manifold are your works! In wisdom have you made them all; the earth is full of your creatures*" (Psalm 104:24). The earth is a marvel. Life is abundant. Nature works in precise cycles. It is the work of breathtaking genius. Yet God *continues* to provide for his creation, daily repeating his goodness. "*These all look to you, to give them their food in due season…when you open your hand, they are filled with good things*" (Psalm 104:27, 28). Creation looks to the Creator to sustain it.

But especially does he provide in this way for man. "*You cause the grass to grow for the livestock and plants for man to cultivate, that he may bring forth food from the earth and wine to gladden the heart of man, oil to make his face shine and bread to strengthen man's heart*" (Psalm 104:14-15). Jehovah does more than just provide food for man. He gives "*wine to gladden the heart of man*"—the rich flavor of grapes that adds joy and richness to his diet. He gives "*oil to make his face shine*"—the produce of olives that has many uses (besides eating) that bless man, including helping him clean himself. He gives "*bread to strengthen man's heart*"—the food we need to provide emotional and physical strength to tackle the problems of life.

The world is an amazing place and human beings hold a unique position in it. The psalmist specifies the three staple crops of Israel—grapes, olives, and grain—as a special blessing for people. Throughout the world, we could add to this list the wonderful things that grow in each region that bless human existence. The point is that God has done more than just sustain us—*he makes our lives enjoyable and pleasant with things outside our control.* For this, we praise him.

One Thing to Think About: How is my life good in ways that are unnecessary to my survival?

One Thing to Pray For: Appreciation for the richness of the small pleasures of life

WEEK 18—WEDNESDAY

Reading: Psalm 105:1-22

When They Were Few in Number

This psalm calls on the worshiper to remember all the good Jehovah has done. "*Sing to him, sing praises to him; tell of all his wondrous works!...Remember the wondrous works that he has done, his miracles, and the judgments he uttered*"(Psalm 105:2, 5). His focus is on God's goodness as revealed to the patriarchs down through the exodus from Egypt. It all began with a freely given promise to Abraham: "*To you I will give the land of Canaan as your portion for an inheritance*"(Psalm 105:11). Because of God's incredible faithfulness, he continues to act on this promise as "*the word that he commanded, for a thousand generations*"(Psalm 105:8).

But the promise, once given, requires God's intervention to fulfill. "*When they were few in number, of little account, and sojourners in it, wandering from nation to nation, from one kingdom to another people, he allowed no one to oppress them; he rebuked kings on their account, saying, 'Touch not my anointed ones, do my prophets no harm!'*"(Psalm 105:12-15). God protects the fledgling family as they follow his circuitous leading, even rebuking kings. "*When he summoned a famine on the land and broke all supply of bread, he had sent a man ahead of them, Joseph, who was sold as a slave*"(Psalm 105:16-17). The psalmist sees Jehovah as the source of the famine—and Jehovah as the source of provision during the famine. God is close by this growing family to ensure that his word to them is fulfilled.

God promised Abraham to make him a great nation—and he will. Yet there is a time "*when they were few in number,*" running for their lives, lying to Pharaoh and Abimelech, desperate and fearful. There is a time when famine forces them out of their land. In every case, Jehovah is there, protecting and guiding to keep his word. While God can clearly save and protect the many, it is refreshing to know that he has his eye on us even when we are "few in number."

One Thing to Think About: Is anything too small or unimportant for God to notice? What might that mean for my problems and anxieties?

One Thing to Pray For: The assurance that God has his eye on me

WEEK 18—THURSDAY

Reading: Psalm 105:23-45

The Grace of Plagues

After the famine, Israel ends up in Egypt. Jehovah is there with them. "*And the LORD made his people very fruitful and made them stronger than their foes. He turned their hearts to hate his people, and to deal craftily with his servants*"(Psalm 105:24-25). God blesses his people in Egypt and they multiply there. But, since God is seen as responsible for every part of this historical situation, he turns the hearts of the Egyptians to hate Israel and enslave them. Now his people are in trouble in a foreign land.

God acts. "*He sent Moses, his servant, and Aaron, whom he had chosen. They performed his signs among them and miracles in the land of Ham*"(Psalm 105:26-27). God's plagues are his gift to bless his people. "*He sent darkness…he turned their waters into blood… he spoke, and there came swarms of flies…he gave them hail for rain…he struck down their vines and fig trees…he spoke, and the locusts came…he struck down all the firstborn*"(Psalm 105:28, 29, 31, 32, 33, 34, 36). Jehovah is directly active. He is at work, intimidating the Egyptians, challenging Pharaoh, and forcing the end of slavery for his people in an unmistakable way. "*Then he brought out Israel with silver and gold, and there was none among his tribes who stumbled. Egypt was glad when they departed, for dread of them had full upon it…So he brought his people out with joy*"(Psalm 105:37-38, 43). The whole process of the plagues is a gift God gives his people.

It is hard to think of plagues as a gift. We think of those who suffer and die in Egypt rather than the joy of Israel. It is helpful to see plagues as a form of judgment on the Egyptians for their evil and stubbornness. God hears the cries of oppression from his people and judges, setting the captives free. The fact that he does this through hardship and suffering is secondary to his desire for their ultimate good. God remains both just and good.

One Thing to Think About: How is God using hardship and suffering to bless his people today?

One Thing to Pray For: Trust in God's desire for my ultimate good

WEEK 18—FRIDAY

Reading: Psalm 119:97-105

A Lamp to My Feet

Psalm 119 is David's love letter to God about his law. "*Oh how I love your law! It is my meditation all the day...How sweet are your words to my taste, sweeter than honey to my mouth!*"(Psalm 119:97, 103). Yet when he writes these words, David is not merely celebrating Bible study. God's law is *God's* words, the expression of his heart and will. With God's wisdom, David is equipped for life. "*Your commandment makes me wiser than my enemies, for it is ever with me. I have more understanding than all my teachers, for your testimonies are my meditation. I understand more than the aged, for I keep your precepts*"(Psalm 119:98-100). As he focuses on God's word, David suddenly grows in wisdom and understanding far beyond his enemies, teachers, and older mentors. He is wise beyond his years—thanks to God.

One of David's favorite ways of describing God's law is with the picture of a path. "*I hold back my feet from every evil way, in order to keep your word. I do not turn aside from your rules, for you have taught me...I hate every false way. Your word is a lamp to my feet and a light to my path*"(Psalm 119:101-102, 104-105). David pictures himself walking along a path in the darkness. On his own, he is unprepared for the twists, turns, and forks in the way. He cannot afford to walk by feel alone; the risk is too great. Yet "*your word is a lamp to my feet and a light to my path.*" God's word illuminates the right way and enables him to "*hold back my feet from every evil way.*" God helps us to see clearly so that we can walk rightly.

Life is a journey. We move from place to place. We move from one stage in life to another. We meet new friends and lose old ones. The blessing is that God teaches us the best way to navigate these movements. He shows us what foolish things to avoid, what dangerous tendencies are forming in ourselves, and where all the paths lead. We do not love God's word because we just enjoy intense study. We love it because it is a perfect guide to life.

One Thing to Think About: At what points in my life have I regretted not listening to God's word?

One Thing to Pray For: Wisdom to see the best way in my present moment

WEEK 19—MONDAY

Reading: Psalm 130:1-8

If You Should Mark Iniquities, Who Could Stand?

This psalm is part of the "Songs of Ascent" that Jews would sing as they traveled up to Jerusalem for the various feast days. It begins with personal desperation and branches out to national need. "*Out of the depths I cry to you, O LORD! O Lord, hear my voice! Let your ears be attentive to the voice of my pleas for mercy!*"(Psalm 130:1-2). The psalmist is sinking in the deep, overwhelmed by his problems. But on what ground can he cry out to God? He knows that he is not innocent; in fact, the "*depths*" may be the result of his own sin. "*If you, O LORD, should mark iniquities, O Lord, who could stand? But with you there is forgiveness that you may be feared*"(Psalm 130:3-4). If Jehovah were to only bless the blameless, who would be worthy? If he holds all people to account for all their sins, who passes the test? But the psalmist is confident that "*with you there is forgiveness,*" encouraging him to reach out despite his weakness and imperfection.

The psalmist then declares that he will wait for Jehovah to save him. "*My soul waits for the Lord more than watchmen for the morning, more than watchmen for the morning*"(Psalm 130:6). Watchmen have the hungry anticipation of the end of their vigil and the passing of danger. Watchmen *know* that the morning is coming and the psalmist *knows* that God will save. He then invites all of Israel to share his faith: "*O Israel, hope in the LORD! For with the LORD there is steadfast love, and with him is plentiful redemption. And he will redeem Israel from all his iniquities*"(Psalm 130:7-8). The only basis for hope in this psalm is a generous, gracious, forgiving, loving God.

At times we grow discouraged by our own unworthiness. We have such intimate knowledge of our own sin that seeing God's righteousness makes us feel that God would never forgive us, care about us, or help us. This psalm helps in that discussion. It reminds us that *unworthiness is true of all people.* The fact that God has anything to do with *any people* means that in some way, he is willing to overlook and work in spite of our sins. This is not an encouragement to sin; it is an invitation to "*hope in the LORD*" even though we are sinners.

One Thing to Think About: What might it mean for me to "wait for the Lord"?

One Thing to Pray For: The discipline to cry out first to God when I am in trouble

Reading: Psalm 136:1-26

His Steadfast Love Endures Forever

Reading Psalm 136 aloud is a unique experience. The consistent repetition of the psalmist's main thought—"*his steadfast love endures forever*"—serves as a foundation for the varying meditations on all that God has done. "*Give thanks to the LORD, for he is good, for his steadfast love endures forever*"(Psalm 136:1). Declaring that God is *good* says more than we might realize. It is to say that Jehovah is not only powerful, wise, and eternal. He does things that benefit us and demonstrate his love. Not only that, but because he is eternal, this aspect of his character "*endures forever.*" He is eternally good to us.

So the psalmist takes us through various demonstrations of God's goodness and steadfast love. We give thanks "*to him who by his understanding made the heavens*"(Psalm 136:5), planning the universe and making earth habitable for life. We give thanks "*to him who struck down the firstborn of Egypt*" and "*brought Israel out from among them*"(Psalm 136:10, 11). All Israel looks back to Jehovah's great deliverance as the beginning point of their great nation. We give thanks "*to him who struck down great kings*"(Psalm 136:17) "*and gave their land as a heritage*"(Psalm 136:21) to Israel. "*It is he who remembered us in our low estate, for his steadfast love endures forever; and rescued us from our foes*"(Psalm 136:23-24). Looking back over even an abbreviated list of all Jehovah has done for us, we are left humbled and thankful.

Each of us can add his or her own experience to this brief tally of the steadfast love of Jehovah. The love of God continues throughout different generations, manifesting itself in all kinds of ways. We have received the tremendous benefits of technology, medicine, and wealth—for his steadfast love endures forever. We live longer and more safely than our forebears—for his steadfast love endures forever. We have unprecedented access to God's word and reap the fruits of centuries of his servants' work to help us understand it—for his steadfast love endures forever. The longer the list grows, the more of God's goodness we see.

One Thing to Think About: Why is it important for us to learn to give thanks?

One Thing to Pray For: Consistency in my attempts to be good to others—like the steadfast love of my God

WEEK 19—WEDNESDAY

Reading: Psalm 145:1-21

You Open Your Hand

David sees part of our function as human beings as praising Jehovah. "*One generation shall commend your works to another, and shall declare your mighty acts*"(Psalm 145:4). And so David adds his praise. "*Every day I will bless you and praise your name forever and ever. Great is the LORD, and greatly to be praised, and his greatness is unsearchable*"(Psalm 145:2-3). Each day brings new opportunities to add *our* thoughts of God's greatness to the great symphony of creation. David even feels that God's "*wondrous works...speak of the might of your awesome deeds*"(Psalm 145:5, 6, 10, 11). The things God builds, creates, sustains, and helps praise him—whether consciously or not.

David stands in awe of God's power: "*Your kingdom is an everlasting kingdom, and your dominion endures throughout all generations*"(Psalm 145:13). God has a heart for the weak: "*The LORD upholds all who are falling and raises up all who are bowed down... The LORD is near to all who call on him*"(Psalm 145:14, 18). All of this bespeaks a life-giving generosity: "*The eyes of all look to you, and you give them their food in due season. You open your hand; you satisfy the desire of every living thing*"(Psalm 145:15-16). David pictures all the living things of the earth with eyes upturned to heaven, seeking God's provision. Jehovah, the source of all life, opens his hand to meet all our needs.

In Deuteronomy, God warns his people that if any of their fellow Israelites becomes poor, "*you shall not harden your heart or shut your hand against your poor brother, but you shall open your hand to him and lend him sufficient for his need*"(Deut 15:7-8). The clenched fist represents greed and selfishness while the open hand signifies willingness to share. God is the God of open hands, freely giving without fear or concern for himself. God expects his people to be generous because we have learned from his generosity.

One Thing to Think About: Do I ever harden my heart or shut my hand against those in need? Why?

One Thing to Pray For: Opportunities to add my praise to that of the rest of creation

WEEK 19—THURSDAY

Reading: Psalm 146:1-10

Jehovah Sets the Prisoners Free

The psalmist is living during an era in which the people are looking to earthly rulers to help them. He seeks to turn them to trust in God instead. "*I will praise the LORD as long as I live; I will sing praises to my God while I have my being. Put not your trust in princes, in a son of man, in whom there is no salvation. When his breath departs, he returns to the earth; on that very day his plans perish*"(Psalm 146:2-4). As people throughout history, when we hitch our wagons to a man's star, we are inevitably disappointed. Even the best of men die—along with their ambitious plans for the world. Jehovah is different.

God not only "*made heaven and earth, the sea, and all that is in them*," but he also "*keeps faith forever*"(Psalm 146:6). Unlike a ruler, the scope of God's power and the eternal consistency of his word inspire our confidence. God is the one "*who executes justice for the oppressed, who gives food to the hungry. The LORD sets the prisoners free; the LORD opens the eyes of the blind. The LORD lifts up those who are bowed down; the LORD loves the righteous. The LORD watches over the sojourners; he upholds the widow and the fatherless, but the way of the wicked he brings to ruin*"(Psalm 146:7-9). God always acts in the best interest of the disadvantaged—giving justice, food, freedom, sight. Rulers (almost) always act in the best interest of the *ruler*. Which one should be trusted?

Setting the prisoners free does not mean that God wants criminals to have free reign. The idea is that he is a God of liberation and freedom, not restraint. God did not make people to be imprisoned; this is not our purpose. God restores us to our rightful role, removing the vestiges of sin and injustice that cling to us as we live in a sin-stained world. "Princes" come and go, serving the agenda of the moment. Jehovah is eternally present to help. Which one should be trusted?

One Thing to Think About: In what ways am I tempted to trust in people?

One Thing to Pray For: God's help with the prisons, blindness, and hunger that plague me

WEEK 19—FRIDAY

Reading: Proverbs 2:1-15

Jehovah Gives Wisdom

Much of the early section of Proverbs is written as a father instructing his son. "*My son, if you receive my words and treasure up my commandments with you, making your ear attentive to wisdom and inclining your heart to understanding...if you seek it like silver and search for it as for hidden treasures, then you will understand the fear of the LORD and find the knowledge of God*" (Prov 2:1-2, 4-5). Solomon wants his son to listen carefully to his instructions and guidance, understanding their great value. The interesting connection here is that by hearing his dad, this son will "*understand the fear of the LORD and find the knowledge of God.*" Parents—especially those who instruct out of their own knowledge of God—can teach their kids to properly fear and know God for themselves.

Solomon sees parent-child relationships as yet another way God blesses the world. "*For the LORD gives wisdom; from his mouth come knowledge and understanding; he stores up sound wisdom for the upright; he is a shield to those who walk in integrity*" (Prov 2:6-7). Jehovah is the source of wisdom. Often that wisdom comes through our connection to other people (parents, mentors, cautionary examples), but Jehovah is its ultimate origin. Wherever we get it, wisdom helps us "*understand righteousness and justice and equity, every good path*" (Prov 2:9). It also shows us every *bad* path: "*delivering you from the way of evil, from men of perverted speech...men whose paths are rooked, and who are devious in their ways*" (Prov 2:12, 15). Wisdom protects us from the hurt and damage evil people can do to us.

We don't enter this world equipped to survive. Others must help us and teach us. Over time, we learn by experience and instruction what is good and bad for us to do. This is wisdom. Occasionally we are able to learn wisdom without having to experience mistakes for ourselves, which is an added blessing. "*The LORD gives wisdom.*" The creator of life knows the best way to live life and graciously shares it with us.

One Thing to Think About: How has Jehovah given me wisdom? In what areas do I need more?

One Thing to Pray For: Wisdom to fulfill my responsibilities in the best, most God-honoring way

WEEK 20—MONDAY

Reading: Proverbs 3:1-12

The Grace of Reproof

Solomon's instructions to his son in this section center around his relationship with God. "*Let not steadfast love and faithfulness forsake you; bind them around your neck; write them on the tablet of your heart. So you will find favor and good success in the sight of God and man*"(Prov 3:3-4). Some character traits please both God and people. Becoming a person of integrity who keeps his commitments will bring blessing "*in the sight of God and man*". "*Trust in the LORD with all your heart, and do not lean on your own understanding. In all your ways acknowledge him, and he will make straight your paths*"(Prov 3:5-6). Trusting Jehovah's word over our own thinking will prompt him to bless us.

This advice extends to finances too. "*Honor the LORD with your wealth and with the firstfruits of all your produce; then your barns will be filled with plenty, and your vats will be bursting with wine*"(Prov 3:9-10). By our giving and our money management, we can show honor (or dishonor) to God. The difficulty is often that we fear giving too much of our money to God's causes will leave us broke; Solomon assures us that if we give, we will have more than we need. "*My son, do not despise the LORD's discipline or be weary of his reproof, for the LORD reproves him whom he loves, as a father in the son in whom he delights*"(Prov 3:11-12). Hardship, discipline, and reproof from God—which often manifest as difficult times in our lives—are not a sign of God's abandonment, but his great love. Like a son, he disciplines us for our good.

Solomon is not promising us that serving God always brings financial blessings and straight paths. In fact, he acknowledges that sometimes we will be disciplined by God. However, he *is* pointing out that the general tenor of God-honoring lives is one of blessing and fruitfulness. Decisions we make to live with integrity, trust God over our own thinking, give to his causes, and press on through difficulty are blessed by him. Even reproof is a gift, reminding us that God is our Father and loves us enough to forge us into the people he calls us to be. Our job is to "*not despise the LORD's discipline*," choosing to see the benefits it brings us and the great love that prompts it.

One Thing to Think About: How has God reproved me?

One Thing to Pray For: The courage to trust God with all my heart and lean not on my own understanding

WEEK 20—TUESDAY

Reading: Ecclesiastes 3:9-15

The Grace of Pleasure in Work

Ecclesiastes is often a dark book. The Preacher assigns himself the mission of discovering what is meaningful in life. He finds that without an eternal dimension, life is meaningless and full of frustration. He applies this perspective to work here: "*What gain has the worker from his toil?*"(Eccl 3:9). We work our fingers to the bone for most of our lives, but what ultimate good does this bring us? We must leave it to another person (Eccl 2:18), sometimes we lose all we should have gotten (Eccl 5:14), and sometimes we can't even enjoy the money we make (Eccl 6:1-2). God "*has put eternity into man's heart, yet so that he cannot find out what God has done from the beginning to the end*"(Eccl 3:11). We have a nagging sense of the eternal, but it is always just tantalizingly beyond us.

What is the solution? "*I perceived that there is nothing better for them than to be joyful and to do good as long as they live; also that everyone should eat and drink and take pleasure in all his toil—this is God's gift to man*"(Eccl 3:12-13). Solomon seems wistful for his old joy—the joy he had in the ordinary pleasures of life before he took on this existential search. He urges his hearers to "*eat and drink and take pleasure in all (our) toil.*" He really means this. He repeats it over and over again throughout the book (Eccl 2:24, 3:12-13, 3:22, 5:18, 8:15, 9:7). The balance to the frustrating vanities and limitations of life is to be joyful in the moment. This is God's gift.

There is a deep satisfaction that comes from a job well done. We take pleasure from things that are well-made and well-maintained. We smile when we look back on a day well-spent. Like God after the creation, we can look at what we have done and declare it good. While we can't afford to let this grow into pride, Solomon here asserts that there is "*nothing better*" than eating, drinking, and enjoying this great blessing. This is God's gift.

One Thing to Think About: What keeps me from taking pleasure in my work?

One Thing to Pray For: A heart to be mentally and spiritually present in my everyday work

WEEK 20—WEDNESDAY

Reading: Isaiah 1:12-20

Though Your Sins Be as Scarlet

Isaiah is prophesying to a corrupt Judah who is on the brink of judgment from a foreign power. It is immediately clear that God is angry with them. "*When you come to appear before me, who has required of you this trampling of my courts? Bring no more vain offerings; incense is an abomination to me. New moon and Sabbath and the calling of convocations—I cannot endure iniquity and solemn assembly*"(Isa 1:12-13). The people are worshiping, but God is angry. He says he hates their worship (Isa 1:14) and will ignore their prayers (Isa 1:15). If they are doing the acts of worship God desires, why is he so upset?

The issue here is the lifestyle of the people. "*Even though you make many prayers, I will no listen; your hands are full of blood*"(Isa 1:15). Worship is not a "get out of jail free" card for evil living. God does not bless and stay in relationship with those who continually rebel against him. So through Isaiah God urges them to "*wash yourselves; make yourselves clean; remove the evil of your deeds from before my eyes; cease to do evil, learn to do good; seek justice, correct oppression; bring justice to the fatherless, plead the widow's cause*"(Isa 1:16-17). Make real change to your lives! Treat people differently! Start living like my people! If they do, God assures them: "*though your sins are like scarlet, they shall be as white as snow; though they are red like crimson, they shall become like wool*"(Isa 1:18). If they turn to him in obedience, God will remove the guilt and make them pure again.

God uses colors here to illustrate his point. Like a blood stain on a white shirt, our sins stick with us. Guilt haunts us, the memory upsets us, the consequences discourage us. Yet here God promises—because of his own grace—that those who turn their hearts toward him in obedience and faithfulness will be cleansed. As Christians, we have come to God with sins like scarlet, only to find the cleansing in Jesus' blood has washed us to make us pure and holy again. God has shown mercy.

One Thing to Think About: Have I ever used worship as an excuse to avoid making real changes in my life?

One Thing to Pray For: God's cleansing for my sins

Reading: Isaiah 25:1-9

He Will Swallow Up Death Forever

These chapters of Isaiah speak to an intense judgment on then nations around Israel—along with sharp words toward God's own people. Yet even in this judgment "*strong peoples will glorify you; cities of ruthless nations will fear you. For you have been a stronghold to the poor, a stronghold to the needy in his distress, a shelter from the storm and a shade from the heat*"(Isa 25:3-4). Jehovah's actions draw the attention of the great nations of the world (he surely must be thinking of Assyria). They acknowledge that God defends and protects the poor and vulnerable, while humbling the great.

A tremendous vision interrupts these thoughts: "*On this mountain the LORD of hosts will make for all peoples a feast of rich food, a feast of well-aged wine, of rich food full of marrow, of aged wine well refined*"(Isa 25:6). Just as on Mount Sinai (Ex 24:9-11), so fellowship with God is pictured as a meal. God provides an abundance of food "*for all peoples*" to enjoy his bounty. "*And he will swallow up on this mountain the covering that is cast over all peoples, the veil that is spread over all nations. He will swallow up death forever; and the Lord GOD will wipe away tears from all faces, and the reproach of his people he will take away from all the earth, for the LORD has spoken*"(Isa 25:7-8). Like a veil that is spread over all people is the grim fact that we are doomed to die. Yet as Jehovah provides this remarkable messianic banquet, so he promises to "*swallow up death forever,*" eliminating the haunting fear that has plagued mankind since the garden. He will wipe away our tears.

Isaiah's words signal God's disposition to bless all the peoples of the world. Judgment and death will not reign forever. He sees the seriousness of our plight—"*the covering that is cast over all peoples, the veil that is spread over all nations*"—and longs to wipe away tears from all faces. As we grapple with death and the fear it produces, these words are most welcome. Christians await the messianic banquet with Jesus (Matt 8:11) and the time when God finally wipes away every tear (Rev 21:4).

One Thing to Think About: What would life be like without death?

One Thing to Pray For: God to wipe away my tears

WEEK 20—FRIDAY

Reading: Isaiah 40:1-11

Comfort, Comfort My People!

This chapter marks a sharp turn in the tone of Isaiah. The previous section focused on God's judgment on the nations and the narrow escape Judah makes through Hezekiah's intervention. Now Isaiah speaks to the people many decades in the future, near the end of Babylonian captivity. "*Comfort, comfort my people, says your God. Speak tenderly to Jerusalem, and cry to her that her warfare is ended, that her iniquity is pardoned, that she has received from the LORD's hand double for all her sins*"(Isa 40:1-2). After years of hardship and bad news, God wants his people consoled. The wars are over, the sin is forgiven, the punishment is complete.

But it gets better. "*A voice cries: 'In the wilderness prepare the way of the LORD; make straight in the desert a highway for our God*'"(Isa 40:3). Christians recognize this verse as applying to John the Baptist, but here it stresses the need to prepare the way because *God is coming*. Like a herald announcing a coming king, so this voice cries that Jehovah is on his way. "*Behold, the LORD God comes with might, and his arm rules for him; behold, his reward is with him, and his recompense before him. He will tend his flock like a shepherd; he will gather the lambs in his arms; he will carry them in his bosom, and gently lead those that are with young*"(Isa 40:10-11). Instead of only appearing in judgment, God now comes in gentleness to give rewards. He is here to tend his flock himself, carrying and leading them with care. They are in good hands.

God knows that sometimes we desperately need *comfort*—someone to speak kindly and reassure us during times of hardship and grief. But whereas some comfort is shallow or contrived, there is real comfort in having *actual good news*. God comforts by promising that he is coming to bless and watch out for his people. Even when we deserve punishment, God is still often disposed to show kindness.

One Thing to Think About: When do I most need comfort?

One Thing to Pray For: The reassurance that God really will take care of me

WEEK 21—MONDAY

Reading: Isaiah 41:14-20

I, Jehovah, Will Answer Them

Jehovah speaks to his people in Babylonian captivity, assuring the people that he intends to bless them. "*Fear not, for I am with you; be not dismayed, for I am your God; I will strengthen you, I will help you, I will uphold you with my righteous right hand*"(Isa 41:10). Though Israel is surrounded by enemies who are angry and aggressive (Isa 41:11-12), Jehovah will strengthen and protect them. "*I am the one who helps you, declares the LORD; your Redeemer is the Holy One of Israel*"(Isa 41:14). Practically, God wants these reminders of his presence and care to eliminate their fear (Isa 41:10, 13, 14).

God then zooms out of the present situation to tell his people that *this is what he always does.* "*When the poor and needy seek water, and there is none, and their tongue is parched with thirst, I the LORD will answer them; I the God of Israel will not forsake them. I will open rivers on the bare heights, and fountains in the midst of the valleys. I will make the wilderness a pool of water, and the dry land springs of water*"(Isa 41:17-18). God responds to needs. The figure here is thirst; when people seek water, Jehovah himself answers and blesses them. He does not provide a trickle, but a fountain; he oversupplies our needs. He responds this way "*that they may see and know, may consider and understand together, that the hand of the LORD has done this, the Holy One of Israel has created it*"(Isa 41:20). God's provision leads all people to consider *just how this came to pass*—and end up praising him.

Americans have a curious relationship with need. We know that we have needs, but we hate the experience of being in need and like to pretend that we are self-sufficient. This passage challenges us because it shows God's preference for acting and showing his glory through our needs. It is only when we are reaching out in desperation that God promises this response of grace and abundance. Instead of seeking to feel comfortable and at ease, we must learn to embrace need as a vehicle for God's grace.

One Thing to Think About: How have I seen God work in my life through my needs?

One Thing to Pray For: Assurance of God's presence—so that I may live without fear

WEEK 21—TUESDAY

Reading: Isaiah 53:1-12

Pierced for Our Transgressions

This section speaks of Jehovah's "servant" who will "*be high and lifted up, and shall be exalted*"(Isa 52:13). Interpretations of this text vary in the extreme. Many believe that the servant is a personification of Israel, having finished its suffering, returning to God's favor. That may be a partial meaning here, yet for Christians, the imagery is remarkably similar to Jesus. "*He was despised and rejected by men, a man of sorrows and acquainted with grief; and as one from whom men hide their faces he was despised, and we esteemed him not*"(Isa 53:3). The shocking part of Isaiah's prophecy is that *the servant is only exalted after a period of intense suffering and rejection.*

The servant suffers *on behalf of others.* "*Surely he has borne our griefs and carried our sorrows; yet we esteemed him stricken, smitten by God, and afflicted. But he was pierced for our transgressions; he was crushed for our iniquities; upon him was the chastisement that brought us peace, and with his wounds we are healed. All we like sheep have gone astray; we have turned—every one—to his own way; and the LORD has laid on him the iniquity of us all*"(Isa 53:4-6). The suffering, piercing, and beatings the servant experiences are not the result of his own sin. Jehovah has laid all of "our" iniquity on him. He willingly bears this burden ("*he opened not his mouth*", Isa 53:7) all the way to the point of death (Isa 53:9, 12). Yet in this suffering comes the servant's glory: "*he shall see his offspring; he shall prolong his days; the will of the LORD shall prosper in his hand*"(Isa 53:10). He will be exalted (Isa 53:12). His greatness is fully revealed by his selfless sacrifice.

In his great grace, God is willing to allow one to suffer for many, then exalt the one and redeem the many. The pattern is humility before glory. Christians see our Savior here too—humbly submitting to a suffering he does not deserve, absorbing the piercing and crushing and beating and wounds that should be ours. I have wandered like a foolish sheep, but God has brought me back to him. The song of the suffering servant leaves us mystified, grateful, and in awe.

One Thing to Think About: How have I "gone astray"?

One Thing to Pray For: Respect and gratitude for God's great love

WEEK 21—WEDNESDAY

Reading: Isaiah 61:1-11

Good News!

We all love good news! "*The Spirit of the Lord GOD is upon me, because the LORD has anointed me to bring good news to the poor; he has sent me to bind up the brokenhearted, to proclaim liberty to the captives, and the opening of the prison to those who are bound; to proclaim the year of the LORD's favor, and the day of vengeance of our God; to comfort all who mourn*"(Isa 61:1-2). The servant, whom we read about suffering on behalf of the people, here is empowered by God's Spirit to bless the hurting, poor, needy, and captive. God has sent him to declare good news—that God is looking on his people with favor once again. As his people languish in Babylonian captivity, this good news is surely most welcome.

Instead of being the workforce for another nation, "*strangers shall stand and tend your flocks; foreigners shall be your plowmen and vinedressers*"(Isa 61:5). God has a greater mission for Israel: "*but you shall be called the priests of the LORD; they shall speak of you as the ministers of our God; you shall eat the wealth of the nations, and in their glory you shall boast*"(Isa 61:6). Israel can return to their vocation as a nation of priests to Jehovah (Ex 19:6). The chapter closes with celebration: "*I will greatly rejoice in the LORD; my soul shall exult in my God, for he has clothed me with the garments of salvation; he has covered me with the robe of righteousness, as a bridegroom decks himself like a priest with a beautiful headdress, as a bride adorns herself with her jewels. For as the earth brings forth its sprouts, and as a garden causes what is sown in it to sprout up, so the Lord GOD will cause righteousness and praise to sprout up before all the nations*"(Isa 61:10-11). God will bring the people back to life as a source of right living, bringing praise to Israel and to Jehovah himself.

Isaiah has shown us that when God speaks, it is not always good news. Yet here we see God loving and showing mercy to a people who has been long downtrodden as a result of their sin. *God still cares, even when we deserve our fate.* And in his grace, he will act to save, bless, and restore—not because we deserve such treatment, but to his own praise and glory. That's good news!

One Thing to Think About: How have I experienced God's mercy—even when I still suffered some of the consequences of my sin?

One Thing to Pray For: God's glory to be known among the nations

WEEK 21—THURSDAY

Reading: Isaiah 65:17-25

New Heavens and a New Earth

The Bible begins with God creating all things. "*In the beginning, God created the heavens and the earth*"(Gen 1:1). Here that same God promises a new creation: "*For behold, I create new heavens and a new earth, and the former things shall not be remembered or come into mind*"(Isa 65:17). This new creation will be so magnificent that the creation we inhabit will be forgotten. He wants to stress to his people that this new promise is *good news*: "*But be glad and rejoice forever in that which I create; for behold, I create Jerusalem to be a joy, and her people a gladness*"(Isa 65:18).

The new heavens and new earth will be free of the limitations of this sin-stained world. "*No more shall be heard in it the sound of weeping and the cry of distress. No more shall there be in it an infant who lives but a few days, or an old man who does not fill out his days…They shall not build and another inhabit; they shall not plant and another eat… They shall not labor in vain or bear children for calamity…The wolf and the lamb shall graze together; the lion shall eat straw like the ox, and dust shall be the serpent's food. They shall not hurt or destroy in all my holy mountain*"(Isa 65:19-20, 22, 23, 25). Peace, long life, absence of hatred and hostility—this will be a place where the world is right-side up. It will be a place truly fit for human habitation.

New Testament authors take up Isaiah's language. Peter stresses that "*we are waiting for new heavens and new earth in which righteousness dwells*"(2 Pet 3:13) and John sees "*a new heaven and a new earth*"(Rev 21:1) descending out of heaven. We see glimpses of this new creation when we see Christians leaving behind old ways and making peace with old enemies (like wolves and lambs grazing together). We see glimpses when Christians live in righteousness. Yet we still await God to re-create the world (in whatever way he chooses) so that righteousness fully dwells where we are—and so that we can dwell where he is.

One Thing to Think About: Can I imagine a world without sin?

One Thing to Pray For: Jesus to come quickly and bring God's plan to completion

WEEK 21—FRIDAY

Reading: Jeremiah 23:1-8

A Righteous Branch

Jeremiah prophesies during the last days before Judah is taken into Babylonian exile. It is a dark time. Jehovah has just condemned the last several kings and now takes them as a whole. "'*Woe to the shepherds who destroy and scatter the sheep of my pasture!' declares the LORD. Therefore thus says the LORD, the God of Israel, concerning the shepherds who care for my people: 'You have scattered my flock and have driven them away, and you have not attended to them. Behold, I will attend to you for your evil deeds, declares the LORD*'"(Jer 23:1-2). The kings who should have led the people—whom Jehovah specifies are *his* people—have instead scattered and ignored them. The leaders have looked after their own needs and desires instead of taking care of the people. God promises to judge them.

But God's greater concern is for the sheep (the people) themselves. He promises to gather the remnant of his flock and bring them back to their fold to dwell in safety (Jer 23:3). "*I will set shepherds over them who will care for them, and they shall fear no more, nor be dismayed, neither shall any be missing, declares the LORD*"(Jer 23:4). But even these shepherds anticipate a greater king: "*Behold, the days are coming, declares the LORD, when I will raise up for David a righteous Branch, and he shall reign as king and deal wisely, and shall execute justice and righteousness in the land. In his days Judah will be saved, and Israel will dwell securely. And this is the name by which he will be called: 'The LORD our righteousness*'"(Jer 23:5-6). God promises an ideal king. He comes from the line of David, but also shares in the righteous character of David (who was also a shepherd). He will reign justly and fairly and usher in an age of security for Jehovah's people.

When Jesus comes, he notices that the people of his day are "*harassed and helpless, like sheep without a shepherd*"(Matt 9:36). When we don't have good leadership, people languish and suffer. Yet God, in his amazing grace, knows this about us and has promised to give us a leader we can depend on. When we follow the Messiah, we "*dwell securely*" and God is our righteousness. Our Savior takes care of us like a shepherd tending his flock, so that we no longer have to wander.

One Thing to Think About: Why is leadership so important?

One Thing to Pray For: Jesus to reign more completely in my life

WEEK 22—MONDAY

Reading: Jeremiah 29:1-14

I Know the Plans I Have for You

Jeremiah writes a letter to the people of Judah whom Nebuchadnezzar has taken into Babylon. Some false prophets have been telling the people that the captivity will be very short, but Jeremiah knows that this is not true. He encourages the people to settle in the land where they are living: "*Build houses and live in them; plant gardens and eat their produce. Take wives and have sons and daughters; take wives for your sons, and give your daughters in marriage, that they may bear sons and daughters; multiply there, and do not decrease. But seek the welfare of the city where I have sent you into exile, and pray to the LORD on its behalf, for in its welfare you will find your welfare*"(Jer 29:5-7). What is notable about these actions—houses, marriages, gardens—is that they speak of a permanence that may be difficult for the people to accept. Yet in settling down, the people wait for Jehovah to act.

Jeremiah assures them that God has not forgotten them where they are. "*For thus says the LORD: When seventy years are completed for Babylon, I will visit you, and I will fulfill to you my promise and bring you back to this place. For I know the plans I have for you, declares the LORD, plans for welfare and not for evil, to give you a future and a hope. Then you will call upon me and come and pray to me, and I will hear you*"(Jer 29:10-12). It will take some time, but Jehovah will bring Judah back into their land. Perhaps most reassuring is that *God insists that he has a plan for them—and that it is good.* He has "*plans for welfare and not for evil, to give you a future and a hope.*" Even when the people are enduring judgment and suffering *that they completely deserve*, God is planning to usher in a new wave of grace for them.

This verse is wildly popular in the religious world—although it is always taken out of context. God does have plans for us, to do us good. But Jeremiah reminds us that this good is often achieved through long periods of hardship. Not all of God's plan is rosy. Like Judah, our struggles are often our own doing. The blessing of a passage like this is the reminder of the relentless desire God has to do us good and win us back to him. He longs to bless us.

One Thing to Think About: How has God given me "a future and a hope"?

One Thing to Pray For: The strength of character to endure periods of difficulty with hope in God

WEEK 22—TUESDAY

Reading: Jeremiah 31:15-25

My Heart Yearns for Him

In this section, Jeremiah prophesies about the return of the northern tribes of Israel, who have been scattered after the Assyrian captivity. "*Thus says the LORD: 'A voice is heard in Ramah, lamentation and bitter weeping. Rachel is weeping for her children; she refuses to be comforted for her children, because they are not more.' Thus says the LORD: 'Keep your voice from weeping, and your eyes from tears, for there is a reward for your work, declares the LORD, and they shall come back from the land of the enemy. There is hope for your future, declares the LORD, and your children shall come back to their own country*'" (Jer 31:15-17). Weeping Rachel, mother of the nation, is told that her sorrow will end. Her children will return and God will bring Israel back to their land. Jehovah speaks to give hope.

Ephraim, the personification of the northern tribes, speaks to God: "*You have disciplined me, and I was disciplined, like an untrained calf; bring me back that I may be restored, for you are the LORD my God*" (Jer 31:18). Jehovah hears. "*Is Ephraim my dear son? Is he my darling child? For as often as I speak against him, I do remember him still. Therefore my heart yearns for him; I will surely have mercy on him, declares the LORD*" (Jer 31:20). Even when God disciplines, he still loves and remembers. Like a father who longs to show kindness to his "*darling child*," God insists that he will have mercy. "*My heart yearns for him.*"

God loves his people even when they are rebellious and unlovable. He loves us enough to discipline us—and enough to reassure and show mercy after discipline. While that grace is often reflected in our circumstances, it is important that we see the heart behind it. God's heart yearns for us.

One Thing to Think About: Do I ever feel unlovable?

One Thing to Pray For: Appreciation for God's great love for me

WEEK 22—WEDNESDAY

Reading: Jeremiah 31:31-40

The Grace of a New Covenant

After Jeremiah's many grim predictions of Babylonian conquest, this section brims with surprising optimism. He gazes beyond the coming exile to the deeper bond hopes to forge with his people. "*Behold, the days are coming, declares the LORD, when I will make a new covenant with the house of Israel and the house of Judah, not like the covenant that I made with their fathers on the day when I took them by the hand to bring them out of the land of Egypt, my covenant that they broke, though I was their husband, declares the LORD*"(Jer 31:31-32). After the exodus, Israel came to Sinai and made a covenant with Jehovah, promising to obey all his commands: "*All the words that the LORD has spoken we will do*"(Ex 24:3). Yet here God reminds them that they have broken this covenant despite his role as faithful husband. Israel's unfaithfulness to the first covenant makes the prospect of a new covenant amazingly gracious.

But this new covenant will also be characterized by God's love and forgiveness. "*For this is the covenant that I will make with the house of Israel after those days, declares the LORD: I will put my law within them, and I will write it on their hearts. And I will be their God, and they shall be my people. And no longer shall each one teach his neighbor and each his brother, saying, 'Know the LORD,' for they shall all know me, from the least of them to the greatest, declares the LORD. For I will forgive their iniquity, and I will remember their sin no more*"(Jer 31:33-34). God will put his law in the *hearts* of the people, producing a new spirit of grateful obedience. He will again take them as his people and be their God, but there will be no need for priestly and prophetic teaching. Everyone will already know Jehovah because he will forgive their sins.

Jeremiah's promise of a new covenant is not fully realized until the coming of Jesus (see Heb 8:6-13). God will do a new thing to overcome the disobedience of his people. This covenant will *always* involve the heart, won over to God by his forgiveness and kindness. He will purify his people from the inside out. Disciples of Jesus are the recipients of this great blessing.

One Thing to Think About: Why is God so intent on giving his people second chances? How have I experienced this?

One Thing to Pray For: God's law to be written in my heart

WEEK 22—THURSDAY

Reading: Lamentations 3:19-33

New Mercies Every Morning

Jeremiah is wandering about the streets of Jerusalem in the aftermath of the brutal Babylonian siege. The city is in ruins. The people are gone. The temple is burned. Lamentations contains Jeremiah's bitter cries at the state of things. Yet here, in the middle of the book, a new tone emerges. "*But this I call to mind, and therefore I have hope: The steadfast love of the LORD never ceases; his mercies never come to an end; they are new every morning; great is your faithfulness. 'The LORD is my portion,' says my soul, 'therefore I will hope in him'*"(Lam 3:21-24). If God's steadfast love truly *never ceases*, Jeremiah reasons, then there is still ground for hope. He is not done with this situation. His mercies are new every morning. He is always planning some new way to show kindness. His faithfulness is great. Musing on God's dependable goodness helps Jeremiah find hope amidst the ashes.

So he resigns himself to wait for Jehovah. "*The LORD is good to those who wait for him, to the soul who seeks him. It is good that one should wait quietly for the salvation of the LORD. It is good for a man that he bear the yoke in his youth*"(Lam 3:25-27). Jeremiah will suffer and wait it out. It is not the passive waiting of one who is out of options, but a confident expectation that God will come through in his own time. His faith is hooked into the character of God: "*For the Lord will not cast off forever, but, though he cause grief, he will have compassion according to the abundance of his steadfast love; for he does not afflict from his heart or grieve the children of men*"(Lam 3:31-33). God's rejection is never permanent, Jeremiah insists, because God does not afflict his people "*from his heart.*" It is never his ultimate intention. So he pledges to wait for a faithful God to show new mercies.

God continually showers his people with goodness. "*His mercies never come to an end; they are new every morning.*" There is a freshness to God's grace that, like the dew on the grass, rejuvenates and restores us. When, like Jeremiah, we are in dark places, our assurance of God's goodwill toward us will give us ground for new hope. Tomorrow is a new day and will contain new mercies.

One Thing to Think About: What new mercies do I see today?

One Thing to Pray For: Praise to God for his great faithfulness

WEEK 22—FRIDAY

Reading: Ezekiel 34:1-24

I Will Seek the Lost

Jehovah likens Israel's leaders to shepherds, then takes them to task for doing a poor job shepherding. They have been feeding themselves instead of the sheep (Ezek 34:2). "*You eat the fat, you clothe yourselves with the wool, you slaughter the fat ones, but you do not feed the sheep. The weak you have not strengthened, the sick you have not healed, the injured your have not bound up, the strayed you have not brought back, the lost you have not sought, and with force and harshness you have ruled them*"(Ezek 34:3-4). The leaders have been using their position for their own gain, refusing to serve and care for the people. A bad shepherd is a double whammy: they are corrupt and evil while the sheep languish and suffer. Worst of all, God declares that "*my sheep were scattered*"(Ezek 34:5).

Yet God does not simply promise to punish these evil, selfish shepherds. "*For thus says the LORD God: Behold I, I myself will search for my sheep and will seek them out-*"(Ezek 34:11). God is emphatic that he *himself* will do this *personally*. He will seek out his sheep and rescue them (Ezek 34:12), bring them out from the places where they are scattered (Ezek 34:13), feed them (Ezek 34:14), and act directly as their shepherd (Ezek 34:15). "*I will seek the lost, and I will bring back the strayed, and I will bind up the injured, and I will strengthen the weak, and the fat and the strong I will destroy. I will feed them in justice*"(Ezek 34:16). Jehovah will go after the sheep who have been driven away by the negligence of corrupt leaders, restoring them to faith and wholeness. He loves each of his people and is determined to intervene for their good.

Practically, God is describing how corrupt, unspiritual leadership in the nation discourages the people and encourages them to drift from him. This is not God's will for leadership. He promises that he will not allow unscrupulous men to have the last word in his relationship with his people. God does not see this task as below him. He will go after his people in loving concern and restore them. He even promises that he will set David over them to be the good shepherd—foretelling the seeking of the lost Jesus will come to accomplish.

One Thing to Think About: What is involved in seeking lost sheep? Why might I be hesitant to do it?

One Thing to Pray For: A heart to serve others instead of exploiting them

WEEK 23—MONDAY

Reading: Ezekiel 36:22-26

I Will Put My Spirit Within You

As God speaks to his people in Babylonian captivity, he both explains why he allowed this situation and why he plans to end it. "*When the house of Israel lived in their own land, they defiled it by their ways and their deeds... So I poured out my wrath upon them for the blood that they had shed in the land, for the idols with which they had defiled it*"(Ezek 36:17, 18). Yet God's name continues to be profaned because Jehovah's people are not allowed to dwell in Jehovah's land (Ezek 36:20). So God will save, though his people don't deserve it. "*It is not for your sake, O house of Israel, that I am about to act, but for the sake of my holy name, which you have profaned among the nations to which you came. And I will vindicate the holiness of my great name*"(Ezek 36:22-23). God's people have no claim on God's mercy; it is sheer grace and to his own glory.

What will he do? He promises to gather the people from their scattering among the nations and "*sprinkle clean water on you, and you shall be clean from all your uncleannesses*"(Ezek 36:24, 25). But he has a deeper plan in mind: "*And I will give you a new heart, and a new spirit I will put within you. And I will remove the heart of stone from your flesh and give you a heart of flesh. And I will put my Spirit within you, and cause you to walk in my statutes and be careful to obey my rules. You shall dwell in the land that I gave to your fathers, and you shall be my people, and I will be your God*"(Ezek 36:26-28). God wants his people to have a new heart and spirit, an entirely new disposition toward him. No longer will they be stubborn and rebellious, kicking against the goads. Their hearts will be flesh again (instead of stone), receptive to his instruction. They will have *his* Spirit—God's own help and strength to continue to obey God's will. God's dream of his people in his land will be fulfilled because he will make it happen.

In our rebellion, we often rebel against the very God who would help us. We stubbornly cling to our own will. The promise of God's Spirit is the promise of his blessing and help—along with a very personal connection we have with him. In the New Testament, this promise takes on added depth and becomes the source of great confidence in God's approval (Rom 8:9-11, 2 Cor 5:4-5).

One Thing to Think About: How does God give us his Spirit yet still preserve our free will?

One Thing to Pray For: A new heart and spirit—to do God's will and not my own

Reading: Ezekiel 37:1-14

Can These Bones Live?

Ezekiel has a vision of a valley full of very dry bones. Jehovah asks him, "'*Son of man, can these bones live?' And I answered, 'O Lord GOD, you know*'"(Ezek 37:3). The obvious answer to the question is no—bones don't just live—yet Ezekiel seems to sense that God has more in mind than what normally happens. God calls on Ezekiel to prophesy to the bones: "*Thus says the LORD God to these bones: Behold, I will cause breath to enter you, and you shall live. And I will lay sinews upon you, and will cause flesh to come upon you, and cover you with skin, and put breath in you, and you shall live, and you shall know that I am the LORD*"(Ezek 37:5-6). Amazingly, Ezekiel watches as the bones rattle and begin to attach together. Sinews form, flesh grows, and skin covers them. He calls the breath (or spirit) to come into the bones, and they begin to live. "*They lived and stood on their feet, an exceedingly great army*"(Ezek 37:10).

What is the point of this strange resurrection? "*Son of man, these bones are the whole house of Israel. Behold, they say, 'Our bones are dried up, and our hope is lost; we are indeed cut off.' Therefore prophesy, and say to them, Thus says the LORD God: Behold, I will open your graves and raise you from your graves, O my people. And I will bring you into the land of Israel*"(Ezek 37:11-12). Jehovah speaks words of comfort and blessing to a disheartened and hopeless people. Desperate and forsaken, they feel like worthless bones. Yet God can speak their regeneration into existence—and promises that he will restore the nation, though they are scattered and broken.

Sometimes we become overwhelmed by negative circumstances. We don't see how God could rescue a person like me—or why he would want to. God's grace enters into this discussion. He is absolutely able to resurrect the dead and make them live again. But more than that, *he is willing to.* Just when we think "*our hope is lost*" and "*we are indeed cut off*" is the moment when God's grace is shown in its sharpest clarity. God can redeem *anything*.

One Thing to Think About: How have I seen God rescue, bless, and restore in ways I could not have expected?

One Thing to Pray For: A renewal of my hope in God

WEEK 23—WEDNESDAY

Reading: Daniel 1:8-21

The Grace of Skill

Daniel and his friends are young Jewish boys growing up in Babylonian captivity. They are "*youths without blemish, of good appearance and skillful in all wisdom, endowed with knowledge, understanding learning, and competent to stand in the king's palace, and to teach them the literature and language of the Chaldeans*"(Dan 1:4). So they are singled out for special food portions and education to prepare them for the king's service.

The focus of this text is on how Jehovah continues to bless them while they are in captivity. Daniel refuses to defile himself with the king's food and wine and asks the king's eunuch for an exemption. "*And God gave Daniel favor and compassion in the sight of the chief of the eunuchs*"(Dan 1:9). This gift leads the eunuch to view Daniel's request favorably, allowing him to avoid defilement, maintain good relations, and remain physically healthy. God gives more gifts: "*As for these four youths, God gave them learning and skill in all literature in wisdom, and Daniel had understanding in all visions and dreams*"(Dan 1:17). God makes them sharp. They are quick studies of the new language and culture. "*And in every matter of wisdom and understanding about which the king inquired of them, he found them ten times better than all the magicians and enchanters that were in all his kingdom*"(Dan 1:20). They are not better because they are Jews—or better because they have worked harder. God has given them skill.

At times we are tempted to take credit for our skills. Each of us has unique talents. We may hone and develop them—we may work hard to add new ones—but Daniel specifies that "*God gave them learning and skill.*" It is vital that we continue to give *God* credit for the things we excel in. These skills help us provide for our families and create valuable things that bless others. But most of all, they give glory to the God who is the source of all good things.

One Thing to Think About: What skills do I have? Who do I feel is responsible for them?

One Thing to Pray For: A heart to use my skills to help others

Reading: Daniel 2:17-30

The Grace of Revealed Mysteries

There is a crisis in the palace. Nebuchadnezzar has had a dream with clear spiritual importance and demands that his wise men tell him not only the interpretation, but the dream itself—under penalty of death. The Babylonian wise men include the Jewish captives Daniel and his three friends. So Daniel "*told them to seek mercy from the God of heaven concerning this mystery, so that Daniel and his companions might not be destroyed with the rest of the wise men of Babylon. Then the mystery was revealed to Daniel in a vision of the night. Then Daniel blessed the God of heaven*"(Dan 2:18-19). After a period of earnest prayer, God shares the mystery with Daniel, who responds in praise of a giving God: "*He gives wisdom to the wise, and knowledge to those who have understanding; he reveals deep and hidden things…you have given me wisdom and might*"(Dan 2:21, 22, 23).

What is notable is Daniel absolutely refuses to take credit for this knowledge. When brought before the king—with a golden opportunity for advancing his own interests—he declares that "*no wise men, enchanters, magicians, or astrologers can show to the king the mystery that the king has asked, but there is a God in heaven who reveals mysteries, and he has made known to King Nebuchadnezzar what will be in the latter days*"(Dan 2:27-28). As if worried he will give the wrong impression, Daniel insists, "*this mystery has been revealed to me, not because of any wisdom I have more than all the living, but in order that the interpretation may be made known to the king, and that you may know the thoughts of your mind*"(Dan 2:30). Daniel is not a brilliant dream-reader. He is not an especially insightful thinker. He is not a wise philosopher. He is a servant of the God who reveals mysteries.

There is so much about the world, our lives, and the future that is a mystery to us. We are limited in our vision and knowledge. Yet God often chooses to lift the veil of our ignorance and show us some of what he has done, is doing, and will do. In his word, we gain insight into his thinking—and often learn something about ourselves as well (see 1 Cor 2:11-13, Eph 3:3-6). This is an invaluable gift.

One Thing to Think About: What has God shown me about the world—and myself—in his word?

One Thing to Pray For: The humility to acknowledge the limits of my knowledge

WEEK 23—FRIDAY

Reading: Daniel 2:36-49

An Indestructible Kingdom

As Daniel interprets Nebuchadnezzar's dream for him, we learn of a divine plan for the kingdoms of the world. *"You, O king, the king of kings, to whom the God of heaven has given the kingdom, the power, and the might, and the glory, and into whose hand he has given, wherever they dwell, the children of man, the beasts of the field, and the birds of the heavens, making you rule over them all—you are the head of gold"*(Dan 2:37-38). Nebuchadnezzar has dreamed of a large four-tiered statue. Daniel informs him that he (as king of Babylon) is the head of gold. Yet this position is one *God has given* him.

Daniel foretells the successive kingdoms that will displace Babylon in years to come, down to the feet of iron and clay. *"And in the days of those kings the God of heaven will set up a kingdom that shall never be destroyed, nor shall the kingdom be left to another people. It shall break in pieces all these kingdoms and bring them to an end, and it shall stand forever"*(Dan 2:44). God promises to do a new thing, independent of the kingdoms of the world. He will establish his own kingdom that is indestructible, but will instead "*break in pieces all these kingdoms.*" It also will not be "*left to another people,*" meaning that where God has given authority to Nebuchadnezzar temporarily (Dan 1:2, 2:38), the indestructible kingdom will feature God himself will do the ruling.

This may not sound like good news to Nebuchadnezzar, but it should to us. The transitions between governments trample people underfoot. Blood is shed and lives are ruined. Tyrants are born and God's purposes are forsaken in the pursuit of power. By promising (and establishing) an indestructible kingdom, God is giving his people the hope of a better way. There is stability, security, and the promise of a king who truly cares about us. Politics will ebb and flow, but God's kingdom stands.

One Thing to Think About: How does the uncertainty of human power help me see my need for God's rule?

One Thing to Pray For: That the peace of Christ would rule in my heart

Reading: Daniel 3:8-30

He Is Able

It is hard to know which makes Nebuchadnezzar angrier—that Shadrach, Meshach, and Abednego don't serve his gods, won't worship his image, or don't pay attention to him (Dan 3:12). When he calls on them to bow down to his statue and they refuse, he breaks into a "*furious rage*"(Dan 3:13). He gives them another chance to bow, but threatens them: "*But if you do not worship, you shall immediately be cast into a burning fiery furnace. And who is the god who will deliver you out of my hands?*"(Dan 3:15). This is about power. Nebuchadnezzar—the most powerful man in the world—refuses to be denied by people or gods.

The three friends see an opening with Nebuchadnezzar's question: "*If this be so, our God whom we serve is able to deliver us out of your hand, O king. But if not, be it known to you, O king, that we will not serve your gods or worship the golden image that you have set up*"(Dan 3:17-18). They insist: *our God is able!* Yet there is a caveat to their confidence: he *may choose not to*. But even if Jehovah does not deliver them, the men declare that they still will not serve Nebuchadnezzar's gods. This makes the king even angrier, so that he overheats the furnace to the point that it kills the servants who throw the men in. In go Shadrach, Meshach, and Abednego, prepared to burn for their faith. Yet they are spared—unbound, walking in the midst of the fire, with a mysterious fourth person among them. They come out unsinged and without even the smell of smoke on them.

It is a story of terrific courage and faith. What impresses me is the maturity of the response. These men feel that they have no claim on God that would force him to save them. "*But if not*," they make the same decision. This paints God's deliverance in exactly the right light. Sometimes God will choose not to save; that is his right. But he is *always* able. So when God does save—when we see him spare our lives, save our marriage, help our kids, fix our financial woes, make things work out for good—then we know it is always as an act of grace.

One Thing to Think About: When have I experienced God's deliverance? When have I *not* experienced it?

One Thing to Pray For: Deeper confidence in God's power

Reading: Daniel 6:10-28

My God Sent His Angel

The Babylonian kingdom has been toppled by the Persians, yet Daniel (now an old man) has retained his high position. His enemies scheme to defeat him by convincing King Darius to issue a decree that no petition or appeal be made to any god or man except the king. Daniel promptly disobeys. "*When Daniel knew that the document had been signed, he went to his house where he had windows in his upper chamber open toward Jerusalem. He got down on his knees three times a day and prayed and gave thanks before his God, as he had done previously*"(Dan 6:10). This is an act of tremendous courage and faith. His enemies accuse him before the king.

For his part, the king does not realize how he has been used. He is "*much distressed and set his mind to deliver Daniel. And he labored till the sun went down to rescue him*"(Dan 6:14), yet he is unable (since Persian laws are immune to good common sense). So he orders Daniel thrown into the lions' den with the prayer, "*May your God, whom you serve continually, deliver you!*"(Dan 6:16). Unable to sleep, the king rushes down early in the morning to learn of Daniel's fate. He is "*exceedingly glad*" to hear Daniel's voice answering him: "*My God sent his angel and shut the lions' mouths, and they have not harmed me, because I was found blameless before him; and also before you, O king, I have done no harm*"(Dan 6:22). Meanwhile his enemies are thrown in the den and the lions' mouths are opened again.

Daniel specifies that "*my God sent his angel.*" Angels are God's messengers and actors in the world. They are always impressive and inspire fear in humans. Yet there is a danger that our fascination with angels distracts us from the important point: *angels are doing God's will.* Angels are "*ministering spirits sent out to serve for the sake of those who are to inherit salvation*"(Heb 1:14). When God acts in our world, he can use his angels, his Spirit, natural processes, or miraculous works. We can't miss the point: however he does it, *God's good works show us God's favor.*

One Thing to Think About: Would I have prayed if I were Daniel? Is prayer my habit *now*—when I am free to do it?

One Thing to Pray For: God to not allow evil people to overcome the righteous

WEEK 24—WEDNESDAY

Reading: Hosea 2:14-23

The Grace of God's Wooing

The book of Hosea compares God's relationship with his people to a marriage—but not a happy marriage. It is a marriage in which the wife has been repeatedly unfaithful and the husband pleads with her to come back to him. At times Hosea acts out this pattern by accepting his own unfaithful wife. Here, after venting his frustration and promising judgment, God's tone changes. "*Therefore, behold, I will allure her, and bring her into the wilderness, and speak tenderly to her. And there I will give her her vineyards and make the Valley of Achor a door of hope. And there she shall answer as in the days of her youth, as at the time when she came out of the land of Egypt*"(Hos 2:14-15). The words "allure" and "speak tenderly" are powerful; they mean to "seduce" and "romance." God wants to woo his people back to him.

God tells his bride of the great blessings of coming back to him. "*You will call me 'My Husband,' and no longer will you call me 'My Baal.' For I will remove the names of the Baals from her mouth*"(Hos 2:16-17). "*And I will abolish the bow, the sword, and war from the land, and I will make you lie down in safety*"(Hos 2:18). "*I will betroth you to me in faithfulness*"(Hos 2:20). God wants his people back! So even though he has been angry, he also gives voice to his great love and desire to bless. The trouble and hardship will not be permanent. They will not suffer for their infidelity forever. All is not lost. God still cares.

Adultery is a horrible breach of trust. There is pain and betrayal and a fractured relationship. When God pictures our sin as adultery, he is describing how it hurts and upsets him. Yet this other side to God—the side in which God is willing to still work on the relationship, to give us second chances, to try again, to speak tenderly—is a sign of his grace and love. God doesn't have to woo us. He could punish us—or speak harshly (we deserve it)—or give up completely. Yet he remains determined to win his bride back.

One Thing to Think About: How much must God love me?

One Thing to Pray For: Faithfulness to my God

WEEK 24—THURSDAY

Reading: Hosea 11:1-9

How Can I Give You Up?

In this part of Hosea, God speaks of his love for his people not as a marriage, but as a parent. "*When Israel was a child, I loved him, and out of Egypt I called my son*"(Hos 11:1). Yet despite God's great father-love, the relationship did not thrive. "*The more they were called, the more they went away; they kept sacrificing to the Baal and burning offerings to idols*"(Hos 11:2). Instead of getting closer, Israel rejected his father. God reminisces like a parent: "*Yet it was I who taught Ephraim to walk; I took them up by their arms, but they did not know that I healed them. I led them with cords of kindness, with the bands of love, and I became to them as one who eases the yoke on their jaws, and I bent down to them and fed them*"(Hos 11:3-4). He remembers early days of holding the arms of his young son, tender moments of affection.

Yet these memories do not change the present situation: "*My people are bent on turning away from me, and though they call out to the Most High, he shall not raise them up at all*"(Hos 11:7). Judgment is coming (Hos 11:5-6). Or is it? God seems to vacillate: "*How can I give you up, O Ephraim? How can I hand you over, O Israel?...My heart recoils within me; my compassion grows warm and tender. I will not execute my burning anger; I will not again destroy Ephraim; for I am a God and not a man, the Holy One in your midst, and I will not come in wrath*"(Hos 11:8-9). Jehovah is unwilling to execute judgment on his dear son. How can I give you up? God will find another way to achieve his purposes. His mercy has overcome his wrath.

I do not believe that God is genuinely changing his mind back and forth. The message here is that *what Israel deserves is at odds with what God wants for Israel.* God cares—and his care prompts compassion for those who will suffer. This gives us insight into why God does not immediately punish us when we do wrong. It is not because wrong isn't wrong, but because God loves us so dearly that he has compassion. His grace helps us see ourselves in exactly the right light: we are sinners in need of help, deserving of punishment and spared only by his grace. The only appropriate response is to humbly repent and seek to do his will.

One Thing to Think About: What do I really deserve?

One Thing to Pray For: Thankfulness for God's compassion on me

WEEK 24—FRIDAY

Reading: Hosea 14:1-9

I Will Heal Their Apostasy

Hosea urges Israel to come back to Jehovah. "*Return, O Israel, to the LORD your God, for you have stumbled because of your iniquity. Take with you words and return to the LORD; say to him, 'Take away all iniquity; accept what is good, and we will pay with bulls the vows of our lips. Assyria shall not save us; we will not ride on horses; and we will say no more, 'Our God,' to the work of our hands. In you the orphan finds mercy*'"(Hos 14:1-3). If they return, Hosea wants them to "*take with you words.*" These are not mere words; they are earnest commitments to a new way of living. Disgusted with their sin, they beg God to take it away. Disappointed by Assyria, they refuse to look to men to save them. They will no longer mistreat orphans. Returning to God will mean real, concrete change for them.

To such repentant people, God promises a robust response. "*I will heal their apostasy; I will love them freely, for my anger has turned from them. I will be like the dew to Israel; he shall blossom like the lily; he shall take root like the trees of Lebanon; his shoots shall spread out; his beauty shall be like the olive, and his fragrance like Lebanon*"(Hos 14:4-6). In the place of anger and judgment, Jehovah offers healing. He will make all the pain and disappointment a thing of the past. He will give rich, new life—"*for from me comes your fruit*"(Hos 14:8). Jehovah heals those who return to him.

Hosea describes sin using the image of physical departure. We have wandered from God and now must return. Sin creates distance between us and separates us from his blessings. Far from God, we feel lonely, forsaken, insufficient, weak, and dirty. Yet Jehovah remains gracious. "*I will heal their apostasy...I will be like the dew to Israel.*" Jehovah heals those who return to him.

One Thing to Think About: What words and commitments have I brought to God?

One Thing to Pray For: The rich fruit of God dwelling in me

WEEK 25—MONDAY

Reading: Joel 2:12-27

He Relents Over Disaster

Joel prophesies judgment on Israel in the form of a locust invasion (or perhaps an army that is like locusts). He calls to mind the utter disaster that locusts caused in the ancient world—and still cause today in agricultural areas. But in this section, Joel urges the people to respond to the threat of judgment with repentance because God can be counted on to be merciful. "'*Yet even now,' declares the LORD, 'return to me with all your heart, with fasting, with weeping, and with mourning; and rend your hearts and not your garments.' Return to the LORD your God, for he is gracious and merciful, slow to anger, and abounding in steadfast love; and he relents over disaster. Who knows whether he will not turn and relent, and leave a blessing behind him, a grain offering and a drink offering for the LORD your God?*"(Joel 2:12-14). Even at this late hour, God might accept their repentance. Instead of tearing their clothes, Jehovah wants them to tear their *hearts*, genuinely upset by the damage their sin has caused. Who knows whether a gracious God will relent even of this?

So Joel pictures the scene: a nationwide fast attended by elders, children, and newlyweds, begging for God's mercy. How might God respond? "*Then the LORD became jealous for his land and had pity on his people*"(Joel 2:18). "*I will remove the northerner far from you*"(Joel 2:20). "*The threshing floors shall be full of grain; the vats shall overflow with wine and oil*"(Joel 2:24). "*You shall eat in plenty and be sastified*"(Joel 2:26). "*My people shall never again be put to shame*"(Joel 2:27). These are the words of a gracious God—giving good things again and again to bless his people.

There is a tension in this text. Joel asks, "*Who knows whether he will not turn and relent, and leave a blessing behind him?*"(Joel 2:14). "Who knows" means that we have no *claim* on God's grace—it is always his choice. Yet we do know that God is "*gracious and merciful*"(Joel 2:13), so even at the last moment, we can turn to him in faith. Even the worst situations—even those of our own doing—can prove the beginning of another great story of God's grace.

One Thing to Think About: How have I seen God "relent over disaster"?

One Thing to Pray For: A heart torn with grief over my sin

WEEK 25—TUESDAY

Reading: Jonah 1:1-17

Salvation by Fish

Jehovah gives Jonah a command to preach to Nineveh. "*But Jonah rose to flee to Tarshish from the presence of the LORD*"(Jonah 1:3). This is high-handed rebellion. As he sails in the opposite direction, "*the LORD hurled a great wind upon the sea, and there was a mighty tempest on the sea, so that the ship threatened to break up*"(Jonah 1:4). This kind of terror is precisely what Jonah deserves for his insolence.

The sailors begin to question one another about what god might be tormenting them. "*And he said to them, 'I am a Hebrew, and I fear the LORD, the God of heaven, who made the sea and the dry land.' Then the men were exceedingly afraid and said to him, 'What is this that you have done?' For the men knew that he was fleeing from the presence of the LORD, because he had told them*"(Jonah 1:9-10). These pagans are shocked at Jonah's audacity. If he serves such an obviously powerful God, how could he try to run away from him? Jonah tells them to throw him into the sea "*for I know it is because of me that this great tempest has come upon you*"(Jonah 1:12). They reluctantly throw him into the ocean—and the storm ends. It appears that Jonah will die—except for one act of tremendous mercy. "*And the LORD appointed a great fish to swallow up Jonah. And Jonah was in the belly of the fish three days and three nights*"(Jonah 1:17). It is salvation by fish.

God's dealings with Jonah show great grace. Jonah's lessons are just beginning. Somehow God does not write him off because he is rebellious and insolent. Like a patient father, God gets his attention by a frightening storm, then prepares a safe landing spot so that he is not ultimately harmed. God's miraculous deliverance here is only an aside to the greater story—how God will do a work to change Jonah's heart.

One Thing to Think About: How has God preserved me when I needed to learn certain lessons?

One Thing to Pray For: A willingness to run to—rather than from—God

WEEK 25—WEDNESDAY

Reading: Jonah 2:1-10

You Brought Up My Life from the Pit

Jonah has run from God's command, suffered a terrifying storm at sea, and been thrown into the ocean to stop God's wrath. Surely he thinks he is dead. Yet "*the LORD appointed a great fish to swallow up Jonah. And Jonah was in the belly of the fish three days and three nights*"(Jonah 1:17). Now, crying out from inside the fish (!), his attitude is completely changed. "*Then Jonah prayed to the LORD his God from the belly of the fish, saying, 'I called out to the LORD, out of my distress, and he answered me; out of the belly of Sheol I cried, and you heard my voice*'"(Jonah 2:1-2). No longer is Jonah obstinate and disobedient; he sees the danger and knows exactly where to turn. He calls out to Jehovah—and, in spite of everything, Jehovah saves him.

His prayer details the experience. "*For you cast me into the deep, into the heart of the seas, and the flood surrounded me; all your waves and your billows passed over me... The waters closed over me to take my life; the deep surrounded me*"(Jonah 2:3, 5). In this great storm, Jonah is perishing. "*Yet you brought up my life from the pit, O LORD my God. When my life was fainting away, I remembered the LORD, and my prayer came to you, into your holy temple*"(Jonah 2:6-7). At the last moment—when all hope of saving himself is lost—Jonah cries out to God. Now he rejoices and prays and promises to worship: "*But I with the voice of thanksgiving will sacrifice to you; what I have vowed I will pay. Salvation belongs to the LORD!*"(Jonah 2:9). Jonah is thrilled to be saved—even if that salvation comes through the belly of a great fish.

Jonah shows us the power in reciting our story. "*You brought my life up from the pit.*" It helps us to remember our deep need, how desperate the situation was, and God's great salvation. It prompts us to worship. It invites others to celebrate with us. It highlights that God is not just powerful, but *good.*

One Thing to Think About: How has God saved and changed my life?

One Thing to Pray For: Joy in reciting my story and glorifying God

WEEK 25—THURSDAY

Reading: Jonah 3:1-10

The Grace of Averted Disasters

This time when Jehovah tells Jonah to go to Nineveh and preach against it, he goes. No fish are required. *"Jonah began to go into the city, going a day's journey. And he called out, 'Yet forty days, and Nineveh shall be overthrown!'"*(Jonah 3:4). It is a prophecy of judgment and imminent disaster. The detail of "forty days" means that there is a specific looming threat. *"And the people of Nineveh believed God. They called for a fast and put on sackcloth, from the greatest of them to the least of them"*(Jonah 3:5). The response is far better than anything Jeremiah gets from God's own people. The Ninevites *believe* God and begin to fast and beg him to avert the disaster.

The king of Nineveh leads the charge, covering himself with sackcloth and ashes. He orders even the *animals* to fast and wear sackcloth. *"Let everyone turn from his evil way and from the violence that is in his hands. Who knows? God may turn and relent and turn from his fierce anger, so that we may not perish"*(Jonah 3:8-9). It may be too late, but they are willing to change their ways. They are not operating on guarantees, but desperate hopes (*"who knows? God may turn"*). They will do whatever is possible to save themselves and their city because they believe God. *"When God saw what they did, how they turned from their evil way, God relented of the disaster that he had said he would do to them, and he did not do it"*(Jonah 3:10). In an act of grace, God spares them.

Jonah's prophecy doesn't come true. He claims that God will destroy the city in forty days—but he doesn't. Instead, God *averts* disaster, changing the plan to show mercy. Jehovah is so willing to turn around the people of Nineveh that he leaves himself open to the charge of changing his mind. Yet, if God wants to change the world to show his grace and pleasure, who are we to complain?

One Thing to Think About: Why do we often respond better to threats than to reason?

One Thing to Pray For: A spirit of repentance to grip our nation

WEEK 25—FRIDAY

Reading: Jonah 4:1-11

Resenting God's Grace

Jonah 3 ends very pleasantly. Jonah has finished with his rebellion to God's commands. The city of Nineveh has repented. The disaster has been averted. That is what makes the next words so jarring. "*But it displeased Jonah exceedingly, and he was angry. And he prayed to the LORD and said, 'O LORD, is not this what I said when I was yet in my country? That is why I made haste to flee to Tarshish; for I knew that you are a gracious God and merciful, slow to anger and abounding in steadfast love, and relenting from disaster*'"(Jonah 4:1-2). Jonah is angry that God is willing to forgive the Ninevites. We learn that this was the reason for his initial rebellion. God's mercy angers Jonah. He feels that some people need to be *punished*, not forgiven.

Jehovah tries to teach Jonah a new perspective. As Jonah sits in the desert outside Nineveh, God causes a plant to grow up and give him shade. But the next day, a worm kills the plant and Jonah is again exposed to the sun. Now he is doubly angry—still angry about Nineveh and now angry about the plant too. He shakes his fist at God, insistent that he is right to be angry. "*And the LORD said, 'You pity the plant, for which you did not labor, nor did you make it grow, which came into being in a night and perished in a night. And should not I pity Nineveh, that great city, in which there are more than 120,000 persons who do not know their right hand from their left, and also much cattle?*'"(-Jonah 4:10-11). Jehovah wants Jonah to learn *pity*—to care about others the way he has cared about the plant. Jehovah does not give grace because he doesn't care about right living; he gives grace because he has pity for people.

Resenting grace strikes us as odd, yet we have to admit that there are some people that we would rather see punished than forgiven. When someone has hurt us, wronged us, disappointed us, or ignored us, we don't want God to let them off the hook. In those moments, grace doesn't seem fair. We need the perspective God shares with Jonah: when we take our own desires out of the equation and truly care for people, we can appreciate God's grace for us *and* others.

One Thing to Think About: Are there people in my life who I don't want to be forgiven? Why might that be?

One Thing to Pray For: Pity

WEEK 26—MONDAY

Reading: Micah 7:14-20

You Will Cast Our Sins into the Sea

Like many of the prophets, Micah has revealed both Jehovah's frustration with the people and his desire to bless them. In this final section, Micah sees the degradation of his society ("*the godly has perished from the earth,*" Micah 7:1) but still finds room for confidence and optimism. "*Rejoice not over me, O my enemy; when I fall, I shall rise; when I sit in darkness, the LORD will be a light to me...He will bring me out to the light; I shall look upon his vindication*"(Micah 7:8, 9). It is in his hope for Jehovah's intervention that Micah prays: "*Shepherd your people with your staff, the flock of your inheritance, who dwell alone in a forest in the midst of a garden land, let them graze in Bashan and Gilead as in the days of old*"(Micah 7:14). Something has convinced Micah that God, though justifiably angry, is not done with his people.

So it is fitting that he closes his book with a meditation on God's nature. It is more than theology; it is what gives him hope in a difficult time. "*Who is a God like you, pardoning iniquity and passing over transgression for the remnant of his inheritance? He does not retain his anger forever, because he delights in steadfast love. He will again have compassion on us; he will tread out iniquities underfoot. You will cast all our sins into the depths of the sea. You will show faithfulness to Jacob and steadfast love to Abraham, as you have sworn to our fathers from the days of old*"(Micah 7:18-20). Jehovah is a God who is willing to pardon, to have compassion, to show steadfast love. When we are unfaithful, he stomps out our sin and throws it into the sea, never to be seen again.

Sin is a burden we carry. We feel bad about what we have done. We know we stand to be punished—by people and by God—for what we have done. Often we compound the sin by covering it up or rationalizing it. God's grace is amazing because he is able and willing to *completely remove sin*—from both his sight and ours—through his great forgiveness. This is not license for unfaithfulness; instead it is a basis for hope for the imperfect but penitent.

One Thing to Think About: Do I ever feel haunted by the poor choices of my past?

One Thing to Pray For: Confidence and optimism in the midst of a degraded society

WEEK 26—TUESDAY

Reading: Matthew 6:1-15

How to Pray to a Gracious God

One of Jesus' primary roles is to reveal the nature of the Father to us (John 1:18). His unique perspective enables him to give us essential instruction as we try to relate to God: "*Beware of practicing your righteousness before other people in order to be seen by them, for then you will have no reward from your Father who is in heaven*"(Matt 6:1). Given the fact that the Father wants to reward us (Matt 6:1, 4, 6), seeking a different reward—the praise of men—will invalidate what we hope to receive from God. The reason, of course, is that we are not doing it to honor God, but to build our own reputations among men. That is the opposite of religion.

Jesus points out some important things to remember about God. First, he stresses that the Father "*sees in secret*"(Matt 6:4, 6). He knows what we are doing, thinking, and desiring even when people don't. Then he reminds us that "*your Father knows what you need before you ask him*"(Matt 6:8). Prayer is not a news flash for God. We will not impress or surprise him. So Jesus teaches us how to pray to a gracious God: privately, sincerely, briefly, and with an emphasis on the most important issues between us and God. Eloquence can be discarded. Honesty is essential. We must be willing to examine ourselves and forgive others.

God longs to bless us, but he also wants to be treated as if he is real and powerful. We come to him seeking favors—daily bread, forgiveness, and deliverance—but we also come offering praise. We want his approval and not merely man's.

One Thing to Think About: In what ways do I tend to do my good deeds to be seen?

One Thing to Pray For: A deeper prayer life

WEEK 26—WEDNESDAY

Reading: Matthew 11:25-30

I Will Give You Rest

In the middle of a great crowd, Jesus' message is largely negative and harsh. He criticizes them for complaining about John the Baptist's approach, then his own approach. Like children in the marketplace, they are never pleased. Then he pronounces woes on several cities who have rejected him and his message. These are not our favorite Jesus sound bites. But they make the positive turn that follows all the more surprising: "*At that time Jesus declared, 'I thank you, Father, Lord of heaven and earth, that you have hidden these things from the wise and understanding and revealed them to little children; yes, Father, for such was your gracious will*'"(Matt 11:25-26). Jesus sees this pattern of rejection and acceptance as part of God's plan. The wise and understanding will opt out of the kingdom, while the "*little children*" will become its heirs.

So he starts calling more little children. "*Come to me, all who labor and are heavy laden, and I will give you rest. Take my yoke upon you and learn from me, for I am gentle and lowly in heart, and you will find rest for your souls. For my yoke is easy, and my burden is light*"(Matt 11:28-30). Those who "*labor and are heavy laden*" are the poor, lowly seekers. They want to do right, but they struggle. They know they cannot keep the law like they should, but they are trying. They are not the great teachers. They do not move in the important circles. The world does not notice them. But they love God. Jesus calls them. He promises that he will be gentle and lowly to the gentle and lowly. He will give them a new yoke and a new path. There are things to learn and work to do, but compared to where they have been, it will be "*easy*" and "*light*." He offers rest.

Jesus is offering to be a teacher and leader to anyone who is willing to come to him. He promises to reveal the Father to anyone who will come (Matt 11:27). He knows the past history and the inner turmoil of the people he addresses—and he wants them anyway. He longs to give us rest.

One Thing to Think About: What does it feel like to "labor" and be "heavy laden"?

One Thing to Pray For: The knowledge Jesus offers

Reading: Matthew 20:1-16

You Have Made Them Equal to Us

Jesus tells this story to reveal what "*the kingdom of heaven is like*"(Matt 20:1), but he is also responding to Peter's question about what followers of Jesus will receive (Matt 19:27). In the story, workers are hired at different times to labor in the vineyard. The owner is very aggressive in bringing in more and more workers throughout the day. The key part of the story comes at the end of the day when they are all paid. Shockingly, the one-hour workers receive a *full day's wage* (Matt 20:9). The others, seeing this, are suddenly excited that they might receive more—perhaps even twelve times as much—than they originally agreed to.

They are disappointed. Everyone is paid the same. They "*grumbled at the master of the house, saying, 'These last worked only one hour, and you have made them equal to us who have borne the burden of the day and the scorching heat*'"(Matt 20:11-12). The treatment seems unfair because "*you have made them equal to us.*" It is an interesting objection because they are not lamenting their pay, but their pay *relative to others*. The master responds: "*Friend, I am doing you no wrong. Did you not agree with me for a denarius?*"(Matt 20:13). His goodness does not *wrong* anyone, it only *blesses* some. "*I choose to give to this last worker as I give to you. Am I not allowed to do what I choose with what belongs to me?*"(Matt 20:14-15). These are grace words. *I choose to give.* God reserves the right to freely give good things to the undeserving. It is only when we feel that we deserve better than others that this bothers us.

This parable spells out how grace can feel scandalous. We are concerned about justice: Do others get what they deserve? And as we try to serve God, we know that we need grace, but we also want a kind of credit for the hard work we do for him. So it is easy to resent God extending grace to the undeserving—and to forget that we ourselves are undeserving. Jesus teaches us that grace is God's right, but that it may require an adjustment in our thinking in the direction of humility.

One Thing to Think About: How do I feel when others get what they don't deserve—or don't get what they do deserve?

One Thing to Pray For: A heart to celebrate God's grace for everyone

WEEK 26—FRIDAY

Reading: Mark 8:1-10

I Have Compassion on the Crowd

These are the days in which Jesus is near the height of his fame. Huge numbers of people are streaming out into the Galilean countryside to hear him teach and experience his healing. *"In those days, when again a great crowd had gathered, and they had nothing to eat, he called his disciples to him and said to them, 'I have compassion on the crowd, because they have been with me now three days and have nothing to eat. And if I send them away hungry to their homes, they will faint on the way. And some of them have come from far away'"*(Mark 8:1-3). Jesus reveals his inner turmoil. As he serves the people, he has "*compassion*" on them, meaning that he deeply feels their difficulty. They have left their homes and jobs to come to him and have patiently followed through three days of hunger. Jesus feels sorry for them.

It is this compassion that prompts him to intervene miraculously. *"And he took the seven loaves, and having given thanks, he broke them and gave them to his disciples to set before the people; and they set them before the crowd...And they ate and were satisfied"*(Mark 8:6, 8). Taking what little food is available, Jesus produces enough that everyone is sated. There are seven baskets full of leftovers. It is easy to allow this amazing act to overshadow the marvelous motive: Jesus feeds 4000 people because he *cares*.

In our selfishness, we often grow cold toward the needs and troubles of others. We focus on how their problems affect *us*. Jesus reminds us of our need for compassion by showing us how God looks at the world. Surrounded by a hungry, desperate world, Jesus has compassion. Every gift, blessing, and encouragement God gives stems from his pity for us.

One Thing to Think About: What needs, struggles, and wounds do those around me have?

One Thing to Pray For: The compassion of Jesus—to care about and feel the pain of others

WEEK 27—MONDAY

Reading: Mark 10:23-31

A Hundredfold Now

The rich young ruler has eagerly approached Jesus, then departed sorrowful. Why? Jesus urges him to sell his possessions and give them to the poor—and he has great possessions. Jesus then turns to the disciples to teach them: "*How difficult it will be for those who have wealth to enter the kingdom of God!...It is easier for a camel to go through the eye of a needle than for a rich person to enter the kingdom of God!*" (Mark 10:23, 25). In commenting on the difficulty of this man, Jesus warns that wealth can be a massive hindrance to entering the kingdom. The disciples are "*amazed*" and "*exceedingly astonished*" at this (Mark 10:24, 26) because conventional wisdom dictates that wealth is a sign of God's favor.

But Peter takes this another way: if wealth is a problem, then the disciples should be in good shape, since they are poor! "*Peter began to say to him, 'See, we have left everything and followed you.' Jesus said, 'Truly, I say to you, there is no one who has left house or brothers or sisters or mother or father or children or lands, for my sake and for the gospel, who will not receive a hundredfold now in this time, houses and brothers and sisters and mothers and children and lands, with persecutions, and in the age to come eternal life*" (Mark 10:28-30). Jesus honors those who have left their families and homes to follow him. He also promises that such will "*receive a hundredfold now in this time, houses and brothers and sisters and mothers.*" God has blessings to give his people *now*.

"A hundredfold now" speaks to the incredible wealth of the kingdom community. We may have a divided family, but in Christ we gain a hundred times more family. We may leave houses, but we share houses with so many more people in the church. When we leave behind something lesser in pursuit of something greater, God will meet our needs and give us "a hundredfold" more through the generosity of our brethren.

One Thing to Think About: How have I seen this principle at work?

One Thing to Pray For: Possessions not to have too great a hold over me

WEEK 27—TUESDAY

Reading: Luke 1:67-79

He Has Visited and Redeemed His People

After the birth of his son John (the Baptist), Zechariah is able to speak again. His first words are a blessing to God (Luke 1:64) prompted by the Holy Spirit (Luke 1:67). "*Blessed be the Lord God of Israel, for he has visited and redeemed his people and has raised up a horn of salvation for us in the house of his servant David, as he spoke by the mouth of his holy prophets from of old*"(Luke 1:68-70). The idea of Jehovah visiting his people has a rich and distinguished history. Jehovah visits Sarah and she conceives Isaac (Gen 21:1). He visits his people in Egyptian slavery (Ex 4:31). He visits his people to give food during famine (Ruth 1:6). Here Zechariah sees the unfolding of God's plan—through John and Jesus—as a way God fulfills his word and visits again, coming near to shower blessings.

Threaded through Zechariah's song is the hope of salvation. God acts "*so that we should be saved from our enemies*"(Luke 1:71) and "*that we, being delivered from the hand of our enemies, might serve him without fear*"(Luke 1:74). He even sings to his own infant son, telling him that his mission is "*to give knowledge of salvation to his people in the forgiveness of their sins*"(Luke 1:77). Salvation implies that there is a grave threat that God's people are facing. But rescuing them from this threat involves "*the forgiveness of their sins.*" God is visiting, but not to give a short-term blessing. He will redeem his people by removing their sins forever.

The births of John and Jesus show God's willingness to intervene in history to bless his people. He has not forgotten about us. Though we are often rebellious against him, he has come near to us (visited) and given himself to pull us out of sin (redeemed).

One Thing to Think About: Why does God care so much about his people?

One Thing to Pray For: The opportunity to "serve him without fear"

WEEK 27—WEDNESDAY

Reading: Luke 6:27-38

He Is Kind to the Unthankful and Evil

As Jesus teaches his disciples how to love, he introduces the radical idea that we do not only love the worthy. "*But I say to you who hear, Love your enemies, do good to those who hate you, bless those who curse you, pray for those who abuse you*"(Luke 6:27-28). The very people who do us wrong are the ones he calls us to love, do good to, bless, and pray for. Not only do we not retaliate in response to their wrongs (turning the other cheek), but we actively do good to them. "*And as you wish that others would do to you, do so to them*"(Luke 6:31).

Jesus challenges the shallowness of basing our behavior on how others treat us. "*If you love those who love you, what benefit is that to you? For even sinners love those who love them*"(Luke 6:32). If our relationships are merely loving those who love us, what difference is religion making in our lives at all? Even evil people can meet that low bar. "*But love your enemies, and do good, and lend, expecting nothing in return, and your reward will be great, and you will be sons of the Most High, for he is kind to the ungrateful and evil*"(Luke 6:35). Loving enemies makes us like God. God is kind even when people don't deserve it. So Jesus urges us to give undeserved kindness—giving and forgiving instead of judging and condemning (Luke 6:37-38). It is an attitude that makes us gracious like God.

There is deep challenge in these words. The worldly pattern of retaliation is strongly ingrained in us. Yet it is God's example that leads us to grow here. God does not deprive people of breath, food, and people because they are evil. Certainly he works through hardship and difficulty to wake them up and bring them back to him, but he also gives them time and opportunity to do so. He is kind to them. People will do us wrong and we will have the choice: will I be like God or like other people?

One Thing to Think About: How has God been kind to me—even when I was evil?

One Thing to Pray For: A heart to love my enemies the way God does

WEEK 27—THURSDAY

Reading: Luke 11:5-13

Ask, Seek, Knock

As Jesus teaches his disciples to pray, he explains something important about the nature of the God they are praying to. He tells the story of a man who goes to his friend at midnight seeking some bread to feed a newly arrived houseguest. The friend is unwilling to help at first. *"I tell you, though he will not get up and give him anything because he is his friend, yet because of his impudence he will rise and give him whatever he needs"*(Luke 11:8). Jesus singles out the man's "*impudence*" (or "*persistence*", NKJV) that prompts him to keep knocking and bothering his friend until he gets out of bed and helps him. Jesus wants us to pray like that.

"And I tell you, ask, and it will be given to you; seek, and you will find; knock, and it will be opened to you. For everyone who asks receives, and the one who seeks finds, and to the one who knocks it will be opened"(Luke 11:9-10). Prayer works, but it must be offered diligently and persistently. Like the man visiting his friend at midnight, we may have to knock long enough to rouse the host. But Jesus is not merely teaching us to annoy God into helping us. *God wants to help and bless.* *"What father among you, if his son asks for a fish, will instead of a fish given him a serpent; or if he asks for an egg, will give him a scorpion? If you then, who are evil, know how to give good gifts to your children, how much more will the heavenly Father give the Holy Spirit to those who ask him!"*(Luke 11:11-13). Like any good father, God wants to give gifts to his kids. The difference is that God *really knows* how to give good gifts—even the Holy Spirit himself. God is itching to bless us, so we should ask, seek, and knock.

Jesus stresses that prayer is *relational rather than transactional.* God wants to bless because he is our Father. Prayer is not a process or a principle of the world that we can leverage into getting stuff. Prayer is our primary way of seeking God's good gifts. God is itching to bless us, so we should ask, seek, and knock.

One Thing to Think About: Why is persistence in prayer difficult?

One Thing to Pray For: Gratitude for God being such a good father to me

WEEK 27—FRIDAY

Reading: Luke 12:22-31

Learning to Trust God's Grace

Teaching in a large crowd, Jesus has been addressing our tendency to focus on money. He rebukes a man who is arguing with his brother over the inheritance for his covetousness (Luke 12:13-15). He then segues into a story about a rich man consumed with what he will do with all his crops, only to discover he loses his life and wealth in one night (Luke 12:16-21). In this text, he addresses the anxiety behind such fixation on money: "*Therefore I tell you, do not be anxious about your life, what you will eat, nor about your body, what you will put on. For life is more than food, and the body more than clothing*"(Luke 12:22-23). The danger is that we will not recognize the real importance of life and our bodies because we are so anxious about how to take care of them.

The answer to this anxiety touches on God's grace. "*Consider the ravens: they neither sow nor reap, they have neither storehouse nor barn, and yet God feeds them. Of how much more value are you than the birds!*"(Luke 12:24). Jesus boldly states that "*God feeds them*," then implies that God will definitely feed us, since we are worth more than birds. "*Consider the lilies, how they grow: they neither toil nor spin, yet I tell you, even Solomon in all his glory was not arrayed like one of these. But if God so clothes the grass, which is alive in the field today, and tomorrow is thrown into the oven, how much more will he clothe you, O you of little faith!*"(Luke 12:27-28). Jesus asserts that God clothes the flowers of the field, short-lived though they are. He will certainly clothe us. Our anxiety is misplaced. "*Your Father knows that you need*" food and clothing (Luke 12:30). If we seek him, he will provide.

Jesus wants us to spend some time considering nature. God takes care of his creation. He gives consistently, repeatedly, and dependably. He gives what is needed to the small and ephemeral animals and plants. God is a giver and provider. Our anxiety belies our hesitancy to trust God to take care of us. God is so good that Jesus wants us to count on his grace. He will be good to us too.

One Thing to Think About: What does anxiety have to do with trust?

One Thing to Pray For: God's help in letting go of anxiety and trusting his provision

WEEK 28—MONDAY

Reading: Luke 12:32-40

The Grace of the Kingdom

Jesus has been addressing his disciples' anxiety, especially with regard to money and the necessities of life. He tells them not to "*seek*" such things (Luke 12:29), setting their focus and hearts on them. "*Instead, seek his kingdom, and these things will be added to you*"(Luke 12:31). Seeking the kingdom means that (unlike the rich fool) we are "*rich toward God*"(Luke 12:21). We focus our attention on God's will and work rather than our own goals and desires. We pursue what is right and good—and in doing so, God will provide the food, clothes, and shelter we need.

"*Fear not, little flock, for it is your Father's good pleasure to give you the kingdom*"(Luke 12:32). Instead of fear, we rejoice because we are the object of our Father's "*good pleasure*" and grace. Daniel prophesies that "*the kingdom and the dominion and the greatness of the kingdoms under the whole heaven shall be given to the people of the saints of the Most High*"(Dan 7:27, see also Dan 7:18, 22). Even though they are a "*little flock,*" this tiny band of Jesus' followers will receive tremendous authority and glory from God. So they do not fear. Instead, Jesus calls on them to "*sell your possessions, and give to the needy. Provide yourselves with moneybags that do not grow old, with a treasure in the heavens that does not fail, where no thief approaches and no moth destroys. For where your treasure is, there will your heart be also*"(Luke 12:33-34). When we trust that God will give us the great gift of the kingdom, we worry much less about what our current financial state is. We focus on saving up heavenly treasures, confident that a wonderful glory awaits us there.

I wish I could detail more about what saints receiving the kingdom entails. Does this mean we will have positions of authority in the age to come? What will our exaltation and glorification look like? Yet my ignorance on some of these things does not detract from the clear message: despite our seeming weakness, God will bless us from his own "*good pleasure.*" We can live free and easy with poverty and hardship now because our treasure is not here.

One Thing to Think About: What do my heart, focus, words, and bank statement show about where my treasure is?

One Thing to Pray For: Wisdom not to grow too attached to material things

WEEK 28—TUESDAY

Reading: Luke 13:6-9

The Grace of Another Chance

This little parable comes in the midst of some ominous pronouncements from Jesus. He tells the crowds that he has come to cast fire on the earth and bring division to families (Luke 12:49-53). He rebukes the people for not discerning the times (Luke 12:54-59) and then interprets some recent tragedies by cautioning them that "*unless you repent, you will all likewise perish*"(Luke 13:3, 5). The fig tree parable offers both grace and warning.

A man plants a fig tree and grows frustrated that there is still no fruit. He complains to his vinedresser: "*Look, for three years now I have come seeking fruit on this fig tree, and I find none. Cut it down. Why should it use up the ground?*"(Luke 13:7). His disappointment is well-founded; what good is a fig tree that gives no figs? Yet the vinedresser—who probably has worked long and hard with the tree—pleads for mercy. "*Sir, let it alone this year also, until I dig around it and put on manure. Then if it should bear fruit next year, well and good; but if not, you can cut it down*"(Luke 13:8-9). Just one more year. The vinedresser will give it special attention, then one more opportunity to produce its fruit. The grace here is in the reprieve and the special attention. The warning is that without change, the tree's time is short.

Throughout the Bible, God's people are often pictured as a vineyard from which God wants to collect certain fruits (see Isaiah 5:1-7, Matt 21:33-44, et al). God wants his people to live in the way he expects and if they do not, he brings judgment and pulls them out of the vineyard. When we fail to live up to our purpose—especially after many years of teaching, effort, and opportunity—we frustrate God. This story helps us see God's frustration—and God's great mercy in giving us another chance. It might even be that the digging and manure here refer to the unique opportunity God's people have as Jesus comes to them. But with this grace always comes the warning—God won't give us other chances forever. We must repent and do God's works *now*—while his grace allows it.

One Thing to Think About: How has God given me extra chances to do what is right?

One Thing to Pray For: Appreciation of the urgency of my obedience to Jesus

WEEK 28—WEDNESDAY

Reading: Luke 13:10-17

The Grace of Loosing Bonds

Whether he will heal on the Sabbath is a source of continual contention between Jesus and the Jewish leaders. Here he is teaching in a synagogue on the Sabbath when a woman in desperate need stumbles in. *"And behold, there was a woman who had had a disabling spirit for eighteen years. She was bent over and could not fully straighten herself. When Jesus saw her, he called her over and said to her, 'Woman, you are freed from your disability'"*(Luke 13:11-12). The woman is crippled and cannot walk erect. She has suffered for a long time and must have slowly come to accept her compromised condition. Impulsively Jesus calls her to him and heals her.

Then the criticism begins. The synagogue ruler complains (Luke 13:14). Jesus explains his reasoning: *"You hypocrites! Does not each of you on the Sabbath untie his ox or his donkey from the manger and lead it away to water it? And ought not this woman, a daughter of Abraham whom Satan bound for eighteen years, be loosed from this bond on the Sabbath day?"*(Luke 13:15-16). No Jew would hesitate to untie his animal to water it on the Sabbath; this may appear to be work, but it is for the benefit of another. Jesus then explains that all he has done is untie this woman ("*loosed*" is the same word for untie) from her satanic bond. How is this not a greater gesture of humanity? She has suffered for 18 years—how much longer must she wait before she can have Satan's bonds on her loosed?

Jesus looses this woman's bonds as an act of grace. He does not promise to heal everyone who is crippled or loose everyone who is bound by Satan. Instead, he assures us that he is aware of our suffering and whatever healing we experience comes from him. *"If you abide in my word, you are truly my disciples, and you will know the truth, and the truth will set you free"*(John 8:31-32). Jesus looses bonds.

One Thing to Think About: In what ways have I been set free?

One Thing to Pray For: Compassion for others who are suffering

WEEK 28—THURSDAY

Reading: Luke 18:1-8

The Grace of Justice

Luke tells us precisely what Jesus hopes to communicate with this story: "*and he told them a parable to the effect that they ought always to pray and not lose heart*"(Luke 18:1). Jesus wants to encourage his disciples to pray consistently, trusting that God really does hear them and will act in his own time. In his story, a widow keeps asking a judge to rule in her favor and against her enemy. The judge is a scoundrel and doesn't care about justice, "*yet because this widow keeps bothering me, I will give her justice, so that she will not beat me down by her continual coming*"(Luke 18:5). True persistence can move mountains.

Yet the message is not that God is like this unethical judge or that we need to annoy him into action. "*And the Lord said, 'Hear what the unrighteous judge says. And will not God give justice to his elect, who cry to him day and night? Will he delay long over them? I tell you, he will give justice to them speedily*"(Luke 18:6-7). If God's chosen people, oppressed and overcome by worldly powers, "*cry to him day and night*," won't God respond? If an evil judge acts because of another's persistence, how much more a good God? Jesus assures that "*he will give justice to them speedily*." Yet he also wonders: "*Nevertheless, when the Son of Man comes, will he find faith on earth?*"(Luke 18:8). When Jesus returns, will there be people with the trust to keep asking for God's intervention?

Repeatedly Jesus describes justice as a gift that God must give. The widow asks the judge to "*give me justice*" and the judge decides that "*I will give her justice.*" "*And will not God give justice to his elect?*" All of us have situations of unfairness and injustice. We trust that we should not take revenge ourselves, but wait for the Lord. When evil seems to win, we beg and plead. Jesus promises that true, ultimate justice is coming—and urges us "*always to pray and not lose heart.*"

One Thing to Think About: How have I seen justice done? What injustices have I seen?

One Thing to Pray For: God to make all the wrongs right

WEEK 28—FRIDAY

Reading: Luke 19:1-10

Today Salvation Has Come to This House

As Jesus passes through Jericho, he encounters an interesting character in the crowd. Zacchaeus is a "*chief tax collector and was rich*"(Luke 19:2), which implies that his special role as a higher-up in the tax system has given him opportunity to enrich himself at his countrymen's expense. The echoes of his sin run throughout the story: the crowd grumbles that he is a sinner and unworthy of Jesus' presence (Luke 19:7), he speaks of his own defrauding (Luke 19:8), and Jesus speaks about saving the lost after their interaction (Luke 19:10).

Yet there are the stirrings of change in Zacchaeus. He is so eager to see Jesus that he climbs a tree. When Jesus tells him he is coming over (!), Zacchaeus "*hurried and came down and received him joyfully*"(Luke 19:6). He then boldly makes a speech to Jesus, "*Behold, Lord, the half of my goods I give to the poor. And if I have defrauded anyone of anything, I restore it fourfold*"(Luke 19:8). Zacchaeus is not stating his regular practice (or else why would anyone grumble about him?), but making a new commitment to deal fairly. Jesus declares that "*today salvation has come to this house, since he also is a son of Abraham. For the Son of Man came to seek and to save the lost*"(Luke 19:9-10). Even in Zacchaeus' house, God is able to save. Even Zacchaeus is a son of Abraham.

Zacchaeus is the inverse of the rich young ruler (Luke 18:18-23). Instead of a righteous man unwilling to change, he is a wicked man willing to change. Instead of feeling sad at being called on to give to others, he is joyful. Grace means that God is willing to save the lost, but that he expects us to have a hunger to really change our lives.

One Thing to Think About: What areas of my life need to change? What are the glaring holes in my service to God?

One Thing to Pray For: A willingness to welcome lost seekers—rather than grumbling about them

WEEK 29—MONDAY

Reading: John 1:1-13

The Grace of God's Family

John's prologue tells the gospel story in a nutshell. "*In the beginning was the Word, and the Word was with God, and the Word was God*"(John 1:1). This "Word," both accompanying God and God himself, is life itself and the light of the world. Next John the Baptist enters the picture. His role is "*as a witness, to bear witness about the light, that all may believe through him*"(John 1:7). Now we are situated in history, with John's forerunning message.

The surprising fact of the gospel is that when the light enters the world, his own creation does not acknowledge him. "*He was in the world, and the world was made through him, yet the world did not know him. He came to his own, and his own people did not receive him*"(John 1:10-11). Much of the story of Jesus' incarnation is the story of rejection, unbelief, and dismissal. "*But to all who did receive him, who believed in his name, he gave the right to become children of God, who were born, not of blood nor of the will of the flesh nor of the will of man, but of God*"(John 1:12-13). Yet to the few who do receive and believe in Jesus, he gives a gift: "*he gave the right to become children of God.*" They are given a place in God's family. John even foreshadows the new birth, stressing that God's children are not born "*of blood nor of the will of the flesh nor of the will of man*" (which most commentators take to mean sexual reproduction) but of God's will. We are both adopted into his family and born again into it—and this is a gift God gives.

Family is a wonderful gift and privilege. No one earns their place in a family. Despite our undeserving nature, God chooses to bring us into his family and make us his sons and daughters. We have a special connection with him and with Jesus, our brother. We stand to inherit great, eternal blessings. We have a new identity and a new family name to aspire to. We belong. When we believe, God's gifts flow out toward us.

One Thing to Think About: What does family mean to me? Why is being a part of God's family better than the family I have known?

One Thing to Pray For: A willingness to receive Jesus and believe in his name

WEEK 29—TUESDAY

Reading: John 1:14-18

From His Fullness We Have All Received

John concludes the prologue to his gospel by explaining how the Word comes down to live among people. "*And the Word became flesh and dwelt among us, and we have seen his glory, glory as of the only Son from the Father, full of grace and truth*"(John 1:14). This eternal Word—who *is* God (John 1:1)—has now become his creation. He takes on flesh, yet even as a man there is a divine glory that attends to him—"*glory as of the only Son from the Father.*" He also shares God's giving nature because he is "*full of grace and truth.*" Jesus' ministry is characterized by gifts of favor and dispensing of true words about man, life, and God.

This incarnation is a gift. "*For from his fullness we have all received, grace upon grace. For the law was given through Moses; grace and truth came through Jesus Christ*"(John 1:16-17). Everyone has experienced God's grace and through Jesus we receive an even richer blessing. Through Moses, God gave the law as a great blessing, but through Jesus, he gives *both grace and truth.* Especially does John want us to know that through Jesus, we know God better. "*No one has ever seen God; the only God, who is at the Father's side, he has made him known*"(John 1:18). The Law taught what God *wants*; Jesus reveals *who God is.*

Jesus' coming is a wonderful sign of God's goodwill toward his creation. Though we are rebellious and recalcitrant, he continues to shower us with blessings. He sends his Son to reveal his mind and heart to us and to open up new avenues for grace to us. "*From his fullness we have all received.*" Every creature constantly benefits from God's goodness. In Jesus, we see "*grace upon grace.*"

One Thing to Think About: How does Jesus help *me* to know God better?

One Thing to Pray For: Spiritual eyes to see Jesus in all his glory

WEEK 29—WEDNESDAY

Reading: John 4:7-15

The Grace of Living Water

Jesus sits by a well in Samaria and asks a Samaritan woman to give him a drink. She is surprised because of the racial and gender climate of the time: *"How is that you, a Jew, ask for a drink from me, a woman of Samaria?"*(John 4:9). Jesus brushes aside the social part and focuses on the asking for a drink: *"If you knew the gift of God, and who it is that is saying to you, 'Give me a drink,' you would have asked him, and he would have given you living water"*(John 4:10). Jesus alludes to a gift God wants to give—and assures her that *he himself* has the power to give it to her. This gift is equated with *"living water"*—an image that draws the woman's interest.

While she is focused on the logistics of living water—how to get it out of the well—Jesus stresses that there is more to it. *"Everyone who drinks of this water will be thirsty again, but whoever drinks of the water that I will give him will never be thirsty again. The water that I will give him will become in him a spring of water welling up to eternal life"*(John 4:13-14). Physical needs like thirst are only satisfied temporarily, but Jesus' water will quench the inner thirst permanently. In fact, he promises to give water that will take root within a person and *"become in him a spring of water welling up to eternal life."* Missing Jesus' soaring language, the woman comments that she will be excited not to have to carry her water jar.

What is this great gift of living water Jesus offers? Living water was a common description of running water that did not grow stagnant. Jews used living water to become ceremonially clean. Jesus brings life and purity to our spirits. As we will see in coming days, Jesus offers spiritual life to his followers in various metaphors. There is also a possibility that he is referring to the indwelling of the Holy Spirit, since he uses water pictures to describe that in John 7:38-39. Whatever the specific reference, *Jesus offers a gift that will bless and sustain us.* We want living water.

One Thing to Think About: How does Jesus quench my thirst?

One Thing to Pray For: Jesus to continue to give me living water—to bless and sustain me

Reading: John 5:19-29

The Grace of Life

Just prior to this section, Jesus has healed an official's son who was at the point of death, then healed a man crippled for 38 years. The Jews in authority, though, criticize him for healing the latter man on the Sabbath, which they consider a violation of God's law. Jesus responds by stressing his close relationship with the Father: "*Truly, truly, I say to you, the Son can do nothing of his own accord, but only what he sees the Father doing. For whatever the Father does, that the Son does likewise*" (John 5:19). Jesus is not breaking ranks with God to do his own thing; he is doing precisely what God has shown him.

But Jesus also wants them to know that his miracles speak to greater things ahead. "*For as the Father raises the dead and gives them life, so also the Son gives life to whom he will*" (John 5:21). Life is a gift. The Father gives it to people and Jesus shares the ability to give life. Part of this is about spiritual life: "*Truly, truly, I say to you, an hour is coming, and is now here, when the dead will hear the voice of the Son of God, and those who hear will live*" (John 5:25). This is those who believe in Jesus (John 5:24) and so emerge from a state of spiritual death into eternal life. But Jesus' great works—and power over physical death—also point to this power. "*Do not marvel at this, for an hour is coming when all who are in the tombs will hear his voice and come out, those who have done good to the resurrection of life, and those who have done evil to the resurrection of judgment*" (John 5:28-29). Jesus' voice not only calls people to eternal life now; it will also jumpstart the physical resurrection. In every circumstance, Jesus is giving and promising life.

Life is a gift. We do not earn it or deserve it. God offers no guarantees about physical life now, but he does promise eternal life—a blessed, joyful existence for eternity—to those who believe in Jesus. Yet even in this, it is God who is the source of life and we are only his beneficiaries. We must learn to be grateful for the measure of life he gives us now and eagerly anticipate the promised life to come.

One Thing to Think About: Why is life so fragile? What can I learn from that fact?

One Thing to Pray For: A desire to respond to Jesus' voice *now*

WEEK 29—FRIDAY

Reading: John 6:27-37

The Grace of True Bread

In this intriguing little scene, the crowds follow Jesus across the Sea of Galilee after he has fed the 5000. Yet Jesus knows that they are not interested in the teaching and miracles, but bread. "*Truly, truly, I say to you, you are seeking me, not because you saw signs, but because you ate your fill of the loaves. Do not work for the food that perishes, but for the food that endures to eternal life, which the Son of Man will give to you*"(John 6:26-27). Jesus wants to give them "*the food that endures to eternal life*," but only if they will stop focusing so much on him giving them more free bread. It is hard to talk about spiritual things with carnally minded people.

Jesus and the crowd banter back and forth. How do we do God's works? Believe in the one he sent. What sign will you do? You know Moses gave bread… "*Jesus then said to them, 'Truly, truly, I say to you, it was not Moses who gave you the bread from heaven, but my Father gives you the true bread from heaven. For the bread of God is he who comes down from heaven and gives life to the world*'"(John 6:32-33). The manna did not satisfy the Israelites forever. God is giving them a greater gift. "*I am the bread of life; whoever comes to me shall not hunger, and whoever believes in me shall never thirst*"(John 6:35). By believing in and following Jesus, our needs are met completely. This is not a promise that we will never be physically hungry or thirsty. Jesus is promising to sustain and satisfy all our spiritual needs. And he will do it *for free*—he will *give us* this true bread.

Hunger and thirst are Jesus' way of describing the aching needs of our hearts. We try to fill them with worldly things—people, experiences, fun, money, status—but always find them lacking. We still feel lonely, still get tired, still get old, still feel lost, still feel bitter. Jesus gives us direction and peace. We have a companion, a hope, and an expectation of a new body. He satisfies our needs so that we can rest easy in him. This is a marvelous gift.

One Thing to Think About: How has Jesus given me peace?

One Thing to Pray For: Wisdom to see the insufficiency of worldly things to satisfy my soul

WEEK 30—MONDAY

Reading: John 10:1-5

He Calls His Own Sheep by Name

Jesus gives the extended metaphor of a shepherd with his sheep to describe his relationship with his disciples. As our studies this year have shown us, this is a very common picture in the Old Testament. For Jesus, it comes in the aftermath of the healing of the man born blind, who is then persecuted for his simple faith in Jesus. He is one of Jesus' sheep. "*Truly, truly, I say to you, he who does not enter the sheepfold by the door but climbs in by another way, that man is a thief and a robber. But he who enters by the door is the shepherd of the sheep*"(John 10:1-2). The fold is a safe enclosure for the sheep to be sheltered. If someone tries to enter the fold without using the door or gate, he is not the legitimate shepherd. Only Jesus has the credentials—power, love, and obedience to God—that prompt us to follow him.

Then Jesus describes taking the sheep out of the fold. "*The sheep hear his voice, and he calls his own sheep by name and leads them out. When he has brought out all his own, he goes before them, and the sheep follow him, for they know his voice*"(John 10:3-4). Shepherds in the Near East often have unique calls that their sheep recognize and follow. Jesus "*calls his own sheep by name and leads them out.*" Each one is uniquely his and he knows them personally. He knows their names. The sheep trust him because "*they know his voice.*" But "*a stranger they will not follow, but they will flee from him, for they do not know the voice of strangers*"(John 10:5). Jesus seems to refer here to people like the blind man (John 9:33) and the crippled man (John 5:11) who endure hostility from the Jewish authorities because they believe in Jesus. Jesus' sheep know his voice—and will *only* follow him.

There is a beauty and intimacy to this picture. It is a simple shepherd loving and watching over his sheep. He has a special name for each one. He knows the difference between them. They are *his*. Our job, as sheep, is simply to follow our shepherd—and no other.

One Thing to Think About: How does it make me feel to know that Jesus knows my name?

One Thing to Pray For: Discernment to know the difference between Jesus' voice and "the voice of strangers"

WEEK 30—TUESDAY

Reading: John 10:7-10

Abundant Life

Jesus has been describing his role as shepherd, characterized by him entering the sheepfold by the door and knowing the sheep by name. Now he plays with the image a bit: "*Truly, truly, I say to you, I am the door of the sheep*"(John 10:7). Most sheepfolds have a door or gate that allows entry and exit, but also protects the sheep from intruders or wild animals. Jesus is that door—allowing both access and safety. "*I am the door. If anyone enters by me, he will be saved and will go in and out and find pasture*"(John 10:9). Approaching God through Jesus means not only salvation, but continued provision—"*pasture.*" Just like this sounds for the sweet life for a sheep, so following Jesus is the height of human existence.

But Jesus contrasts these blessings with others who claim to lead people and speak for God. "*All who came before me are thieves and robbers, but the sheep did not listen to them*"(John 10:8). Many have attempted to lead God's people, but Jesus' sheep know the difference in the shepherd and the thief. "*The thief comes only to steal and kill and destroy. I came that they may have life and have it abundantly*"(John 10:10). Motives matter. Corrupt leaders are out for themselves; Jesus longs to bless and take care of the sheep. He wants us to "*have life and have it abundantly*"—to experience what it means to *truly live*. He wants us to fulfill the original purpose God had for all people when he created us.

Jesus uses the word "life" here to denote far more than mere physical existence. We can continue to live without *truly living*. Jesus has come to provide spiritual life that begins now and extends through eternity. His blessings ensure we will forever have far more than we need to *truly live*.

One Thing to Think About: Do I really believe that Jesus has my best interests at heart?

One Thing to Pray For: Abundant life—the capacity to truly live

WEEK 30—WEDNESDAY

Reading: John 10:11-18

I Lay Down My Life for the Sheep

Jesus claims to be the "good shepherd" for a number of reasons, but one stands above the rest. "*The good shepherd lays down his life for the sheep*"(John 10:11). He envisions a scenario in which a predator approaches the sheep and the shepherd has a choice to make—to save his sheep or save his own skin. "*He who is a hired hand and not a shepherd, who does not own the sheep, sees the wolf coming and leaves the sheep and flees, and the wolf snatches them and scatters them. He flees because he is a hired hand and cares nothing for the sheep*"(John 10:12-13). If we are just doing a job—like a hired shepherd—then we will not risk our lives to save sheep. Jesus speaks of many would-be leaders who don't love their followers and are not really motivated by helping them.

Jesus is different. "*I am the good shepherd. I know my own and my own know me, just as the Father knows me and I know the Father; and I lay down my life for the sheep*"(John 10:14-15). Jesus' familiarity with his people means that he won't run from danger but will offer himself to spare them. "*For this reason the Father loves me, because I lay down my life that I may take it up again. No one takes it from me, but I lay it down of my own accord*"(John 10:17-18). Some of the images don't directly translate—the crucifixion is not about wolves attacking us, nor do shepherds regularly take up their lives again after dying. But the sense is clear: Jesus offers himself for the good of his sheep. Laying down his life is the permanent proof that he is not in this for himself.

As we study God's grace this year, this is a gift that stands above the others. Jesus does not merely give us a blessing; he gives something that deeply costs him. He lays down his own life for our good. If some person died for us, we would feel tremendously grateful and be deeply affected by their act. How much more Jesus?

One Thing to Think About: Who would I be willing to die for? What does this say about Jesus' feelings for me?

One Thing to Pray For: A sacrificial love for others

WEEK 30—THURSDAY

Reading: John 10:22-30

The Grace of Security

Jesus' parable about the shepherd and the sheep is interrupted by some hostile reactions (John 10:19-21). Some of the Jews, meanwhile, want to end all the metaphors and convince Jesus to say something incriminating. "*How long will you keep us in suspense? If you are the Christ, tell us plainly*"(John 10:24). Jesus sidesteps their trap but insists that the problem here is not that they lack information. "*I told you, and you do not believe. The works that I do in my Father's name bear witness about me, but you do not believe because you are not among my sheep*"(John 10:25-26). Here's the rub: these people are not really following God, so they cannot hear his Son (see John 8:42, 47).

But this leads Jesus to say more about his sheep. "*My sheep hear my voice, and I know them, and they follow me. I give them eternal life, and they will never perish, and no one will snatch them out of my hand. My Father, who has given them to me, is greater than all, and no one is able to snatch them out of the Father's hand*"(John 10:27-29). Jesus *gives* his sheep eternal life as they follow him. They have pasture and abundant life. But because Jesus gives them this gift, "*they will never perish*" and "*no one will snatch them out of my hand.*" In the language of the sheep, no wolves or thieves can take them away from the shepherd. When we follow Jesus, we need not fear that we will be lost. We can rest secure.

John's gospel speaks frequently of persecution and opposition. The blind man, the lame man, and Lazarus are targeted because they receive Jesus' healing. The world will hate Jesus' people (John 15:18-20). Yet here he gives us a gift—the certainty that none of these outside attacks can sever our relationship with him. They will not snatch us away. If we follow Jesus, we need fear no one.

One Thing to Think About: Why does it matter if we feel secure? Why do we struggle so much with this?

One Thing to Pray For: The faith to rest secure in Jesus

WEEK 30—FRIDAY

Reading: John 14:1-4

I Go to Prepare a Place for You

Judas has already left the room to betray Jesus. The cross is looming. Darkness hovers over this night and the disciples feel it. Jesus tells the disciples that he will be leaving them soon: "*Where I am going you cannot follow me now, but you will follow me afterward*"(John 13:36). Peter is distressed and confused. Jesus comforts him: "*Let not your hearts be troubled. Believe in God; believe also in me. In my Father's house are many rooms. If it were not so, would I have told you that I go to prepare a place for you?*"(John 14:1-2). While it is natural for them to be sad because Jesus is leaving them, he insists that this leaving is for their good. He is going, but he is going to prepare a place for them among the "many rooms" in the Father's house. He asks them to trust him.

"*And if I go and prepare a place for you, I will come again and will take you to myself, that where I am you may be also. And you know the way that I am going*"(John 14:3-4). Just as assuredly as he is leaving, Jesus assures them that "*I will come again.*" This is a clear promise of Jesus' second coming. When he comes, he will take his disciples with him. The goal is for Jesus and his people to live together *permanently*—"*that where I am you be may be also.*" Jesus' departure is a necessary part of the unfolding of God's plan to live with his people forever.

When Jesus promises, "*I go to prepare a place for you,*" it is possible to read with the emphasis on *place*. This means that Jesus will make an eternal habitation for us that cannot be taken from us or assaulted by any outside force. But we can also read it with emphasis on *you*—"*I go to prepare a place for you.*" This reminds us of the remarkable gift of God—to make special preparation for *me* to live with him eternally.

One Thing to Think About: How does this promise take the sting out of Jesus' physical absence?

One Thing to Pray For: The time when I can truly and fully be with Jesus

WEEK 31—MONDAY

Reading: John 14:15-17

The Grace of a Helper

Jesus is having a long talk with his disciples to prepare them for the time when he is no longer with them. *"If you love me, you will keep my commandments. And I will ask the Father, and he will give you another Helper, to be with you forever, even the Spirit of truth"*(John 14:15-16). Even when he is not physically present, Jesus expects his disciples to continue to follow his commands. Yet as they follow him, Jesus promises that the Father will (at his request) "*give you another Helper.*" The word helper here has many nuances. It can mean a comforter, an advocate, or a counselor. It is someone who is called alongside another to perform a special service. The Holy Spirit will come and help, comfort, counsel, and advocate for them. Jesus will be gone, but the disciples will not be on their own.

Jesus explains that this helper is "*the Spirit of truth, whom the world cannot receive, because it neither sees him nor knows him. You know him, for he dwells with you and will be in you*"(John 14:17). The Spirit is connected with truth because part of his role is to reveal God's will (particularly through the preaching of the apostles). They receive him because they belong to Jesus, not the world. The Spirit "*dwells with you and will be in you*"—a part of their hearts, thinking, and words. Jesus similarly says that "*if anyone loves me, he will keep my word, and my Father will love him, and we will come to him and make our home with him*"(John 14:23). Dwelling and making his home within us speak to a special relationship that empowers and blesses us as we do God's will.

There is a lot of mystery about the working of the Spirit. The apostles possessed the Spirit in a unique way because God used them as his messengers to reveal the word and record Scripture. Yet all believers are indwelled by the Spirit of God (Rom 8:9). How does he work? What are the specifics of the indwelling? I can't answer all the questions I have, but I know that Jesus intends the Spirit as a helper to us. He provides us with strength, produces his fruit, and is an assurance of eternal life. He is a tremendous gift.

One Thing to Think About: Do I ever feel like I need a helper?

One Thing to Pray For: A deeper understanding and awareness of the work of the Holy Spirit

WEEK 31—TUESDAY

Reading: John 14:25-31

The Grace of Peace

Jesus is preparing his disciples for his departure. "*These things I have spoken to you while I am still with you. But the Helper, the Holy Spirit, whom the Father will send in my name, he will teach you all things and bring to your remembrance all that I have said to you*"(John 14:25-26). Things are moving fast for the disciples at the moment. Everything is turning upside down and a pall has been cast over the whole night. Jesus assures them that the coming Spirit will help them to understand and remember all that is important about what is happening. They will not be limited by their imperfect understanding, faulty memory, or overwhelming emotion.

Then Jesus offers a gift: "*Peace I leave with you; my peace I give to you. Not as the world gives do I give to you. Let not your hearts be troubled, neither let them be afraid*"(-John 14:27). "Peace" (shalom) is the typical Jewish greeting for both hello and goodbye. Jesus is saying goodbye, but is also urging them to truly be at peace within. Their hearts are settled by the awareness that Jesus is going to the Father, but will also come back to them (John 14:28). What will happen in the coming days will test their faith, but Jesus wants them to trust that it is not the end of their connection with God. In the shadow of the cross, he is at peace—and he wants them to be too.

Jesus stresses that he *gives* peace. This is not about meditating for a sufficient amount of time to quiet our own minds. It is the assurance that because we are at peace with God, whatever happens to us is not as important of what he thinks about us. He also stresses that "*not as the world gives do I give to you.*" Worldly peace is circumstantial; it comes and goes depending on the situation. Jesus gives us peace that is deeper, stronger, and more permanent.

One Thing to Think About: Am I at peace? Why—or why not?

One Thing to Pray For: The peace of Christ to rule in my heart (Col 3:15)

WEEK 31—WEDNESDAY

Reading: Acts 4:23-37

The Grace of Boldness

We have moved forward to the early church. Jesus has ascended to heaven and the Spirit has come, as Jesus promised. Yet Peter and John have been arrested and threatened not to speak or teach anymore in Jesus' name (Acts 4:18). Now they gather with the other believers and pray. They remember together the prophecy of Psalm 2 that rulers and kings will oppose the Messiah—and they now feel the force of that passage personally. "*And now, Lord, look upon their threats and grant to your servants to continue to speak your word with all boldness, while you stretch out your hand to heal, and signs and wonders are performed through the name of your holy servant Jesus*"(Acts 4:29-30). They ask this favor of God: that he empower them to continue to preach and not be cowed by their persecutors.

God answers. "*And when they had prayed, the place in which they were gathered together was shaken, and they were all filled with the Holy Spirit and continued to speak the word of God with boldness*"(Acts 4:31). God gives them a gift, presumably through the Holy Spirit, and they are newly bold. Not only that, but this response seems to unleash a new burst of energy in the Christian community. "*There was not a needy person among them, for as many as were owners of lands or houses sold them and brought the proceeds of what was sold and laid it at the apostles' feet, and it was distributed to each as any had need*"(Acts 4:34-35). They are bound together in their boldness and advocacy for Jesus. They share in their goods. Luke summarizes all of this by saying that "*great grace was upon them all*"(Acts 4:33).

Peter and John have already been singled out by the ruling authorities because of their boldness (Acts 4:13). Boldness involves courage, persistence, and a willingness to jeopardize relationships in order to say what needs to be said. Yet boldness is not pictured here as merely a natural gift some have and some do not. It is a gift of God, there for our asking. If we want to speak what is right and good, God will empower us to do it.

One Thing to Think About: How bold am I? How could God help me here?

One Thing to Pray For: That I might speak God's word with all boldness

WEEK 31—THURSDAY

Reading: Acts 10:34-43

Grace without Partiality

Peter has come into the house of a Roman centurion, which is a notable occurrence in itself. Many Jews felt at this time that entering a Gentile's home defiled them, and it has taken a vision, the Spirit's reassurance, and the presence of an angel to convince Peter. Yet here he is, with a fresh realization to declare: "*Truly I understand that God shows no partiality, but in every nation anyone who fears him and does what is right is acceptable to him*"(Acts 10:34-35). The stress of this statement is on God's *openness* to accepting people of all kinds, provided that they are willing to serve him. God has already said as much to Cornelius (Acts 10:4), but Peter now understands.

Yet Cornelius still needs to hear about Jesus and be saved through faith in him. So Peter preaches to him about Jesus. He specifies that Jesus is "*Lord of all*"(Acts 10:36), not just Jews. He recaps how Jesus "*went about doing good and healing all who were oppressed by the devil, for God was with him*"(Acts 10:38). Yet the Jewish leaders condemned and executed him. God raised Jesus, showed him in certain appearances to the apostles, and sent them to testify to the world. "*To him all the prophets bear witness that everyone who believes in him receives forgiveness of sins through his name*"(Acts 10:43). Forgiveness is available to everyone—*everyone*—who believes in him.

In Jesus, God has offered forgiveness to sinful mankind. But that offer is not based on our works or our race. *Everyone* who believes can receive this gift—even if they come from a distant land or have lived an awful life previously. God is so generous that he is willing to give this forgiveness utterly without partiality.

One Thing to Think About: Why do I hesitate to give without partiality?

One Thing to Pray For: Praise to God for accepting me despite everything I am

WEEK 31—FRIDAY

Reading: Acts 11:19-26

Seeing the Grace of God

After Peter's visit to Cornelius' house, Jewish Christians begin to get involved in the spread of the gospel to Gentiles. A group of them come to Antioch and "*spoke to the Hellenists also, preaching the Lord Jesus. And the hand of the Lord was with them, and a great number who believed turned to the Lord*"(Acts 11:20-21). Jesus' hand is with them and the gospel finds a rich audience in these Gentiles. "*The report of this came to the ears of the church in Jerusalem, and they sent Barnabas to Antioch*"(Acts 11:22). Wanting to encourage this new mission field, the Jerusalem church sends Barnabas—a noted encourager—to help ground the young converts.

"*When he came and saw the grace of God, he was glad, and he exhorted them all to remain faithful to the Lord with steadfast purpose, for he was a good man, full of the Holy Spirit and of faith. And a great many people were added to the Lord*"(Acts 11:23-24). Barnabas arrives and "*saw the grace of God.*" It is clear to him that Jesus is doing a great work in this place. He puts his own hands to the work, exhorting the new believers. A positive spirit abounds among them and many more eagerly join them. Barnabas even sees a role in Antioch for Saul, so he travels to Tarsus to bring him back to Antioch. "*For a whole year they met with the church and taught a great many people*"(Acts 11:26). God's word thrives.

I am intrigued by the idea that Barnabas "*came and saw the grace of God.*" He has spiritual eyes to see what others might overlook. Worldly people would simply see a pointless change of religion; Barnabas sees that God is at work, giving gifts. Barnabas sees the boundless potential of a life-changing message in a major city among a new demographic. We would do well to see God's grace in our everyday lives. Instead of desperate, doomed situations—instead of noticing all that is imperfect—instead of dismissing good things as unimportant—we need to notice God's grace. Infected with that vision, we can exhort others, involve others in working with God, and build the kingdom to God's glory.

One Thing to Think About: Do I have trouble seeing God's grace? Why might that be?

One Thing to Pray For: A heart to exhort

WEEK 32—MONDAY

Reading: Acts 13:42-48

The Rejection of Grace

While visiting the synagogue in Antioch of Pisidia, Paul is invited to speak and preaches about Jesus. "*Let it be known to you, therefore, brothers, that through this man forgiveness of sins is proclaimed to you, and by him everyone who believes is freed from everything from which you could not be freed by the law of Moses*"(Acts 13:38-39). There is freedom and hope in this message, yet Paul also adds a foreboding warning from Habakkuk about unbelief (Acts 13:40-41). It is this rejection of grace that forms the heart of our text.

After this initial sermon, there is general excitement as the Jews want to hear more about Jesus. "*And after the meeting of the synagogue broke up, many Jews and devout converts to Judaism followed Paul and Barnabas, who, as they spoke with them, urged them to continue in the grace of God*"(Acts 13:43). They respond favorably to the message of grace and Paul pushes them to continue in it. Yet the next Sabbath a great crowd gathers to hear the gospel and the Pisidian Jews grow jealous and argue with Paul. Recognizing their hard-heartedness, Paul makes a decision to move on. "*It was necessary that the word of God be spoken first to you. Since you thrust it aside and judge yourselves unworthy of eternal life, behold, we are turning to the Gentiles*"(Acts 13:46). For their part, the Gentiles are thrilled, "*rejoicing and glorifying the word of the Lord, and as many as were appointed to eternal life believed*"(Acts 13:48).

Not everyone wants God's gifts. God offers freedom and forgiveness and some of his own people refuse him. Yet the reason matters too. They have become jealous of the attention Paul is getting and of the presence of the Gentiles. They do not reject the gospel as much as personally resent the way things are playing out. Often our emotions—jealousy, disappointment, bitterness, anger—lead us to reject God's good gifts. This is a terrible tragedy.

One Thing to Think About: How do other people influence the way I think about God's gifts? Do I ever feel jealous of what God has given others?

One Thing to Pray For: God's freedom and forgiveness

WEEK 32—TUESDAY

Reading: Acts 14:1-7

The Grace of Signs and Wonders

After the majority of the Jews in Pisidian Antioch grew hostile to Paul and raised up persecution to them, they have moved on to Iconium. Their initial foray here meets success: "*Now at Iconium they entered together into the synagogue and spoke in such a way that a great number of both Jews and Greeks believed*"(Acts 14:1). Many of the Jews accept Jesus as the promised Messiah, but there are also many Greeks (presumably those who are interested in Judaism) who also believe. "*But the unbelieving Jews stirred up the Gentiles and poisoned their minds against the brothers*"(Acts 14:2). Unsatisfied to simply reject the message for themselves, some of the unbelievers try to cause trouble among the Gentile officials of the city.

In this challenging climate of hostility and faith, Paul decides to stay and keep teaching. "*So they remained for a long time, speaking boldly for the Lord, who bore witness to the word of his grace, granting signs and wonders to be done by their hands*"(Acts 14:3). Not only is the gospel itself "*the word of his grace,*" but Jesus gives more grace, "*granting signs and wonders to be done by their hands.*" Paul and Barnabas are able to demonstrate the true power of their message, establishing faith and lending them credibility. Though they do not become a permanent fixture in Iconium, God's grace enables them to do faith-building work in difficult territory.

Signs and wonders are always done at God's discretion. Even the apostles can only ask God to do special works—and he can always say no. Yet when God chooses to give signs and wonders, they are often spectacular confirmations of his power, wisdom, and goodwill that echo through the centuries. His signs also establish the prophetic credibility of his spokesmen, encouraging us to trust that Paul's word really is inspired. Rather than lamenting why God doesn't always give signs and wonders today, our time is better spent appreciating what God has already given.

One Thing to Think About: Why might God not always use miracles to reach mankind?

One Thing to Pray For: Confidence in the power of God's words to convince and convict

Reading: Acts 14:8-18

He Did Good

Paul and Barnabas have moved on to Lystra and are preaching there when Paul notices a crippled man. "*Seeing that he had faith to be made well*" (Acts 14:9), Paul tells him to stand up and, in doing so, heals him. The crowd is astounded and immediately conclude that Paul and Barnabas are gods who have come down in human flesh (a common occurrence in the Greek pantheon). They declare Barnabas Zeus (perhaps he is a larger man?) and Paul Hermes (because he is the more prominent speaker).

This is all amusing until they start to prepare to sacrifice to them. Barnabas and Paul tear their clothes and begin to plead with the people: "*We are also men, of like nature with you, and we bring you good news that you should turn from these vain things to a living God, who made the heaven and the earth and the sea and all that is in them*" (Acts 14:15-16). He is, of course, implying that Zeus and Hermes are *not* living gods while Jehovah is. But Paul insists that any theology that would leave us sacrificing to people is "*vain.*" One God is the maker of heaven, earth, and sea. This God "*did not leave himself without witness, for he did good by giving you rains from heaven and fruitful seasons, satisfying your hearts with food and gladness*" (Acts 14:17). Even the Greeks should know this God, since has offered his own testimony throughout the ages. "*He did good*"—and the good in the world, from the food we eat to the joy that makes us laugh, is his doing.

There is so much good in the world. While it is true that there is also evil that corrupts and harms, there is also good. Where does it come from? Paul argues that the evidence for God's existence comes from all the good we see and experience. Even a sin-stained world is good enough that we are surprised, frustrated, and disappointed when we don't regularly see good. The goodness in other's character, the satisfaction of good work, the joy of human relationships, the sweet taste of good food, the thrill of a good night's sleep, the beauty in a sunset, the chance to see someone smile—these are gifts from a good God.

One Thing to Think About: What good is there in my life right now?

One Thing to Pray For: Worship to God that is worthy of his goodness to me

Reading: Acts 15:1-11

Relief from the Yoke of the Law

Some of the Jewish Christians come down to Antioch and warn the Gentile believers there that there is more they need to do to be saved by Jesus. "*Unless you are circumcised according to the custom of Moses, you cannot be saved*" (Acts 15:1). The argument is that they are not saved just by their obedient faith; they must now submit to circumcision and a life of keeping the Law of Moses. "*It is necessary to circumcise them and to order them to keep the Law of Moses*" (Acts 15:5). The strong implication is that they are not acceptable to God as they are—the way Jews would be.

In the ensuing debate, Peter reminds them that he was the first to acknowledge God's acceptance of Gentiles in the house of Cornelius. "*And God, who knows the heart, bore witness to them, by giving them the Holy Spirit just as he did to us, and he made no distinction between us and them, having cleansed their hearts by faith*" (Acts 15:8-9). Thinking back to that scene, Peter recalls that God "*cleansed their hearts by faith*" and gave them the Holy Spirit without their circumcision or law-keeping. He draws a conclusion from this: "*Now, therefore, why are you putting God to the test by placing a yoke on the neck of the disciples that neither our fathers nor we have been able to bear? But we believe that we will be saved through the grace of the Lord Jesus, just as they will*" (Acts 15:10-11). To insist on circumcision and law-keeping—to "Judaize" Gentile converts—is to test God and place an unbearable yoke on them. The contrast to that yoke is *grace*—grace that saves both Jew and Gentile believers.

Peter declares that "*neither our fathers nor we have been able to bear*" the yoke of perfect law-keeping. The law makes constant demands and insists on perfection. It is too much for imperfect humans to live up to. Yet grace is a relief. Instead of perfection, there is forgiveness. God still expects obedience, but his favor is no longer dependent on our goodness.

One Thing to Think About: How is perfect law-keeping like a yoke? Have I ever experienced this?

One Thing to Pray For: A heart that makes no distinctions between people—like God

WEEK 32—FRIDAY

Reading: Acts 17:22-25

Life and Breath and Everything

Paul is addressing a group of philosophers in Athens as he stands on the Areopagus, a large rock in the shadow of the Parthenon and many temples to Greek gods. "*Men of Athens, I perceive that in every way you are very religious. For as I passed along and observed the objects of your worship, I found also an altar with this inscription, 'To the unknown god.' What therefore you worship as unknown, this I proclaim to you*"(Acts 17:22-23). Paul compliments their religious interest. They are a very spiritually aware people, but the gods they serve are the problem. Somewhere in the city Paul has noticed an altar to "the unknown god." This altar is probably the product of concern that neglecting some god would lead him to be angry and inflict some disaster on the city.

But Paul explains who this "unknown god" really is: "*The God who made the world and everything in it, being Lord of heaven and earth, does not live in temples made by man*"(Acts 17:24). Paul declares that the universe is not the result of titanic warfare, but God's creation. This God is also the Lord of his creation, reigning over and sustaining it. As such, he does not live in something his creatures build for him. "*Nor is he served by human hands, as though he needed anything, since he himself gives to all mankind life and breath and everything*"(Acts 17:25). Unlike these other gods, the true God is not dependent on people. Man does not give to him; *he gives to man.* He gives man "*life and breath and everything.*" He gives life and maintains life—from life's first cry to final breath. It is all a gift from him.

God doesn't need us; we need him. We do not sustain him; he sustains us. These facts make his grace all the greater. "*He himself gives to all mankind life and breath and everything.*" I am alive today by the grace of God. Each breath I take is a gift from him. Everything I have and am is—in one way or another—his.

One Thing to Think About: How am I using the time—life and breath—that God has given me?

One Thing to Pray For: A constant awareness of God's sustaining of my life

WEEK 33—MONDAY

Reading: Acts 17:26-29

That They Should Seek God

Paul is still speaking to the philosophers of Athens on the Areopagus, explaining the "unknown God" they worship. Not only has God created the world—including mankind—but he has sustained it down to the present. *"And he made from one man every nation of mankind to live on all the face of the earth, having determined allotted periods and the boundaries of their dwelling place, that they should seek God, and perhaps feel their way toward him and find him"*(Acts 17:26-27). Just as he made the heavens and the earth, so he has made the full race of mankind, assigning them appropriate nations, boundaries, and times of flourishing. The goal of such nations and cultures is *"that they should seek God"* and *"feel their way toward him and find him."* God is willing to be sought and found by his creatures. He wants people of all backgrounds to search for him. This is our purpose.

Since God is spirit, *"he is actually not far from each one of us"*(Acts 17:27). He does not live in temples people build (Acts 17:24). Instead, *"'in him we live and move and have our being'; as even some of your own poets have said, 'For we are indeed his offspring'"*(Acts 17:27-28). Since God is the creator of all people and wants them to seek him, it should not surprise us that people in all cultures feel this need to reach out for God. Paul cites two Greek poets who confirm this impulse—that we derive our being from God and that we are his offspring. If this is the case, then God is not *"like gold or silver or stone, an image formed by the art and imagination of man"*(Acts 17:29). We can seek God, but he is not to be found in man's works and imaginations.

Paul's picture of God is of a benevolent creator who longs to be known by his creation. He is close to us. We are his offspring. We have our being in him. He gives us life and breath and all things. This desire for his people—despite the sin we commit and the ways we fall short of his glory—is a part of God's great grace.

One Thing to Think About: How am I seeking God?

One Thing to Pray For: A hunger to know the God who gives me life

Reading: Acts 26:12-23

The Help that Comes from God

Paul has been arrested and is now testifying before Governor Festus and King Agrippa. As he often does, Paul takes the opportunity to tell the story of the great change in his life that started with a vision of Jesus. "*I myself was convinced that I ought to do many things in opposing the name of Jesus of Nazareth*"(Acts 26:9). Previously, he thought that the only course for a faithful Jew was fighting against this new movement. This is why he was traveling to Damascus when he saw a bright light and a voice asking, "*Saul, Saul, why are you persecuting me? It is hard for you to kick against the goads*"(Acts 26:14). Where Paul believed he was persecuting a misguided movement, he now realizes that he was fighting a *person*—and an incredibly powerful one at that.

Jesus commissions Paul to preach to the Gentiles "*to open their eyes, so that they may turn from darkness to light and from the power of Satan to God, that they may receive forgiveness of sins and a place among those who are sanctified by faith in me*"(Acts 26:18). As part of that work, Jesus also promises that he will continue "*delivering you from your people and from the Gentiles*"(Acts 26:17). So even when the Jews seize Paul in the temple—and even now he is in state custody—he can declare that "*to this day I have had the help that comes from God, and so I stand here testifying both to small and great, saying nothing but what the prophets and Moses said would come to pass*"(Acts 26:22). Through all the danger, all the work, all the arguments, all the difficulty in changing his heart and practice, Paul has had "*the help that comes from God.*" God does a mighty work through Paul—permanently changing the world—but even in the moment, Paul knows that he is not working alone.

Paul does not specify or diagram what he means by "*the help that comes from God.*" It is something more than a sense of his own personal destiny, yet something less than constant miracles protecting him from vulnerability. God is real and with him, helping. It is important that disciples of Jesus acknowledge that when we do the work of Jesus, we never work alone. As an expression of his grace, we too have "*the help that comes from God.*"

One Thing to Think About: How has God protected, strengthened, changed, and helped me?

One Thing to Pray For: God's help in the crises I have yet to face

WEEK 33—WEDNESDAY

Reading: Romans 2:1-5

Presuming on Grace

Paul's goal in this section of Romans is to convince both Jews and Gentiles that they are all guilty before God despite different paths to disobedience. Chapter 1 describes the Gentiles' descent into evil, idolatry, sexual sin, and a society that is the fruit of the "*debased mind.*" Yet Paul also knows that the Jews in his audience might be thinking they are exempt from this condemnation. "*Therefore you have no excuse, O man, every one of you who judges. For in passing judgment on another you condemn yourself, because you, the judge, practice the very same things*"(Rom 2:1). It is tempting to look down on others for their sin because it makes us feel better about ourselves. But if we practice the same things as they do, what room do we have to condescend?

Paul confronts this hypothetical hypocrite. "*Do you suppose, O man—you who judge those who practice such things and yet do them yourself—that you will escape the judgment of God? Or do you presume on the riches of his kindness and forbearance and patience, not knowing that God's kindness is meant to lead you to repentance?*"(Rom 2:3-4). God is a just judge. Will he ignore my sin and condemn another's sin? What is really happening is that we "*presume on the riches of his kindness and forbearance and patience.*" We assume that God will have mercy for *us*—but earnestly hope he will not have mercy for *others*. God will always grade me on a curve! God knows my heart! We study passages on God's grace and feel better, but we miss the point of God's grace: "*God's kindness is meant to lead you to repentance.*" All of God's goodness, manifested throughout the centuries and crystalized in Jesus, is intended to get us to *change our evil ways*. Any other response is missing the point and setting us up for a terrifying judgment (Rom 2:5).

Sometimes we get overly concerned about other people. We constantly evaluate their behavior, complain about their sins, and feel justified in our superiority. This passage is a warning. Knowledge of God's grace does not mean that we have the proper attitude toward it. I am a sinner too. Having experienced God's kindness, forbearance, and patience, *am I different now?*

One Thing to Think About: How might I be tempted to presume on God's grace?

One Thing to Pray For: To continually have a "broken and contrite heart"—the heart of sincere repentance

WEEK 33—THURSDAY

Reading: Romans 3:21-26

A New Way to God

Having demonstrated that both Jew and Gentile are lost and condemned (Rom 3:9), Paul has set an appropriate stage for the good news about Jesus. Gentiles have lost their way by ignoring God's nature as revealed in creation and digressing into deeper and deeper rebellion. Jews, meanwhile, have failed to live up to the perfection their law demands. "*But now the righteousness of God has been manifested apart from the law, although the Law and the Prophets bear witness to it—the righteousness of God through faith in Jesus Christ for all who believe*"(Rom 3:21-22). Through Jesus, God has revealed a new way to attain his righteousness. It is no longer through Moses' Law—meaning that ethnicity, circumcision, and perfection are not requirements. It is "*through faith in Jesus Christ for all who believe.*"

In the same way that "*all have sinned and fall short of the glory of God,*" so all can be "*justified by his grace as a gift, through the redemption that is in Christ Jesus*"(Rom 3:23, 24). Paul doubles his language to emphasize his point: we are declared right "*by his grace as a gift.*" Part of the gift is that God gave Jesus "*as a propitiation by his blood, to be received by faith*"(Rom 3:25), meaning that God uses Jesus' sacrifice to atone for and remove our sins. "*It was to show his righteousness at the present time, so that he might be just and the justifier of the one who has faith in Jesus*"(Rom 3:26). God's grace enables him to both remain just and declare us just despite our sins. He is "*just and the justifier.*"

Jesus opens up a new way to God. Even after the intervening centuries, it is still hard for us to wrap our minds around the idea. God is not willing to save the best people—or the people closest to his standard—or the people who work the hardest. He justifies, redeems, and passes over the sins of *those who believe*. This is pure grace—something we could never earn or be worthy of. It only leaves us in awe of God's great love—and desperate to follow (and tell others about) this new way.

One Thing to Think About: Am I still tempted to think that God will save the best people? Why?

One Thing to Pray For: Gratitude for the undeserved access I have to God

WEEK 33—FRIDAY

Reading: Romans 4:1-4

The Grace Abraham Found

Abraham is revered by the Jewish people as a forefather and hero of faith. So when Paul brings him into the discussion of how Christians are saved by faith instead of works, he is working from familiar common ground. "*What then shall we say was gained by Abraham, our forefather according to the flesh? For if Abraham was justified by works, he has something to boast about, but not before God*"(Rom 4:1-2). Being saved by our works gives us room for boast: look what I've done! I earned God's blessing! This is the natural extension of the mindset that seeks to be saved by being a good person. Yet Paul asks: is that really what happened with Abraham?

"*For what does the Scripture say? 'Abraham believed God, and it was counted to him as righteousness*'"(Rom 4:3). Scripture actually says that Abraham became righteous *because he believed*, not because he worked his way to God's favor. But God—as an act of grace—took his faith and counted it to him as if it was righteousness. "*Now to the one who works, his wages are not counted as a gift but as his due*"(Rom 4:4). We do not consider our paycheck a gift from our boss; we have *earned* it. In the same way, if we rely on our works to save us, then we are saving ourselves and there is no room for grace. But if, like Abraham, we believe God and allow him to *count* that as righteousness, we become recipients of God's grace.

The issue here is that when we are trying to be good enough for God to accept us, we leave no room for his grace. *It's all about us*. But Abraham shows us that there is (and has always been) a different path to God: the path of trusting obedience. On this path, we rely on God's goodwill. We receive his favor as a gift, never as our due. Abraham is a timeless example for us because he believed God—and so found his grace.

One Thing to Think About: In what ways am I tempted to rely on myself for salvation?

One Thing to Pray For: To boast in God's goodness—and not in myself

WEEK 34—MONDAY

Reading: Romans 4:5-8

The Grace David Found

Paul has been discussing Abraham's faith, which God counted as righteousness. He is highlighting the difference between salvation by works and salvation by grace through faith. "*Now to the one who works, his wages are not counted as a gift but as his due. And to the one who does not work but believes in him who justifies the ungodly, his faith is counted as righteousness*"(Rom 4:4-5). The wording here can be confusing because it sounds like Paul is warning us not to do *anything*—which contradicts his examples, his own teaching, and his personal life. "*The one who works*" is one who is attempting to be good enough for God to save him on his own merit while "*the one who does not work but believes*" is the one who trusts God to save him despite his own imperfection. We can either seek for God to give us what we deserve (works) or to give us what we do not deserve (grace).

Yet all of this can seem awfully abstract, so Paul illustrates through the mouth of David. In Psalm 32, David is celebrating the huge relief he feels after reluctantly confessing his sin. "*David also speaks of the blessing of the one to whom God counts righteousness apart from works: 'Blessed are those whose lawless deeds are forgiven, and whose sins are covered; blessed is the man against whom the Lord will not count his sin*'"(Rom 4:6-8). The blessing here is the blessing of *forgiveness, not perfection*. This is what salvation by grace looks like: seeking God's forgiveness instead of stubbornly relying on our own goodness. David is happy that God has forgiven him; he has found grace. Paul affirms that God has grace for us in the same way.

Sin is an oddly universal experience. After a certain age, we all know what it is to do wrong. We know the shock of guilt, the disappointment in ourselves, the impulse to hide what we have done, and the temptation to lie about it. It is uniquely unpleasant. Yet David sees something new: when he quit fighting and asked God to save him, his sins were covered. God gave him favor he did not deserve. So he rejoices and is able to smile again. Paul affirms that God has grace for us in the same way.

One Thing to Think About: How has forgiveness brought me relief?

One Thing to Pray For: A heart willing to trust God rather than myself

WEEK 34—TUESDAY

Reading: Romans 4:9-16

A Promise Resting on Grace

Paul is discussing how Jesus presents a new path to God—not based on the Law, our own perfection, or our bloodlines. He presents Abraham as an example and cites David's description of the blessing of salvation by forgiveness instead of perfect law-keeping. "*Is this blessing then only for the circumcised, or also for the uncircumcised? For we say that faith was counted to Abraham as righteousness. How then was it counted to him? Was it before or after he had been circumcised? It was not after, but before he was circumcised*"(Rom 4:9-10). Are Gentiles also allowed to be right with God? Paul goes back to Abraham, the father of the Jewish nation. Circumcision—the dividing line between Jew and Gentile—began with God's covenant to Abraham. Yet Paul reminds us that Genesis 15—when God declares Abraham's faith as righteousness—comes before Genesis 17—when God declares circumcision. It is not his circumcision but his faith that God uses to declare Abraham righteous.

This may seem obscure to us, but Paul insists that it is vital. These facts make Abraham the father of *all* believers—both Jew and Gentile (Rom 4:11-12)—and not simply ethnic Jews. "*For the promise to Abraham and his offspring that he would be heir of the world did not come through the law but through the righteousness of faith*"(Rom 4:13). Abraham received promises (Gen 12:1-3), but they are not based on his law-keeping, nor do those who receive the promises do so through the Law. "*That is why it depends on faith, in order that the promise may rest on grace and be guaranteed to all his offspring—not only the adherent of the law but also to the one who shares the faith of Abraham, who is the father of us all*"(Rom 4:16). Now all nations can be blessed as they share the faith Abraham has—and become recipients of God's grace.

Paul's reasoning here is ingenious because he shows us that Abraham's own life reveals God's grace (as opposed to Abraham working a law). God gave promises freely, acknowledged and accepted Abraham's faith, and foretold of future blessings to his descendants. Paul sees the children of Abraham as far more than the Jewish nation—*all* believers of *every* nation. When we come to faith in Jesus, we join Abraham's long line and stand ready to inherit God's rich promises.

One Thing to Think About: How am I like Abraham?

One Thing to Pray For: A sense of the tremendous promises I stand to inherit

WEEK 34—WEDNESDAY

Reading: Romans 5:1-8

God's Love Poured Into Our Hearts

Having discussed salvation by grace at length, Paul moves from past to present. "*Therefore, since we have been justified by faith, we have peace with God through our Lord Jesus Christ*"(Rom 5:1). While our actions should have made us God's enemies (see Rom 5:10), *his* actions have made peace with us. The great problem of our lives—the punishment we deserve for our sins—has been solved. "*Through him we have also obtained access by faith into this grace in which we stand, and we rejoice in hope of the glory of God*"(Rom 5:2). We also are now able to stand in God's grace, with its attendant assurance that he will continue to justify us when we sin (provided that we repent, as we will see in chapter 6). All of this produces great relief, joy, and hope.

Even our *sufferings* serve only to reinforce this joy, because suffering builds endurance, which builds character, which builds hope (Rom 5:3-4). This hope is rooted in the incontrovertible fact of God's love for us, shown through the cross. "*Hope does not put us to shame, because God's love has been poured into our hearts through the Holy Spirit who has been given to us*"(Rom 5:5). The Spirit has told us of the love for God and poured that love into our hearts. Even the gift of the indwelling of the Spirit is a sign of God's great love and grace. "*God shows his love for us in that while we were still sinners, Christ died for us*"(Rom 5:8). Whatever sufferings we endure, we continue to hope. If God loves us that much, how will he not keep all of us his promises to us?

God has not begrudgingly forgiven us, like some Scrooge who feels bound to help those less fortunate. He has sacrificed his precious Son to bless his greatest enemies. He has given us his Spirit so that we can—now and forever—live in vibrant relationship with him. His love has been poured into our hearts—overwhelming our need and inadequacy, changing our character and attitude, and leading us to respond in love to him.

One Thing to Think About: Do I believe that I am worthy of God's love and grace?

One Thing to Pray For: God's love to transform my relationships with others

WEEK 34—THURSDAY

Reading: Romans 5:12-17

Undoing Adam's Sin

In attempting to magnify the incredible reality of what God has done for us in Jesus, Paul makes a comparison between Jesus and Adam. "*Therefore, just as sin came into the world through one man, and death through sin, and so death spread to all men because all sinned*"(Rom 5:12). He takes us back to Adam, who—despite God's warning that if he ate the fruit, he would die—disobeyed God and brought death into the world. He envisions death spreading throughout mankind, emphasizing how universal this death is: "*so death spread to all men because all sinned.*" Even over those who did not sin in precisely the same way Adam did (Rom 5:14), sin and death still reigned. This is the story of human history.

Yet Jesus undoes Adam's sin. "*But the free gift is not like the trespass. For if many died through one man's trespass, much more have the grace of God and the free gift by the grace of that one man Jesus Christ abounded for many*"(Rom 5:15). Where Adam's sin affected far more people than himself, so Jesus' sacrifice affects far more than himself. "*And the free gift is not like the result of that one man's sin. For the judgment following one trespass brought condemnation, but the free gift following many trespasses brought justification*"(Rom 5:16). It is truly sad to look at the spiritual carnage Adam began—judgment and condemnation that spread to all man—yet it is a source of indescribable joy to look at the spiritual rejuvenation Jesus began.

Man's universal plight since the garden has been this (seemingly) inescapable cycle of sin and death. Stuck in our own sins, rightly condemned to our own death, we were helpless and hopeless. Yet God mercifully sent his Son to change the whole direction of humanity. Now we have help and hope and holiness—a rich gift from a gracious God.

One Thing to Think About: How have sin and death affected me?

One Thing to Pray For: Praise to God for his goodwill toward his creatures

WEEK 34—FRIDAY

Reading: Romans 5:17-21

Grace Reigns

Paul is chewing on the fact that Adam's sin affected far more than just himself. "*For if, because of one man's trespass, death reigned through that one man, much more will those who receive the abundance of grace and the free gift of righteousness reign in life through the one man Jesus Christ*"(Rom 5:17). By giving sin an entry point into the world, Adam allowed death to "*reign*" over his descendants who likewise followed his rebellion against God (Rom 5:12). Yet Jesus' act allows for a different kind of reigning—those who receive his gift "*reign in life through the one man Jesus Christ.*" The reign of terror has ended.

Surprisingly, the Law of Moses did not break the reign of sin and death. "*Now the law came in to increase the trespass, but where sin increased, grace abounded all the more, so that, as sin reigned in death, grace also might reign through righteousness leading to eternal life through Jesus Christ our Lord*"(Rom 5:20-21). The law served to "*increase the trespass,*" adding to our awareness of our sin, shame, and death without dealing with them definitively. But into that dark world of evil, corruption, and death comes Jesus. He gives righteousness as a gift based on his atonement on the cross. Now "*grace also might reign through righteousness leading to eternal life.*" The human experience is fundamentally changed. The reign of terror has ended. Now grace abounds all the more.

The reign of grace means that God's goodwill has overruled and overcome the mess that we have made of the world. Instead of living in the contamination of sin with only the fear of coming death, now we live in righteousness with the hope of eternal life to come. We can now interpret all of life as a function of God's grace.

One Thing to Think About: How have I seen good overcome evil?

One Thing to Pray For: God's grace to reign in more and more hearts

WEEK 35—MONDAY

Reading: Romans 6:1-11

Can We Keep Sinning?

Since God has shown his willingness to forgive us, an odd formula develops. "*Where sin increased, grace abounded all the more*"(Rom 5:20). Sin's increase has led to the increase of grace. "*What shall we say then? Are we to continue in sin that grace may abound?*"(Rom 6:1). Paul takes this idea to its logical conclusion: can we just keep sinning? He recoils at the idea. "*By no means! How can we who died to sin still live in it? Do you not know that all of us who have been baptized into Christ Jesus were baptized into his death? We were buried therefore with him by baptism into death, in order that, just as Christ was raised from the dead by the glory of the Father, we too might walk in newness of life*"(Rom 6:2-4). Our conversion to Christ was not the beginning of sin, but its end. We have *died* to sin and *buried* that old man and now live a *new* life.

Paul details how our baptism pictures Jesus' death, burial, and resurrection. We are buried "*with him*"(Rom 6:4) and "*united with him in a death like his*"(Rom 6:5) and "*crucified with him*"(Rom 6:6). It is certainly a symbolic act, but Paul argues that it is not *merely symbolic*. A real change takes place at conversion—a real death and a real rebirth. We are "*no longer enslaved to sin*"(Rom 6:6) but now look forward to the idea that "*we shall certainly be united with him in a resurrection like his*"(Rom 6:5). This anticipation means that in the present moment we "*consider (ourselves) dead to sin and alive to God in Christ Jesus*"(Rom 6:11). We can't just keep sinning.

While it seems unlikely to me that people were actually arguing that we should keep sinning to increase grace, his words challenge the mentality that takes advantage of God's kindness. Whenever we hesitate to address weakness and sin in our lives—whenever we indulge with the thought that we'll repent later—whenever we put off until tomorrow what could be done today—Paul would take us back to baptism. Didn't you die with Jesus? Aren't you a new person? Instead of sinning, we now rejoice in being "*alive to God in Christ Jesus.*"

One Thing to Think About: Does God's grace ever lead me to think that sin is not that big a deal?

One Thing to Pray For: A continual reminder that I am dead to—and free from—sin

Reading: Romans 6:12-19

No Dominion

Throughout this section of Romans, Paul has repeatedly used terms of reigning and dominion to describe the nature of sin and grace. Previously, "*death reigned*"(Rom 5:14, 17), but now "*grace also might reign through righteousness*"(Rom 5:21). Jesus has been raised from the dead and so now "*death no longer has dominion over him*"(Rom 6:9). But this shift is not just about mankind generally; it is also deeply personal. Since we have participated in his death and resurrection through baptism, we are free. "*Let not sin therefore reign in your mortal body, to make you obey its passions…For sin will have no dominion over you, since you are not under law but under grace*"(Rom 6:12, 14). Each person has someone or something that *reigns* in their lives, directing their behavior. Paul insists that Christians no longer let sin have dominion over them. We have been set free.

Part of the insight here is that sin is not just something we do; it actively enslaves us. "*Do you not know that if you present yourselves to anyone as obedient slaves, you are slaves of the one whom you obey, either of sin, which leads to death, or of obedience, which leads to righteousness? But thanks be to God, that you who were once slaves of sin have become obedient from the heart to the standard of teaching to which you were committed, and, having been set free from sin, have become slaves of righteousness*"(Rom 6:16-18). When we decide to sin, we become its slaves, bound to commit more sin and destined for the fate (death) it brings. Yet the grace of God is that we have been set free to become slaves of what is right. Practically, this means that while Christians may still sin occasionally, we can never allow sin to again dominate and enslave us. We must ruthlessly eliminate sin—apologizing, changing, confessing—with the fear a freed slave might have of going back under the chain.

This section pushes us toward introspection. Who is in charge of my life? What does the pattern of my life show about my allegiances? How am I living as a servant of righteousness today? Are there sins I am allowing to control or dominate me? Am I free?

One Thing to Think About: How can I show that I am a servant of righteousness today?

One Thing to Pray For: Determination to not let sin reign in my body

WEEK 35—WEDNESDAY

Reading: Romans 6:20-23

The Grace of Eternal Life

As Paul works to convince Christians to live in a new, sin-free way, he reminds them that all lifestyles lead somewhere. "*For just as you once presented your members as slaves to impurity and to lawlessness leading to more lawlessness, so now present your members as slaves to righteousness leading to sanctification*"(Rom 6:19). One path takes us to more and more lawlessness, the other leads to holiness. He then reminds us that we have spent some time on the first path. "*For when you were slaves of sin, you were free in regard to righteousness. But what fruit were you getting at that time from the things of which you are now ashamed? For the end of those things is death*"(Rom 6:20-21). We used to have no commitment to do right. How did that go for us? We were ashamed of what we did and got nothing good out of our lives—other than the temporary pleasure of sin.

But now, through Jesus, we have stepped onto a different path. "*But now that you have been set free from sin and have become slaves of God, the fruit you get leads to sanctification and its end, eternal life*"(Rom 6:22). Now instead of doing things we are ashamed of, we see ourselves becoming holier. And we know that at the end of the path of righteousness and holiness is eternal life, the promise of the righteous and holy God we serve. "*For the wages of sin is death, but the free gift of God is eternal life in Christ Jesus our Lord*"(Rom 6:23). Death is what sin *deserves*; eternal life is what God *gives freely*. This eternal life is forever-existence in the presence of God, something we do not deserve and could never earn. Why would we not choose this path?

God graciously extends to us a free gift that is worth far more than what we should receive for our conduct. He sets us free from the awful tyranny of sin, regret, and death, to make us into a people who have a purpose, purity, and a perfect destination. Why would we not choose this path?

One Thing to Think About: What awful actions from my past am I ashamed of? How has Jesus changed this?

One Thing to Pray For: Sanctification

WEEK 35—THURSDAY

Reading: Romans 7:21-25

Who Will Deliver Me?

Driving this section is Paul's surprising realization that the Law of Moses did not actually help him overcome sin. The Law identifies sin ("*you shall not covet*," Rom 7:7), but this information does not empower us to avoid it. "*But sin, seizing an opportunity through the commandment, produced in me all kinds of covetousness*"(Rom 7:8). The Law is still good (Rom 7:12), but it shows man to be sinful. Not only that, but once sin takes root, the Law only continues to convict us of our own sinfulness. Even when we *want* to do right, we lack the strength. "*For I have the desire to do what is right, but not the ability to carry it out*"(Rom 7:18). We need an entirely new way to be right with God. We are slaves who need to be delivered.

But is there any torment like wanting desperately to do right, yet finding oneself a slave to do wrong? "*For I delight in the law of God, in my inner being, but I see in my members another law waging war against the law of my mind and making me captive to the law of sin that dwells in my members. Wretched man that I am! Who will deliver me from this body of death?*"(Rom 7:22-24). This is the bitter cry of all who serve God under the Law of Moses: we are deeply aware of our sin but utterly incapable of removing it. We cry out for a Savior. "*Thanks be to God through Jesus Christ our Lord!*"(Rom 7:25). Now God has not only convicted us of sin, but definitively removed it through Jesus. Now we are free.

Paul's words here do not (or at least should not) describe Christians who have been redeemed. Yet his words powerfully resonate, taking us back to the time when we were spiritually aware enough to know that we were wrong but unable to fix our problem. Only when we recall the desperation of slavery and the futility of all our efforts to "be better" do we see the surpassing value of Jesus' sacrifice. Until we know we are lost, we don't see how much we need a Savior.

One Thing to Think About: How have I experienced this war between mind and body?

One Thing to Pray For: A healthy memory of where I used to be—and what God has done to deliver me

WEEK 35—FRIDAY

Reading: Romans 8:9-11

Life to Your Mortal Bodies

Because Jesus has delivered us from slavery to sin, we now "*walk not according to the flesh but according to the Spirit*"(Rom 8:4). Disciples of Jesus adopt an entirely new set of behaviors and mindsets because we no longer follow the dictates of our flesh, but the Spirit God has given to us. "*You, however, are not in the flesh but in the Spirit, if in fact the Spirit of God dwells in you. Anyone who does not have the Spirit of Christ does not have God*"(Rom 8:9). Paul not only insists that the Spirit indwells Christians, but that this is a vital indicator of whether we "*have God*" at all.

Why does the Spirit's indwelling matter so much? "*But if Christ is in you, although the body is dead because of sin, the Spirit is life because of righteousness*"(Rom 8:10). The Spirit teaches us a new way to live—the way of life and righteousness. Following the dictates and impulses of our bodies has led us to slavery and death; following the Spirit guides us into righteousness, holiness, and life. The indwelling Spirit means that we are "*debtors*" to follow the one who has given us so much and always wants our good (see Rom 8:12-13). But there is more: "*If the Spirit of him who raised Jesus from the dead dwells in you, he who raised Christ Jesus from the dead will also give life to your mortal bodies through his Spirit who dwells in you*"(Rom 8:11). This is a promise that the indwelling will lead to our resurrection. Our "*mortal bodies*" are subject to sickness and death, but the God with power over death indwells us. He guarantees a future grace; "*he will give life.*" All that he has done so far—the sending of Jesus, the deliverance from sin, the giving of the Spirit, the revelation of his will—is a down payment on this future gift. Our dying bodies will be given true life.

Resurrection-hope is the key to Christian faith. Without it, all our faith is a pointless temporary exercise. Here Paul makes the promise explicit. He also ties it to our present behavior, reminding us that who we follow and listen to now indicates whether the Spirit is indwelling us. To simple people who listen to and obey him, God will give the greatest gift.

One Thing to Think About: Is the Spirit living in me? How do I know?

One Thing to Pray For: Confidence in God's power over death

Reading: Romans 8:31-39

If God Is for Us, Who Can Be against Us?

Paul takes a step back from all the technical arguments of the last several chapters to consider what this all means. "*What then shall we say to these things? If God is for us, who can be against us?*"(Rom 8:31). Jesus' coming and death demonstrate that *God is for us*. He wants to save us. He loves us despite our sins. He has offered himself for us and given his Spirit to guide us and give us life. If he is favorable to us, what other person or entity do we need to fear? More, his past grace promises future grace: "*He who did not spare his own Son but gave him up for us all, how will he not also with him graciously give us all things?*"(Rom 8:32). If God is such a giver, what will he withhold?

But Paul is also thinking about how God's grace takes the sting out of human opposition. "*Who shall separate us from the love of Christ? Shall tribulation, or distress, or persecution, or famine, or nakedness, or danger, or sword?*"(Rom 8:35). God's goodness does not guarantee that these hardships will not come (see Rom 8:36), yet they cannot "*separate us from the love of Christ.*" Many people can be against us, but "*who can be against us?*" means that their opposition can never jeopardize our standing with God. "*For I am sure that neither death nor life, nor angels nor rulers, nor things present nor things to come, nor powers, nor height nor depth, nor anything else in all creation, will be able to separate us from the love of God in Christ Jesus our Lord*"(Rom 8:38-39). Nothing anyone ever does to us—no circumstance we ever encounter—no bad news we ever receive—no threat to us can ever take us away from God's love. God is determined to bless us. Who can stand in his way?

Paul is not thinking of whether Christians can lose faith or lapse into a life of sin. Certainly we can leave the Lord if we want to. His point is that *no person or situation can force us away from Jesus*. So many forces are beyond our control. Many possible future scenarios frighten us. God's grace gives us confidence. If he is for us, who can be against us?

One Thing to Think About: What circumstances do I most fear? How does God's grace to me give me confidence in those circumstances?

One Thing to Pray For: Perspective—that people and their actions are less important than God's goodwill

WEEK 36—TUESDAY

Reading: Romans 9:1-13

God's Grace to Israel

In the next several chapters, Paul wrestles with the question of why so many of the Jews have rejected the gospel message proclaiming Jesus as Messiah. As an ethnic Jew, it disturbs Paul greatly: *"I have great sorrow and unceasing anguish in my heart. For I could wish that I myself were accursed and cut off from Christ for the sake of my brothers, my kinsmen according to the flesh"*(Rom 9:2-3). He proceeds to enumerate the tremendous blessings of being a native Israelite—God's gifts to the people. *"They are Israelites, and to them belong the adoption, the glory, the covenants, the giving of the law, the worship, and the promises. To them belong the patriarchs, and from their race, according to the flesh, is the Christ, who is God over all, blessed forever"*(Rom 9:4-5). Adopted as God's own son, blessed with the glorious presence of God, bound to him by covenant, pursuing him by a divinely handcrafted law, worshiping by an elaborately revealed system, holding on to future promises of blessing the world, God has tremendously blessed them.

Yet these blessings beg the question: what is going on now, in Paul's day? Has all God has done for them and promised them failed? Paul protests: *"But it is not as though the word of God has failed. For not all who are descended from Israel belong to Israel, and not all are children of Abraham because they are his offspring"*(Rom 9:6-7). God's word and promise can be fulfilled *in a different way than just Abraham's physical descendants.* Paul argues that God fulfilled his word to Isaac (not Ishmael) and Jacob (not Esau). There are *physical* descendants of Abraham and *spiritual* descendants who inherit the promises. He also stresses that this status is not something earned (Rom 9:11), but is God's gift, given on terms *he* decides. It just so happens that he now chooses to adopt believers in Jesus (from all nations) as spiritual Israel (see Rom 9:30-32).

The tragic irony of this passage is that God blesses Israel so richly—adoption, glory, covenants, etc—yet they still find reasons to reject his Son. It is possible for us to receive so much from God that we begin to take his favor for granted, assuming that we deserve his blessings, growing spoiled and frustrated with any hardship, and rejecting his appeals for us to change.

One Thing to Think About: Have I ever allowed blessings and good times to make me spiritually complacent?

One Thing to Pray For: Stronger faith that God will fulfill his promises

WEEK 36—WEDNESDAY

Reading: Romans 9:14-24

Is God Unfair?

Grace often opens God up to accusations of unfairness. In Jesus' parable of the workers in the vineyard, some resent the master being gracious to some and not others. Similarly, as Paul describes God choosing Jacob over Esau without regard to their works, some might protest. "*What shall we say then? Is there injustice on God's part? By no means! For he says to Moses, 'I will have mercy on whom I have mercy, and I will have compassion on whom I have compassion.' So then it depends not on human will or exertion, but on God, who has mercy*"(Rom 9:14-16). Doesn't God have the free right to show mercy on those he chooses?

The challenge comes when Paul mentions Pharaoh as someone he *hardens*: "*So then he has mercy on whomever he wills, and he hardens whomever he wills*"(Rom 9:18). This does come closer to unfairness, since God is all-powerful (Rom 9:19). Yet Paul opens up the possibility that what seems like unfairness in the moment can actually be a way God brings about the fullness of his plans. "*What if God, desiring to show his wrath and to make known his power, has endured with much patience vessels of wrath prepared for destruction, in order to make known the riches of his glory for vessels of mercy, which he has prepared beforehand for glory—even us whom he has called, not from the Jews only but also from the Gentiles?*"(Rom 9:22-24). God can use people (like Pharaoh or physical Israel) without endorsing their behavior. And he can work through them to fulfill his word and plan in a way he desires but we do not expect—by calling a new people by faith.

Paul's reasoning here rests on the foundation he has laid in the rest of Romans: sin brings death (Rom 6:23) and we are saved from that death by faith in Jesus (Rom 3:21-26). God never unfairly condemns us. Yet the way God demonstrates his grace is *always his choice.* We might like him to save more (or perhaps fewer!) people. We might prefer him do it in different ways. But if God is unfair, it is because he is unfairly *good* to those who believe.

One Thing to Think About: Does God ever seem unfair to me?

One Thing to Pray For: Awe at the genius of God

Reading: Romans 9:25-33

Stumbling Over the Stone

In light of the fact that many Jews in Paul's day have rejected Jesus, he is answering the objection that this means God's promises to Israel have been broken. Here he actually quotes several prophets who foretold this exact scenario: Jews rejecting God and Gentiles accepting him. Hosea says that "*those who were not my people I will call 'my people*'"(Rom 9:25), but Isaiah repeatedly sees unbelief in Israel's future. "*Only a remnant of them will be saved*"(Rom 9:27), they will be nearly wiped out as Sodom and Gomorrah (Rom 9:29). Rather than God breaking his word, present circumstances show God *keeping* his word, to the letter.

The irony of this is not lost on Paul. "*What shall we say then? That Gentiles who did not pursue righteousness have attained it, that is, a righteousness that is by faith; but that Israel who pursued a law that would lead to righteousness did not succeed in reaching that law. Why? Because they did not pursue it by faith, but as if it were based on works. They have stumbled over the stumbling stone*"(Rom 9:30-32). Gentiles who previously were not interested in doing right are now *declared* right; Jews who previously pursued the law are now shown to have not reached it. The difference is faith. God accepts those who believe, regardless of their pursuit of law. In Jesus, Paul sees the age-old prophecy of Isaiah fulfilled: "*Behold, I am laying in Zion a stone of stumbling, and a rock of offense; and whoever believes in him will not be put to shame*"(Rom 9:33). Jesus is the stone that trips up the Jews. He is not a list of laws to keep. He is not pursued by more doing. They must believe in him—the very thing they refuse to do—and so they stumble.

It is surprising that what is good news of grace to one group causes another to stumble. God's grace challenges us to abandon the belief that we are good enough—that we can accomplish everything if we just work harder—that the way we've always done things is sufficient. Accepting God's favor as a gift means we must leave behind the pride and self-sufficiency that Americans love. If we continue to work to earn our place, we too will stumble over the stone.

One Thing to Think About: Does it surprise—or bother—me that sincere, devout Jews do not attain righteousness (Rom 9:31)?

One Thing to Pray For: The humility to believe

WEEK 36—FRIDAY

Reading: Romans 10:1-4

Zeal Is Not Enough

As Paul laments that many of his countrymen have not responded to the good news about Jesus, he explains the tremendous good he sees in them. "*Brothers, my heart's desire and prayer to God for them is that they may be saved. For I bear them witness that they have a zeal for God, but not according to knowledge*"(Rom 10:1-2). Paul has seen their zeal firsthand. As a devout Pharisee, he had been zealous for the law to the point of persecuting Christians (perhaps following the model of Phinehas in Numbers 25). Their passion to serve God is an undeniably good thing; it is just not enough because it is "*not according to knowledge*."

The problem with zeal on its own is that it may not be aimed in the right direction. "*For, being ignorant of the righteousness of God, and seeking to establish their own, they did not submit to God's righteousness*"(Rom 10:3). God has revealed a new way of being right (Paul sometimes calls it "*the righteousness of God*", see Rom 3:22) that is not through lawkeeping, but grace. This is *God's* righteousness, but many Jews insist on pursuing their *own* righteousness. They continue to frantically pursue a law that they can never attain in hopes that God will accept them. God has laid out a different path: "*For Christ is the end of the law for righteousness to everyone who believes*"(Rom 10:4). Faith in Jesus as Messiah is the endpoint of righteousness and a death-blow for attempts to be good on our own.

Zeal is a good thing. It is only natural for us to passionately pursue the things that matter most. The danger is that we mistakenly think that serving God is about *me*—my righteousness, my goodness, my growth. God has inverted this. We "*submit to God's righteousness*" and leave behind our own. Any righteousness that we have is *given* to us rather than earned by us. We respect zeal—both in ourselves and others—but must ensure that it is "*according to knowledge*."

One Thing to Think About: Have I ever been zealous for the wrong thing? How did I learn better?

One Thing to Pray For: The knowledge I need to follow God's will properly

WEEK 37—MONDAY

Reading: Romans 10:5-13

Bestowing His Riches

In this section, Paul argues that salvation through Jesus is more available and accessible than under Moses' Law. "*For Moses writes about the righteousness that is based on the law, that the person who does the commandments shall live by them*"(Rom 10:5). Eternal life was possible under Moses' Law, provided that one "*does the commandments*" perfectly. But faith proceeds differently. It is not so far above us that we must ascend to heaven, so far below us that we must descend into the abyss, or so challenging that we can never accomplish it. It is "*in your mouth and in your heart*"(Rom 10:8), which Paul explains as the simplicity of confessing with the mouth and believing with the heart. God has brought salvation down to us and made it possible even for imperfect people.

This fits with the witness of the Old Testament. "*For the Scripture says, 'Everyone who believes in him will not be put to shame'*"(Rom 10:11). Paul focuses on the *everyone* in this text, which stresses God's willingness to accept even Gentiles. "*For there is no distinction between Jew and Greek; for the same Lord is Lord of all, bestowing his riches on all who call on him. For 'everyone who calls on the name of the Lord will be saved'*"(Rom 10:12-13). God accepts the faith of all people, since "*the same Lord is Lord of all.*" More, he is wonderfully gracious to all, "*bestowing his riches on all who call on him.*" God keeps giving gifts—independent of our race or the worthiness of our actions—when we reach out to him.

God has always had a people, but in Jesus he opens up membership in his people to anyone willing to believe. God is remarkably rich, but he yearns to give his riches to his people. All that he expects is that we call on his name—for salvation, for blessing, and for whatever we need.

One Thing to Think About: Is it possible for God's rich blessings to make me lazy?

One Thing to Pray For: A heart to bestow my riches on others

WEEK 37—TUESDAY

Reading: Romans 10:14-21

Found by Those Who Did Not Seek Me

Paul continues to muse on the Jews' surprising rejection of the gospel. If "*everyone who calls on the name of the Lord will be saved*"(Rom 10:13), why haven't the Jews called on him? Paul runs through a series of questions: "*How then will they call on him in whom they have not believed? And how are they to believe in him of whom they have never heard? And how are they to hear without someone preaching? And how are they to preach unless they are sent?*"(Rom 10:14-15). One by one he checks off their potential excuses: someone has been sent to them, has preached to them about Jesus, has told them enough to believe and thus to call on the Lord. Yet "*they have not all obeyed the gospel*"(Rom 10:16). The fault does not lie with God.

Yet God has also signaled—centuries prior—that he would reach out to the Gentiles. "*But I ask, did Israel not understand? First Moses says, 'I will make you jealous of those who are not a nation; with a foolish nation I will make you angry.' Then Isaiah is so bold as to say, 'I have been found by those who did not seek me; I have shown myself to those who did not ask for me'*"(Rom 10:19-20). God would have dealings with another nation to *make Israel jealous* (Paul will return to this in chapter 11). A threat to their relationship with God would be used to wake them up. Then God declares that he will be "*found by those who did not seek me.*" He will take a new people and save them—not as a reward for their seeking, but as an act of pure grace.

Paul is building toward explaining God's cosmic plan to bring Jew and Gentile together. But God being "*found by those who did not seek me*" intrigues me. We all have periods in life where we lose our way and our desire to do right. We know what it is to not seek God and his righteousness—and we often have scars and regrets to show for it. Yet God does not give up on us. Even when we don't seek him, he is willing to be found.

One Thing to Think About: Have I had times of spiritual lostness? How did God reach me then?

One Thing to Pray For: Gratitude to God for not giving up on me

WEEK 37—WEDNESDAY

Reading: Romans 11:1-6

A Remnant Chosen by Grace

Paul has been stressing that Israel's rejection of the gospel—and the subsequent bringing in of the Gentiles—was foretold long before. Yet that raises a question: "*I ask, then, has God rejected his people?*"(Rom 11:1). The question here is whether the current state is permanent and universal. Is God just done with the nation he chose? "*By no means! For I myself am an Israelite, a descendant of Abraham, a member of the tribe of Benjamin. God has not rejected his people whom he foreknew*"(Rom 11:1-2). Wholesale rejection would exclude even Paul. Something more is going on here.

To explain, he reaches back to a depressed Elijah bemoaning how he is the only righteous one left in Israel. "*But what is God's reply to him? 'I have kept for myself seven thousand men who have not bowed the knee to Baal.' So too at the present time there is a remnant, chosen by grace*"(Rom 11:4-5). In Elijah's day, when the vast majority of Israelites were evil (following King Ahab), there were still some leftover righteous people. This "remnant" kept true religion alive in a dark time and stayed connected to God. Paul argues that there are still faithful Israelites who have come to believe in Jesus—a modern remnant. Yet they are chosen by grace, not perfect law-keeping: "*But if it is by grace, it is no longer on the basis of works; otherwise grace would no longer be grace*"(Rom 11:6). It is not the best Jews who are the remnant; it is the Jews who believe in Jesus.

It is difficult to be one of the faithful few. The tension of going against the grain of culture permeates Paul's words throughout this section. Yet he continues to stress that this is *God's gift*—he has been chosen by grace, not his works. The encouragement is in knowing that God knows those who are his, that he always has a people, and that our place in his favor is not something that rests on our perfection.

One Thing to Think About: In what ways do I find it difficult to swim against the current of my world?

One Thing to Pray For: Strength from knowing that I am not alone

Reading: Romans 11:7-16

Prompting a Holy Jealousy

As Israel has largely rejected the gospel, Paul has argued that they have "*stumbled over the stumbling stone*"(Rom 9:32). Why has this happened and is it the end of God's dealings with them? "*What then? Israel failed to obtain what it was seeking. The elect obtained it, but the rest were hardened, as it is written, 'God gave them a spirit of stupor, eyes that would not see and ears that would not hear, down to this very day*'"(Rom 11:7-8). God has hardened Israel and given them a stupor—but Paul is confident that this is not their final state. There is more to come and he sees himself as instrumental in the process.

"*So I ask, did they stumble in order that they might fall? By no means! Rather through their trespass salvation has come to the Gentiles, so as to make Israel jealous*"(Rom 11:11). The Jews' rejection has given an opening to the Gentiles. Paul sees God as using this new people as "*(making) Israel jealous,*" motivating them to reconsider. If even their *fall* has blessed others, how much more their *restoration* (Rom 11:12)? As apostle to Gentiles, Paul insists, "*I magnify my ministry in order somehow to make my fellow Jews jealous, and thus save some of them*"(Rom 11:13-14). He talks up what God is accomplishing through him among the Gentiles. He longs to prompt a holy jealousy in his people. As they see God at work among Gentiles—pouring out his Spirit, changing lives, glorifying his name and word—they long to be a part of it in this new, deeper way. Paul holds out hope for his people.

The grace in this text is *stupor*—"*God gave them a spirit of stupor*"(Rom 11:8)—which strikes us as quite odd. God has a plan to bring Jew and Gentile together, which requires a temporary blindness for the Jews. Yet even this, Paul argues, brings about blessings to both Jew and Gentile. Much like a marriage can be revitalized when a mate gains a healthy jealousy, so God is reaching out to his people to bond to them more deeply. God loves us enough to make us jealous when we take him for granted.

One Thing to Think About: Am I ever jealous of others' relationship with God? How might that be bad? How might it be good?

One Thing to Pray For: Deeper understanding of God's plans

WEEK 37—FRIDAY

Reading: Romans 11:17-24

The Grace of Grafting

Paul uses the picture of an olive tree to describe God's people. Many of the Jews—the "natural branches"—have rejected Jesus and therefore have been cut off the tree. So Paul cautions the Gentiles: "*But if some of the branches were broken off, and you, although a wild olive shoot were grafted in among the others and now share in the nourishing root of the olive tree, do not be arrogant toward the branches*"(Rom 11:17-18). God, in his grace, has been willing to graft in branches from another tree—a "*wild olive shoot*"—and make them a part of his people. He has accepted Gentiles by faith as an act of grace and placed them right alongside faithful Jews.

But this blessed state holds some warnings. "*Then you will say, 'Branches were broken off so that I might be grafted in.' That is true. They were broken off because of their unbelief, but you stand fast through faith. So do not become proud, but fear. For if God did not spare the natural branches, neither will he spare you*"(Rom 11:19-21). Believers cannot allow God's grace to make us haughty. We are not better than others, nor are we automatically guaranteed a place in God's favor. We must continue in faith, grateful for our unearned place, and hopeful that the natural branches will come to faith as well. "*Note then the kindness and severity of God: severity toward those who have fallen, but God's kindness to you, provided you continue in his kindness. Otherwise you too will be cut off*"(Rom 11:22). God shows himself kind and gracious, but his grace is not to be assumed. He expects continual faith in Jesus.

Sometimes those of us who are Gentile believers lose the sense of this rich blessing. We read Old Testament descriptions of the Jews and think of ourselves as like them. We describe ourselves easily as God's chosen people. Yet what claim do we have on such exalted blessings? They are merely the fruit of God's rich grace toward us. We cannot be haughty—thinking we are great, condescending to others, or assuming God approves of all we do—but must fear.

One Thing to Think About: Why does being a part of God's people seem less important to modern Christians?

One Thing to Pray For: The humility and fear appropriate to God's goodness and severity

WEEK 38—MONDAY

Reading: Romans 11:25-36

Riches, Wisdom, and Knowledge

Why has Israel rejected Jesus and now the message of salvation in his name? Does this mean that God's promises of blessing to Israel are void? Paul concludes his extended discussion here. "*Lest you be wise in your own sight, I do not want you to be unaware of this mystery, brothers: a partial hardening has come upon Israel, until the fullness of the Gentiles has come in. And in this way all Israel will be saved, as it is written, 'The Deliverer will come from Zion, he will banish ungodliness from Jacob;' 'and this will be my covenant with them when I take away their sins*'"(Rom 11:25-27). Part of Israel has been temporarily hardened against the gospel to allow Gentiles entry into God's favor. Paul also foresees a time when more Jews, driven to jealousy, will also come to faith. But he argues that this plan is how all God's promises to save Israel will be fulfilled: "*and in this way all Israel will be saved.*" This "Israel" includes the faithful from both Jews and Gentiles (see Rom 2:28-29, 9:6, etc).

Paul then takes a moment to marvel at how God has accomplished all of this—using the Jews' disobedience to open the door to disobedient Gentiles, then obedient Gentiles to create obedient Jews. "*Oh, the depth of the riches and wisdom and knowledge of God! How unsearchable are his judgments and how inscrutable his ways!*"(Rom 11:33). God's riches, wisdom, and knowledge are far above ours. None of the people who lived through it had any idea of what God was accomplishing through them and for them. No one could have guessed it. God has given man the ability to choose, redeemed man from his sin, and faithfully kept his word in a completely unpredictable way.

There should be a place for us to exclaim with Paul: "*Oh, the depth of the riches and wisdom and knowledge of God! How unsearchable are his judgments and how inscrutable his ways!*"(Rom 11:33). All of God's goodness and genius are directed *toward us*, for our good. This gives us comfort when we are confused and trust when we struggle with his commands.

One Thing to Think About: How have I observed God's genius?

One Thing to Pray For: Confidence that God will keep his promises—even if I don't see how

WEEK 38—TUESDAY

Reading: Romans 12:3-8

The Grace of Personal Gifts

Paul expresses concern that the different talents and skills we have can lead to pride and division between us and other Christians. "*For by the grace given to me I say to everyone among you not to think of himself more highly than he ought to think, but to think with sober judgment, each according to the measure of faith that God has assigned*"(Rom 12:3). Paul's apostleship is "*the grace given to me,*" not anything he has earned. So he encourages all of us to not become proud because of the gifts we have received, but instead acknowledge that they are gifts. "*For as in one body we have many members, and the members do not all have the same function, so we, though many, are one body in Christ, and individually members of one another*"(Rom 12:4-5). Our differences are—as in the parts of our physical bodies—a way to make the whole more versatile and capable. Instead of separating us, they encourage us to band together and grow stronger.

Paul then calls on us to acknowledge and use the personal gifts each of us has. "*Having gifts that differ according to the grace given to us, let us use them: if prophecy, in proportion to our faith; if service, in our serving; the one who teaches, in his teaching; the one who exhorts, in his exhortation; the one who contributes in generosity; the one who leads, with zeal; the one who does acts of mercy, with cheerfulness*"(Rom 12:6-8). It is clear that there are other gifts Paul has left off the list, but there is enough here to spark the imagination. God has given us things we do well—leadership, generosity, prophecy, mercy. Let's identify where we excel and—instead of growing proud and condescending to others—use those gifts to enthusiastically serve one another.

It is essential that we acknowledge that our personal gifts—intelligence, money, social skills, patience, physical strength—are not of our own doing. While we may develop them, they don't originate with us. They are gifts that belie a giver. And with those gifts comes God's expectation that we use them to bless and strengthen others.

One Thing to Think About: What gifts do I have?

One Thing to Pray For: Clarity in how to use my gifts to build up and serve others

Reading: Romans 12:17-21

Giving to Our Enemies

Paul acknowledges our strong tendency toward revenge when others wrong us. Whether we can directly harm them back or not, we long for them to hurt the way they have hurt us. Paul strictly forbids this approach: "*Repay no one evil for evil, but give thought to do what is honorable in the sight of all. If possible, so far as depends on you, live peaceably with all*"(Rom 12:17-18). He stresses that we should be at peace with others as much as we can, implying that we should never be the *cause* of trouble with others. "*Beloved, never avenge yourselves, but leave it to the wrath of God, for it is written, 'Vengeance is mine, I will repay, says the Lord*'"(Rom 12:19). God himself is on the job. He will right whatever wrongs need to be addressed in a completely fair and impartial way. We need to let him do it.

But in the meantime, there is a way we can respond to evil that is far more reflective of God's nature: "*To the contrary, 'if your enemy is hungry, feed him; if he is thirsty, give him something to drink; for by so doing you will heap burning coals on his head.' Do not be overcome by evil, but overcome evil with good*"(Rom 12:20-21). When others become our enemies, Paul urges to *give* to them. Show grace. Give them what is needed—food and drink. "Heaping burning coals on his head" is not about finding a backdoor to revenge; he is arguing that this type of grace can defuse the conflict. When we allow someone else's wrong to cause us to retaliate and do them wrong back, we are "*overcome by evil.*" But when we give to our enemies, we "*overcome evil with good.*"

It is extremely difficult to give to people who have done us wrong. It feels like adding insult to injury. Yet grace has a way of transforming both giver and recipient, drawing them together. People who have hurt me still get hungry and thirsty. They still need things. I can still help them. In doing so, I let go of my hurt, show the love of God, and become more like my Father.

One Thing to Think About: How do I typically respond when someone wrongs me?

One Thing to Pray For: A new determination to overcome evil with good

WEEK 38—THURSDAY

Reading: Romans 13:1-7

The Grace of Government

Paul is writing to the Christians in Rome, the seat of a powerful world empire. He urges them to "*be subject to the governing authorities,*" but not just for self-preservation. "*For there is no authority except from God, and those that exist have been instituted by God. Therefore whoever resists the authorities resists what God has appointed, and those who resist will incur judgment*"(Rom 13:1-2). Government is a gift from God, so part of our submission to God means submission to governing authorities. God empowers rulers to be "*not a terror to good conduct, but to bad*"(Rom 13:3). The ruler is "*the servant of God, an avenger who carries out God's wrath on the wrongdoer*"(Rom 13:4). By checking evil, government blesses the world and helps protect God's people. This makes him "*God's servant for your good*"(Rom 13:4)

All of this means that Christians should "*be in subjection, not only to avoid God's wrath but also for the sake of conscience*"(Rom 13:5). Submission both keeps us out of trouble and honors God. Acknowledging the good that government does, we pay taxes (Rom 13:6). "*Pay to all what is owed to them: taxes to whom taxes are owed, revenue to whom revenue is owed, respect to whom respect is owed, honor to whom honor is owed*"(Rom 13:7). Instead of a defiant stinginess, we willingly give our rulers their due.

The fact that God gives us government does not mean that all rulers acknowledge God, that God endorses their every action, or that God always handpicks the best person to rule. The point here is broader: government is a blessing to mankind and God's people acknowledge this blessing by submitting. If this was true in Paul's day—a day of widespread corruption, tyranny, and brutality by the government—it remains true for Christians under imperfect governments today. We can thank God that we do not live in anarchy.

One Thing to Think About: How often do I thank God for government?

One Thing to Pray For: "That we may lead a peaceful and quiet life, godly and dignified in every way"(1 Tim 2:2)

WEEK 38—FRIDAY

Reading: Romans 14:1-12

The Grace of Welcoming

The Roman Christians have some differences of opinion that are threatening to divide the group. Paul encourages them to welcome each other. "*As for the one who is weak in faith, welcome him, but not to quarrel over opinions*"(Rom 14:1). "*Welcome him*" encompasses a whole range of behaviors. There is initial acceptance; he doesn't need to change something about himself and his opinions to be my brother. There is ongoing relationship; I don't "pass judgment" on him as if he is less than me (Rom 14:4). But this welcome hinges on *God's welcome*: "*Let not the one who eats despise the one who abstains, and let not the one who abstains pass judgment on the one who eats, for God has welcomed him*"(Rom 14:3). If "*God has welcomed him,*" how can I not?

The issues under discussion here—questions of diet, observance of days, and the like—are not the fundamentals of the faith. They are issues of personal discernment about the precise way to live before Jesus. "*The one who observes the day, observes it in honor of the Lord. The one who eats, eats in honor of the Lord, since he gives thanks to God, while the one who abstains, abstains in honor of the Lord and gives thanks to God*"(Rom 14:6). To properly welcome one another, it is vital that we understand that *we are all simply trying to honor Jesus.* Someone might make a choice to honor Jesus that I would not; someone might abstain from something I deem perfectly reasonable to honor Jesus. Paul urges us to see the good in them and remember that it is *Jesus'* judgment of them that matters (Rom 14:4).

Welcoming is hard. We struggle when we discover that someone else thinks differently from us. It is hard to watch someone doing something that bothers us—or abstaining from something that seems fine to us. We tend to not open our arms quite as wide. Yet God has welcomed us—has put away our sins and made us his children—and so we learn to extend that tremendous gift to others.

One Thing to Think About: Whom do I have trouble accepting?

One Thing to Pray For: A deeper appreciation for the faith of others—even those I disagree with

WEEK 39—MONDAY

Reading: Romans 14:13-23

The Grace of Forgoing

Paul's advice here about how we handle disagreements on nonessential matters hinges on understanding the importance of my brother. He is "*the one for whom Christ died*"(Rom 14:15) whom I can "*destroy.*" He is "*the work of God*"(Rom 14:20) whom I can "*destroy.*" I can "*put a stumbling block or hindrance in the way of a brother*"(Rom 14:13). God has blessed, welcomed, saved, and sanctified my brother—and I can undo what God is doing. Paul shifts our perspective from thinking only about our own rights and preferences to focusing on my brother and the God who is working on him.

Paul's advice, then, is to "*decide never to put a stumbling block or hindrance in the way of a brother*"(Rom 14:13). He urges us, "*do not let what you regard as good be spoken of as evil*"(Rom 14:16). He presses us, "*do not, for the sake of food, destroy the work of God*"(Rom 14:20). Probably everyone would agree with these statements, so Paul finally tells us what we should actually *do*: "*It is good not to eat meat or drink wine or do anything that causes your brother to stumble*"(Rom 14:21). We can *forgo* our rights, willfully ceding them for the good of our brothers. We can *give up* what we know God has no problem with. As Paul says in another context: "*if food makes my brother stumble, I will never eat meat, lest I make my brother stumble*"(1 Cor 8:13). By forgoing the action that troubles or encourages my brother to do wrong, I give him a gift.

Americans have a long history of insisting on rights. We demand rights and fight for them. It is extremely rare for us to willingly *give up* rights. Yet God's grace changes us. We are no longer focused solely on living the life we prefer. We are looking to others and how our behavior affects them. In light of all God has given me, can't I give up something to bless my brothers?

One Thing to Think About: What types of nonessential things might I need to forgo—or downplay—to help my brothers?

One Thing to Pray For: An awareness that my brother is the work of God

WEEK 39—TUESDAY

Reading: Romans 15:1-7

The Grace of Bearing with the Weak

As we deal with differences of opinions with others, Paul urges a heart of patience and sacrifice. "*We who are strong have an obligation to bear with the failings of the weak, and not to please ourselves. Let each of us please his neighbor for his good, to build him up*"(Rom 14:1-2). Acting only to "*please ourselves*" means that we are focused on exercising our rights, loudly proclaiming our opinions, and pushing others to accept our behavior. The alternate path is to "*bear with*" those who are weaker, to "*please (our) neighbor for his good*" and acting "*to build him up.*" This is a gift we give others.

Yet it is a gift that we learn from Jesus. "*For Christ did not please himself, but as it is written, 'The reproaches of those who reproached you fell on me*'"(Rom 15:3). Jesus never acted for his own pleasure, but instead endured reproach for us. This selflessness is a gift he gives us—and one that we can then learn to give to our brothers and sisters. As we mutually give grace to each other, the church is unified so that "*together you may with one voice glorify the God and Father of our Lord Jesus Christ*"(Rom 15:6). Our oneness and kindness glorify God. "*Therefore welcome one another as Christ has welcomed you, for the glory of God*"(Rom 15:7).

People can be frustrating. They don't always see and think about things the way we do. Sometimes they cramp our style. We are tempted to abandon them in search of new, better people. We are tempted to fight tooth and nail for our rights. Paul urges a different approach: give others the gift of selflessness, sacrifice, and patience. This is the grace Jesus gives us.

One Thing to Think About: Who do I have trouble "bearing with"? How can I build them up?

One Thing to Pray For: Unity among God's people

WEEK 39—WEDNESDAY

Reading: 1 Corinthians 1:4-9

Not Lacking in Any Gift

Paul has a lot of frustrations with the Corinthian church, but that does not stop him from celebrating what God is doing in them. *"I give thanks to my God always for you because of the grace of God that was given you in Christ Jesus, that in every way you were enriched in him in all speech and all knowledge"*(1 Cor 1:4-5). Every Christian represents an opportunity to praise God. Each Christian represents a lost soul that God has reached, reformed, and redeemed. But Paul sees God's grace going further with the Corinthians: *"that in every way you were enriched in him in all speech and all knowledge."* He is probably referring to spiritual gifts here—gifts of speaking and miraculous knowledge. God has never limited his grace to salvation (as wonderful as it is); he keeps giving so that his people have all that they need to know to know him.

He is confident that *"you are not lacking in any gift, as you wait for the revealing of our Lord Jesus Christ, who will sustain you to the end, guiltless in the day of our Lord Jesus Christ"*(1 Cor 1:7-8). "Gifts" are specific manifestations of God's grace in people. Paul assures them that they are *"not lacking"* and are completely sufficient for the task of continual battle with sin and service to Jesus. God uses those gifts to *"sustain you to the end, guiltless in the day of our Lord Jesus Christ."* They are a part of his provision in successfully moving us from now into eternity in spiritual fellowship with him.

These verses ring with the assurance that God has provided everything we need to follow and know him. While there is certainly more information about God and his will that we would *like*, there is nothing we *need* that we lack. While we might prefer to have more gifts, there is no gift that we lack that will keep us from the Lord. In fact, many of the things we lack personally, God has provided in the church. The proper reaction is confidence in him and a commitment to using our gifts to glorify God and bless others.

One Thing to Think About: Do I ever feel like I'm missing something? Why might that be? How do these verses help?

One Thing to Pray For: Gratitude to God for my brethren

Reading: 1 Corinthians 1:18-31

The Grace of a Foolish Message

Paul meditates on the irony of a gospel message that is rejected by the wise and accepted by the foolish. "*For the word of the cross is folly to those who are perishing, but to us who are being saved it is the power of God*"(1 Cor 1:18). The same message can be foolish to many and brilliant to others. It exposes our motives. "*For Jews demand signs and Greeks seek wisdom, but we preach Christ crucified, a stumbling block to Jews and folly to Gentiles*"(1 Cor 1:22-23). Since it does not fit their preferences, everyone has a problem with the message of Jesus' death. Yet to believers, the gospel is "*Christ the power of God and the wisdom of God*"(1 Cor 1:24).

Practically, this means that most believers are not the world's elites. "*For consider your calling, brothers: not many of you were wise according to worldly standards, not many were powerful, not many were of noble birth*"(1 Cor 1:26). Yet even this is part of God's design, "*so that no human being might boast in the presence of God*"(1 Cor 1:29). He humbles the proud and exalts the humble all in one fell swoop. This is great news—tremendous grace—for those of us whose only hope of greatness is for it to be given to us.

It is hard to overstate the brilliance of God's "foolish message." *No one can accept the gospel and remain proud.* We do not achieve it by our wisdom. It does not appeal to our senses. It humiliates us and exposes our sin. It leaves us only glorifying God. By giving a deathblow to our pride, God gives us a great gift.

One Thing to Think About: How has the gospel humbled me?

One Thing to Pray For: "Let the one who boasts, boast in the Lord"

WEEK 39—FRIDAY

Reading: 1 Corinthians 2:6-16

The Grace of Revelation

The message of the good news about Jesus is not what anyone—Jew or Gentile—expected. It has a counterintuitive brilliance to it because it is not derived from human wisdom. "*But we impart a secret and hidden wisdom of God, which God decreed before the ages for our glory. None of the rulers of this age understood this, for if they had, they would not have crucified the Lord of glory*"(1 Cor 2:7-8). This wisdom was "*secret and hidden*," which allowed for events to transpire in the way God intended without the knowledge of the actors.

In a similar way, God has more great things planned for his people. "*But, as it is written, 'What no eye has seen, nor ear heard, nor the heart of man imagined, what God has prepared for those who love him'—these things God has revealed to us through the Spirit. For the Spirit searches everything, even the depths of God*"(1 Cor 2:9-10). God has prepared blessings for his people that are beyond our imaginings. But he has given us a further gift by revealing many of them to us through his Spirit and the message of the apostles. "*For who knows a person's thoughts except the spirit of that person, which is in him? So also no one comprehends the thoughts of God except the Spirit of God*"(1 Cor 2:11). Since God's thoughts are both his alone and incomprehensible to us, his willingness to reveal himself is a great gift. "*Now we have received not the spirit of the world, but the Spirit who is from God, that we might understand the things freely given us by God*"(1 Cor 2:12). Only by this revelation are we able to learn of God's great grace toward us—"*the things freely given us by God.*"

God does not have to communicate with mankind, especially since we have so often rebelled against him and his will. Left to our own devices, we could only guess at God's opinion of us—although our guilty conscience would surely convince us that he is justifiably angry. It is only through the revelation of his mind—through the Spirit's inspiration of men throughout history—that we learn of our sinfulness, God's love, and our eternal destiny.

One Thing to Think About: If God never revealed himself, how would it change my life?

One Thing to Pray For: A deeper understanding of "what God has prepared for those who love him"

WEEK 40—MONDAY

Reading: 1 Corinthians 6:12-20

You Were Bought with a Price

Some of the Corinthian Christians seem to be justifying fornication—perhaps even with pagan temple prostitutes—under the guise of Christian freedom. "'*All things are lawful for me,' but not all things are helpful. 'All things are lawful for me,' but I will not be dominated by anything*"(1 Cor 6:12). Paul agrees that, in one sense, all things are lawful for Christians, but not if neutral things lead to damage or addiction. However, "*the body is not mean for sexual immorality, but for the Lord, and the Lord for the body*"(1 Cor 6:13). God has not created our bodies for us to be sexually promiscuous. Using the gospel to justify such is a misunderstanding and abuse.

Paul gives several reasons why Christians should avoid sexual immorality. Our bodies are members of Christ and should not be joined with prostitutes (1 Cor 6:15). We become one flesh with a prostitute—a relationship that implies a marriage commitment in any other situation (1 Cor 6:16-17). Fornication is uniquely a sin against our own bodies (1 Cor 6:18). But the most powerful argument, in my view, is his last: "*Or do you not know that your body is a temple of the Holy Spirit within you, whom you have from God? You are not your own, for you were bought with a price. So glorify God in your body*"(1 Cor 6:19-20). Our physical bodies are a temple in which the Holy Spirit dwells, so we must not defile them. "*You are not your own*" means that we are not unilateral actors. "*You were bought with a price*" takes us back to the cross, in which a blood-ransom was paid for us, and then pushes us to live for the one who died for us. How can we accept salvation from past sins and then proceed to sin further?

The word-picture here is of redemption from slavery. If someone paid a great price to set us free from slavery, wouldn't we feel a sense of loyalty to them? Grace is not merely a gift to be accepted; it is a blessing that re-forms the entirety of our lives from this point forward. I am no longer my own.

One Thing to Think About: How does the fact that my body is a temple of the Holy Spirit change my view of my body?

One Thing to Pray For: Loyalty to Jesus because of what he has done for me

WEEK 40—TUESDAY

Reading: 2 Corinthians 1:3-11

The God of All Comfort

Paul has had a harrowing experience that he wants to use to teach the Corinthians. "*For we do not want you to be unaware, brothers, of the affliction we experienced in Asia. For we were so utterly burdened beyond our strength that we despaired of life itself. Indeed, we felt that we had received the sentence of death. But that was to make us rely not on ourselves but on God who raises the dead. He delivered us from such a deadly peril, and he will deliver us*"(2 Cor 1:8-10). He doesn't describe the experience itself, instead focusing on its impact on him. He was "*so utterly burdened beyond our strength that we despaired of life itself,*" convinced that he was going to die. Yet in this overwhelmed state he sees blessings: "*that was to make us rely not on ourselves but on God who raises the dead.*" God gives gifts even in our hardship.

That is why Paul stresses that God is "*the Father of mercies and God of all comfort, who comforts us in all our affliction, so that we may be able to comfort those who are in any affliction, with the comfort with which we ourselves are comforted by God*"(2 Cor 1:3-4). God has comforted him in his trouble and desperation and now Paul can pass that comfort on to others. When we attempt to comfort someone without any firsthand knowledge of grief and loss, our words often sound shallow and empty. Yet when God comforts us, "*we may be able to comfort those who are in any affliction.*" Thus begins a chain in which comfort, blessings, and love pass from brother to brother, to God's glory.

Comforting others is hard. Some thoughts and words comfort us and not others; sometimes we are unable to give comfort while other times we cannot find it ourselves. Paul teaches us to look upward for comfort—seeking out God's perspective, God's will, and God's people. As time passes, our wounds heal, and the intensity of the moment subsides, we praise God for bringing us through the sadness and making us grow deeper along the way.

One Thing to Think About: What people in my life need comfort right now?

One Thing to Pray For: Reliance on God rather than myself

WEEK 40—WEDNESDAY

Reading: 2 Corinthians 3:1-6

Our Sufficiency is from God

Paul has encountered some opposition among the Christians in Corinth. They seem determined to interpret all his actions in the worst way—that his "yes" is not "yes" (2 Cor 1:17), that he lords it over their faith (2 Cor 1:24), and that he is self-promoting (2 Cor 3:1). "*Are we beginning to commend ourselves again? Or do we need, as some do, letters of recommendation to you, or from you? You yourselves are our letter of recommendation, written on our hearts, to be known and read by all*"(2 Cor 3:1-2). He balks at the prospect of needing someone *else* to recommend him to them, since he considers *them* the proof that he is doing the work of Christ. "*And you show that you are a letter from Christ delivered by us, written not with ink but with the Spirit of the living God*"(2 Cor 3:3). This is a lofty view of the Corinthians—and of himself.

Paul acknowledges that even this could be taken the wrong way. "*Such is the confidence that we have through Christ toward God. Not that we are sufficient in ourselves to claim anything as coming from us, but our sufficiency is from God, who has made us sufficient to be ministers of a new covenant, not of the letter but of the Spirit*"(2 Cor 3:4-6). It is not on Paul's own merit that he is capable of ministering God's covenant, delivering Christ's "letter," and preaching the gospel. "*Not that we are sufficient in ourselves*" means that Paul acknowledges his own weakness and unworthiness for his great work. Yet that is not the end of the story. God, in his grace, "*has made us sufficient.*" He helps us to be capable of the tasks that he places before us so that he receives the glory (not us).

In moments of honesty, we can be overwhelmed by the immensity of the tasks before us and our lack of strength, stamina, wisdom, patience, and willpower to accomplish them. We need not fear. God has not chosen us because we are the best and brightest. He *makes us sufficient.* Because we belong to him, we have all that we need to face the difficulties of the day.

One Thing to Think About: What events, demands, or needs make me feel insufficient?

One Thing to Pray For: Remembrance that God has made me sufficient for my tasks

WEEK 40—THURSDAY

Reading: 2 Corinthians 3:7-11

Even More Glory

Paul uses a lesser-to-greater comparison to show the richness of what is in store for believers in Jesus. "*Now if the ministry of death, carved in letters on stone, came with such glory that the Israelites could not gaze at Moses' face because of its glory, which was being brought to an end, will not the ministry of the Spirit have even more glory?*"(2 Cor 3:7-8). At Sinai Jehovah made a covenant with Israel, engraving his laws "*in letters on stone.*" Moses' face shone with the brightness of the glory of proximity to Jehovah. Yet this encounter and the resultant law ultimately produced only death for those unable to fulfill its requirements. With all this majesty, it was only that "*which was being brought to an end.*" If such glory attended it, "*will not the ministry of the Spirit have even more glory?*". We anticipate even greater things.

In fact, Paul—who was raised an observant and dedicated Jew—describes how Jesus' coming has overshadowed the glory of the Law. "*Indeed, in this case, what once had glory has come to have no glory at all, because of the glory that surpasses it. For if what was being brought to an end came with glory, much more will what is permanent have glory*"(2 Cor 3:10-11). Next to Jesus, the Law seems to have no glory at all; it has been outshone. With every jaw-dropping miracle Jesus performs, every world-changing teaching, and his eternal act of sacrifice for others, we see far more than Moses' face shining.

God gave his people a great gift when he delivered the Law of Moses. He not only taught his people how to live, but also impressed on them the seriousness and importance of holiness and righteousness. There was great glory. Yet now he has gone far beyond, giving us a much greater gift. Now we behold God's glory in the person of Jesus, are transformed by his message, and hold promise of an even greater personal glorification in the age to come.

One Thing to Think About: What will it be like for me to be glorified?

One Thing to Pray For: A fresh reminder of God's power and glory

WEEK 40—FRIDAY

Reading: 2 Corinthians 3:12-18

The Grace of Transformation

Since God has given Christians a deeper understanding of himself through Jesus (and a hope of a greater glory), we have confidence. "*Since we have such a hope, we are very bold, not like Moses, who would put a veil over his face so that the Israelites might not gaze at the outcome of what was being brought to an end*"(2 Cor 3:12-13). While great glory attended God's revelation to Moses, there was still a barrier between God and his people, symbolized by Moses' veil. We have no such veil, but in Christ are able to live "*with unveiled face, beholding the glory of the Lord*"(2 Cor 3:18). As recipients of such wonderful access, "*we are very bold.*"

Paul argues that this veil is also symbolic of the inability of many of the Jewish people to see God's glory revealed in Jesus. "*For to this day, when they read the old covenant, that same veil remains unlifted, because only through Christ is it taken away. Yes, to this day whenever Moses is read a veil lies over their hearts. But when one turns to the Lord, the veil is removed*"(2 Cor 3:14-16). There is much more to the Old Testament than we can discover without Jesus and the revelation he brought. Christians, empowered with this knowledge, approach God confidently. "*And we all, with unveiled face, beholding the glory of the Lord, are being transformed into the same image from one degree of glory to another. For this comes from the Lord who is the Spirit*"(2 Cor 3:18). Seeing Jehovah directly, we "*are being transformed into the same image.*" His Spirit works in us, making us more and more like our Father.

The longer we are in relationship with God through Jesus, the more we are changed. We become different people, bearing the fruits of the Spirit's work within us. He smooths out our rough edges, challenges the idols in our hearts, and floods our hearts with the knowledge that we are welcomed as his sons and daughters. We learn to treat people differently, no longer feeling threatened by them, no longer competing, no longer jealous, no longer insecure. This is God's work in us—and a tremendous gift.

One Thing to Think About: How am I different from when I began to follow Jesus?

One Thing to Pray For: God to do his work in me through his Spirit

WEEK 41—MONDAY

Reading: 2 Corinthians 4:7-18

From Grace to Gratitude

As Paul describes his ministry, he emphasizes his own insufficiency. "*But we have this treasure in jars of clay, to show that the surpassing power belongs to God and not to us*"(2 Cor 4:7). Instead of entrusting his word to supermen who never struggle or need help, God has placed the incredible treasure of his life-changing message in fragile, unworthy vessels. This demonstrates his brilliance and power while humbling us. His awareness of this great gift buoys Paul through the hardships he suffers as an apostle ("*persecuted, but not forsaken*", 2 Cor 4:9).

Paul also maintains a focus on the people he is teaching, hoping earnestly that his sufferings will be a blessing to others. "*So death is at work in us, but life in you*"(2 Cor 4:12). "*knowing that he who raised the Lord Jesus will raise us also with Jesus and bring us with you into his presence. For it is all for your sake, so that as grace extends to more and more people it may increase thanksgiving, to the glory of God*"(2 Cor 4:14-15). The more people who respond to the gospel—the farther God's grace extends—the more gratitude goes up to God. God is glorified more and more. The world opens its eyes to its great need and its Creator. God rescues more people from the devastation of sin. We learn just how richly we have been blessed—and we give thanks.

Grace and gratitude come from the same root word. When we receive gifts properly, we are grateful. If we are ungrateful, it is probable that we do not feel we have been given good gifts. Ingratitude is often a first step on a path away from God (see Rom 1:21-32). But Paul's vision here of cosmic gratitude shows that he wants all mankind to see his goodwill toward them and respond to him in faithful obedience and praise. It is what we were made for.

One Thing to Think About: How many good things have I already received from God today?

One Thing to Pray For: Thanks to God for all the manifestations of his grace

WEEK 41—TUESDAY

Reading: 2 Corinthians 5:1-10

Swallowed Up by Life

Paul has been musing on God's strange decision to place his precious gospel in "*jars of clay*"—frail, imperfect people who are sometimes targeted for their faith. Yet he remains confident that "*he who raised the Lord Jesus will raise us also with Jesus*"(2 Cor 4:14). Death is not an end, but a part of the transition to a better body. "*For we know that if the tent that is our earthly home is destroyed, we have a building from God, a house not made with hands, eternal in the heavens*"(2 Cor 5:1). Our present bodies are merely a "*tent*"—a temporary dwelling—while they will soon be transformed into a "*building from God*"—a permanent place to live, a body no longer subject to death and infirmity.

This produces an emotion in us: "*For in this tent we groan, longing to put on our heavenly dwelling, if indeed by putting it on we may not be found naked. For while we are still in this tent, we groan, being burdened—not that we would be unclothed, but that we would be further clothed, so that what is mortal may be swallowed up by life*"(2 Cor 5:2-4). We groan, yearning for the full life that is to come. We groan, weary from the weakness, sadness, and death of mortal life. We groan, helpless in the face of aches, pains, threats, and afflictions. We don't want to shed our bodies ("*be unclothed*"), but to have perfected bodies ("*further clothed*"). We want our mortality to be washed under by immortality—"*swallowed up by life.*"

Christians lament the pains of aging and the terrible fragility of life because we know that this is not God's intention for us or our bodies. Yet each groan and frustration increases our anticipation for his great gift to us—the ending of our mortality and redemption of our bodies (Rom 8:23). Soon and very soon, what is mortal will be swallowed up by life.

One Thing to Think About: In what ways do I groan for immortality?

One Thing to Pray For: The proper balance between mourning our present state and anticipation of future blessings

Reading: 2 Corinthians 9:6-15

Seed for the Sower

Giving does tremendous good. Paul is encouraging the Corinthians to prepare a gift to send to needy Christians in Jerusalem by describing God's view of givers. "*The point is this: whoever sows sparingly will also reap sparingly, and whoever sows bountifully will also reap bountifully. Each one must give as he has decided in his heart, not reluctantly or under compulsion, for God loves a cheerful giver*"(2 Cor 9:6-7). We reap what we sow because God is witness to our giving and makes it so. But God also "*loves a cheerful giver*"—presumably because *he* is such a giver. For those who are afraid that their giving will mean that they do not have enough for themselves, Paul reassures: "*And God is able to make all grace abound to you, so that having all sufficiency in all things at all times, you may abound in every good work*"(2 Cor 9:8). God is capable of giving so that we have enough even as we give. We can't outgive God.

But looking at God's giving nature produces confidence and willingness to give ourselves. "*He who supplies seed to the sower and bread for food will supply and multiply your seed for sowing and increase the harvest of your righteousness. You will be enriched in every way to be generous in every way, which through us will produce thanksgiving to God. For the ministry of this service is not only supplying the needs of the saints but is also overflowing in many thanksgivings to God*"(2 Cor 9:10-12). Just as God gives seed to the sower *and* bread for food—blessing the process of farming at every step—so he will supply our "seed" and increase our "harvest." Paul envisions a beautiful chain of giving, sharing, and gratitude that begins with God, channels through us, passes on to others, from them back to God as thanksgiving. The only thing that shortchanges the process is our own stinginess or ingratitude.

When we are called on to give, many thoughts run through our heads. Where will the money come from? What about what I had planned to do with that? How will it be spent? Paul directs our attention to other questions: what has God given me? What does God want me to do? What do others need? Just as God keeps giving seed to the sower, providing food and blessing to all mankind, so he will ensure that givers do not give themselves empty. We can't outgive God.

One Thing to Think About: Whom will I give to help today?

One Thing to Pray For: Gratitude for all the good things I have received

WEEK 41—THURSDAY

Reading: 2 Corinthians 12:7-10

The Grace of Thorns

Though Paul has received special revelations from God, he is not without hardship. "*So to keep me from becoming conceited because of the surpassing greatness of the revelations, a thorn was given me in the flesh, a messenger of Satan to harass me, to keep me from becoming conceited*"(2 Cor 12:7). Paul does not describe his thorn and our speculation is useless. We know only that it is a physical problem ("*flesh*") that creates pain and inconvenience for him ("*harass*"). It is not clear who gives Paul this "gift"; it is a "*messenger of Satan*" but also has the purpose of keeping him humble (certainly not Satan's goal). What is clear is that Jesus refuses to eliminate the thorn, although he has the power to do so. "*Three times I pleaded with the Lord about this, that it should leave me. But he said to me, 'My grace is sufficient for you, for my power is made perfect in weakness'*"(2 Cor 12:8-9). Jesus refuses, highlighting the gifts he has *already* given Paul (there are many). God reserves the right to say no to our requests, or else grace is no longer grace.

But Paul takes something else positive from Jesus' statement to him. If Jesus' "*power is made perfect in weakness*," then weakness becomes a good thing because it gets him closer to Jesus. "*Therefore I will boast all the more gladly of my weaknesses, so that the power of Christ may rest upon me. For the sake of Christ, then, I am content with weaknesses, insults, hardships, persecutions, and calamities. For when I am weak, then I am strong*"(2 Cor 12:9-10). It is not only thorns, but all kinds of weaknesses and difficulties that Paul learns to live with. My imperfections and limitations give Jesus an opportunity to shine.

When we are wise, healthy, strong, complete, and impressive, we feel little need for God. As much as we dislike obstacles and troubles, they humble us and "*keep (us) from becoming conceited.*" As much as we want Jesus to take them away, they connect us to him and form the basis of our most powerful moments, stories, and songs. I cannot say that Jesus is the *source* of Paul's thorn, but allowing it to remain is part of his *grace*. If God took away all the hardship, he would take away our greatest opportunities for growth and connection to him. Leaving thorns is a grace.

One Thing to Think About: What thorns are there in my life? What good can they produce in me?

One Thing to Pray For: Contentment with circumstances that are less than ideal

WEEK 41—FRIDAY

Reading: Galatians 2:15-21

Nullifying God's Grace

Paul has been dressing Peter down for his hypocrisy. When influential Jewish Christians came to Antioch, Peter stopped associating with his Gentile brothers to mollify them. Paul sees this as a reversion to lawkeeping (since many Jews felt distance from Gentiles necessary for ritual purity). "*We ourselves are Jews by birth and not Gentile sinners; yet we know that a person is not justified by works of the law but through faith in Jesus Christ, so we also have believed in Christ Jesus, in order to be justified by faith in Christ and not by works of the law, because by works of the law no one will be justified*"(Gal 2:15-16). Jewish Christians are not right before God because of their good works. They are accepted by faith just like Gentiles. This means that salvation for all believers—Jew and Gentile—is not something deserved, but an act of God's grace.

Paul warns against accepting God's gift, then going back to our old ways. "*For if I rebuild what I tore down, I prove myself to be a transgressor. For through the law I died to the law, so that I might live to God*"(Gal 2:18-19). There has been a firm break with our past—including, crucially, past ways of attempting to be righteous. We have died to that life and way of thinking. "*I have been crucified with Christ. It is no longer I who live, but Christ who lives in me. And the life I now live in the flesh I live by faith in the Son of God, who loved me and gave himself for me. I do not nullify the grace of God, for if righteousness were through the law, then Christ died for no purpose*"(Gal 2:20-21). We cannot literally nullify God's grace; that is not up to us. Yet when we live as if we can be righteous on our own merits, we declare grace unnecessary. We don't need God. We don't need anyone. He can keep his gifts. There is no need for Jesus to die. This attitude invalidates God's grace for ourselves.

While it is tough to find an exact parallel to the situation Paul is describing, we can recognize this mentality. We take great pride in being self-made, pulling ourselves up by our bootstraps, and doing our own thing. It is a short step from here to convincing ourselves that we don't need God or anyone. *This pride nullifies God's grace*—and it tarnishes our theology.

One Thing to Think About: Do I find it challenging to accept gifts? Why?

One Thing to Pray For: The humility to accept God's righteousness instead of trying to do it all myself

WEEK 42—MONDAY

Reading: Galatians 3:10-14

Redeemed from the Curse

Paul walks us step-by-step through the problem of the curse of the law and how Jesus saves us from it. *"For all who rely on works of the law are under a curse; for it is written, 'Cursed be everyone who does not abide by all things written in the book of the Law, and do them'"*(Gal 3:10). When God gave his law through Moses, he attached curses for disobedience which express the wrath of God. Paul works from the assumption that no one "*(abides) by all things written in the book of the Law.*" So all who attempt to follow it rest under the curse. *"Now it is evident that no one is justified before God by the law, for 'The righteous shall live by faith.' But the law is not of faith, rather 'The one who does them shall live by them'"*(Gal 3:11-12). Law and faith are two distinct approaches to God. One rests on our perfect obedience while the other trusts that God will give us what we cannot attain on our own merit.

So what is to be done for those who have tried to follow the Law and gotten only a curse and condemnation for themselves? *"Christ redeemed us from the curse of the law by becoming a curse for us—for it is written, 'Cursed is everyone who is hanged on a tree'—so that in Christ Jesus the blessing of Abraham might come to the Gentiles, so that we might receive the promised Spirit through faith"*(Gal 3:13-14). Jesus takes on a curse on our behalf on the cross. He does not deserve the curse of disobedience, yet he accepts the curse of hanging on a tree. His sacrificial act redeems us from the curse of Law and sin.

Our sins merit God's wrath—the curse. Yet Jesus willingly suffers a curse for us, redeeming us from the judgment due us. This does not mean that God punished or judged Jesus, but that he accepts undeserved shame and suffering to save us from our fate. Thanks to him, we are free.

One Thing to Think About: What response from God do my actions deserve?

One Thing to Pray For: A deeper faith in the saving power of Jesus' sacrifice

WEEK 42—TUESDAY

Reading: Galatians 3:23-4:7

The Grace of Adoption

Paul likens God's use of the Law of Moses to a young man in a wealthy family growing up under a guardian. "*So then, the law was our guardian until Christ came, in order that we might be justified by faith. But now that faith has come, we are no longer under a guardian, for in Christ Jesus you are all sons of God, through faith*"(Gal 3:24-26). The law helped shepherd the people while in an immature state. But now that Christ has come, everything has changed and we are sons of God. Not only that, but because we are "*in Christ*"(Gal 3:26) and "*have put on Christ*"(Gal 3:27) and are "*one in Christ Jesus*"(Gal 3:28), we are also the heirs of the promise to Abraham (Gal 3:29).

Paul continues with his comparison: "*I mean that the heir, as long as he is a child, is no different from a slave, though he is the owner of everything, but he is under guardians and managers until the date set by his father*"(Gal 4:1-2). A son can look like a slave before he matures. "*But when the fullness of time had come, God sent forth his Son, born of woman, born under the law, to redeem those who were under the law, so that we might receive adoption as sons. And because you are sons, God has sent the Spirit of his Son into our hearts, crying, 'Abba! Father!*'"(Gal 4:4-6). When the right time came for these children to become sons instead of slaves, God sent his Son to redeem us. Now we can "*receive adoption as sons,*" including God's Holy Spirit who comes into our hearts to confirm to us that we are children. God just keeps giving!

Adoption means that we have a place and status that is *given* to us. We have no natural claim on it. God does not merely enlist us as his servants (although that metaphor is common in the NT), but wants us to feel the closeness and acceptance of being *his own sons and daughters.* We stand to inherit as full members of the family. We bear the family resemblance. We know who we are.

One Thing to Think About: How does being God's son or daughter make me bold? How does it give me pause?

One Thing to Pray For: A sense of God's acceptance of me

WEEK 42—WEDNESDAY

Reading: Galatians 5:1-6

Fallen Away from Grace

Paul has strong words for the Galatian Christians who are considering adding circumcision and the Law of Moses to their service to Jesus. "*For freedom Christ has set us free; stand firm therefore, and do not submit again to a yoke of slavery*"(Gal 5:1). They are in danger of returning to the slavery Jesus freed them from. Part of the reason is that the Law of Moses is not pursued in half-measures. "*I testify again to every man who accepts circumcision that he is obligated to keep the whole law*"(Gal 5:3). There is more in the Law than they realize—diets and priests' garments and feasts and sacrifices. We do not dabble in law-keeping; either we do it with our whole hearts or we don't do it at all.

But Paul is especially concerned about the impact this has on their relationship with Jesus. "*If you accept circumcision, Christ will be of no advantage to you...You are severed from Christ, you who would be justified by the law; you have fallen away from grace*"(Gal 5:2, 4). These statements are parallel to his earlier statement that "*if righteousness were through the law, then Christ died for no purpose*"(Gal 2:21). Believing that we can keep a law perfectly enough to earn our salvation means that Jesus didn't have to die. We don't need God's grace. We don't need Jesus at all. This spirit severs us from Christ. We fall from grace—because we are no longer hoping for salvation through grace. We lose the very thing Jesus has given us. Paul then reaffirms the need for faith over against law-keeping: we await the hope of righteousness "*by faith*"(Gal 5:5) and put no value in circumcision but "*only faith working through love*"(Gal 5:6).

This passage merits careful thought in two directions. First, it is clearly possible for us to be severed from Christ and fall away from his grace. This is such a clear and present danger to Paul that he warns about it in several ways and it consumes this entire letter. Christians must live aware of their need to maintain connection to Jesus. Second, falling away here occurs *when Christians believe that they can be righteous on their own*. They build their own systems of righteousness and gain confidence for salvation because of their own actions. For all practical purposes, they feel they don't need Jesus. The great danger that separates people from Christ (in this text) is *reliance on ourselves*.

One Thing to Think About: Am I ever tempted to believe that I can be righteous on my own?

One Thing to Pray For: A stronger dependence on Jesus

WEEK 42—THURSDAY

Reading: Ephesians 1:3-6

Every Spiritual Blessing

Paul begins this letter by praising God for what he has done for his people. It is a story of grace. "*Blessed be the God and Father of our Lord Jesus Christ, who has blessed us in Christ with every spiritual blessing in the heavenly places*"(Eph 1:3). God has, through Jesus, given his people "*every spiritual blessing*," providing for their every need and, in fact, many things we did not know we needed. These blessings are "*in the heavenly places*," meaning that they connect us with the powerful spiritual realm (Eph 2:6), yet are also a present reality for us. Paul then begins to enumerate God's rich gifts: "*even as he chose us in him before the foundation of the world, that we should be holy and blameless before him*"(Eph 1:4). God has been planning for this for a long time—"*before the foundation of the world*" and "*predestined*"(Eph 1:5) point at this. He has made us into the holy and blameless people we were not, just because he wanted to.

God also acted as Father: "*in love he predestined us for adoption as sons through Jesus Christ, according to the purpose of his will*"(Eph 1:5). He slated us to be his new sons and daughters, adopted into the family of God. This adoption is not something we earn or deserve, but is "*according to the purpose of his will.*" All of this is "*to the praise of his glorious grace, with which he has blessed us in the Beloved*"(Eph 1:6). Our new status as God's children—our holiness and blamelessness—our election and predestination—all lead us to praise God's unspeakable goodness. We praise his glorious grace.

We tend to think more easily of *physical* blessings than spiritual ones. Yet Paul directs our attention to deeper realities than money, food, and shelter. *What do I deserve from God?* I deserve God's wrath and punishment for my sins. Yet this is not at all what I receive. I am instead given everything I do not deserve. God makes me into the person I should have been all along, receives me as his child, and invites me to participate in his plan for the world. I praise his glorious grace.

One Thing to Think About: Do I tend to overlook blessings when they are spiritual rather than physical? Why might that be?

One Thing to Pray For: Praise to God for his glorious grace

WEEK 42—FRIDAY

Reading: Ephesians 1:7-10

The Grace of Redemption

Paul is enumerating the rich spiritual blessings God has given to believers. "*In him we have redemption through his blood, the forgiveness of our trespasses, according to the riches of his grace, which he lavished on upon us*"(Eph 1:7-8). In the ancient world, a slave could be set free once the appropriate price was paid to the owner. The slave would be "redeemed" and liberated. Here Paul speaks of the price Jesus freely paid—"*through his blood*"—that ends our slavery to sin. We experience this redemption as "*the forgiveness of our trespasses,*" confident awareness that the evils we have committed are put away and we stand clean before him.

Not only did God do this for us, but he also blessed us by "*in all wisdom and insight making known to us the mystery of his will, according to his purpose, which he set forth in Christ as a plan for the fullness of time, to unite all things in him, things in heaven and things on earth*"(Eph 1:8-10). God has revealed the mystery of his will for us and given us glimpses of where things go from here, including his goal to "*unite all things in him, things in heaven and things on earth.*" We have closure and peace with the past and hope for the future.

Appreciating redemption hinges on deeply understanding our slavery to sin. There is a tragic desperation to the plight of a slave who will never have enough to buy his own freedom, but merely continues dully plodding forward in his work, year after year. We have experienced the frustration of slavery to sin and our futile attempts to leave it behind. We try to feel better about our lives; we grasp about for a sense of purpose; we try to wash ourselves clean; we try to do better; at the end we only lapse exhausted into further despair. *We need to be bought out of our sins.* And when we are, we sing the praise of a Savior who bought us. We live for him.

One Thing to Think About: What has God saved me from?

One Thing to Pray For: A constant awareness that I am not my own, but I was bought with a price (1 Cor 6:19-20)

WEEK 43—MONDAY

Reading: Ephesians 1:11-14

The Grace of Inheritance

When Israel entered the land of Canaan, land was ascribed to different tribes and passed on within families by inheritance. Christians have something similar: "*In him we have obtained an inheritance, having been predestined according to the purpose of him who works all things according to the counsel of his will*"(Eph 1:11). Inheritance combines the ideas of acceptance, provision, and optimism about the future. Some versions translate this passively, making Christians themselves *God's inheritance*, his portion. Whatever the precise meaning, it is clear that it is a blessing that helps us face the future confidently.

Yet God also gives *another* gift to ensure that we remain anchored in anticipation of *this* gift! "*In him you also, when you heard the word of truth, the gospel of your salvation, and believed in him, were sealed with the promised Holy Spirit, who is the guarantee of our inheritance until we acquire possession of it, to the praise of his glory*"(Eph 1:13-14). The "*you also*" here shows that the blessing of inheritance includes Gentiles who believe. When people hear the gospel and believe in Jesus, they are "*sealed with the promised Holy Spirit,*" signifying God's ownership of them. The Spirit is also "*the guarantee of our inheritance,*" a down payment on the future blessings we are promised. The fact that God has given his Spirit to indwell and refine his people speaks to more, richer blessings to come.

Christians are "*heirs of God and fellow heirs with Christ, provided we suffer with him in order that we may also be glorified with him*"(Rom 8:17). We have an inheritance that we do not deserve. No person can take it from us. We await transformation and eternal fellowship with God—and the presence of God's Spirit within us is proof that God will finish what he has begun in Christ. Someday we will inherit even more great gifts from God!

One Thing to Think About: How should Christians feel about the future? How do I feel?

One Thing to Pray For: Assurance that God works all things according to the counsel of his will

WEEK 43—TUESDAY

Reading: Ephesians 1:15-23

I Pray for More

Paul frequently begins his letters by telling the church that he is praying for them. "*For this reason, because I have heard of your faith in the Lord Jesus and your love toward all the saints I do not cease to give thanks for you, remembering you in my prayers*"(Eph 1:15-16). Paul's vibrant prayer life includes frequent mention of his brothers and sisters, expressing gratitude for them to God. But what does he ask for them? "*that the God of our Lord Jesus Christ, the Father of glory, may give you the Spirit of wisdom and of revelation in the knowledge of him*"(Eph 1:17). He prays for more for them: more wisdom, more revelation, more knowledge.

Specifically, he wants the Ephesians to understand more deeply what they have already begun to learn: "*having the eyes of your hearts enlightened, that you may know what is the hope to which he has called you, what are the riches of his glorious inheritance in the saints, and what is the immeasurable greatness of his power toward us who believe*"(Eph 1:18-19). These are things they already know; Paul prays that they may *know* them. He wants God to grant them deeper understanding of the richness of the great gospel. He wants them to feel the majesty of the hope they hold. He wants them to value how God promises them an inheritance—and how they are God's inheritance. He wants them to grasp the incredible power he has directed toward our good. All the things that God has done through Jesus—resurrection, exaltation, dominion (Eph 1:20-23)—he wants the Ephesians to have revealed to them. He prays for more.

Paul's prayer reveals his deep desire for others to continue to grow stronger in Christ. Yet there is no sense that he is getting greedy—that Christians should just be content with our current spiritual state. Instead, this prayer for more is healthy, showing the passionate hunger that drives disciples closer to God. God does not grow tired of blessing his people. We do not need something new and interesting, but more understanding, appreciation, and passion about what we already know. I pray for more.

One Thing to Think About: How often do I pray for the spiritual growth of my brothers and sisters?

One Thing to Pray For: The eyes of my heart to be enlightened, grasping the greatness of the gospel

WEEK 43—WEDNESDAY

Reading: Ephesians 2:1-10

Not Your Own Doing

How should believers think about their salvation? Paul takes us back through what happened when we accepted the gospel. "*And you were dead in the trespasses and sins in which you once walked...we all once lived in the passions of our flesh, carrying out the desires of the body and the mind, and were by nature children of wrath, like the rest of mankind*"(Eph 2:1-2, 3). He mixes metaphors: we were dead, were enslaved, we were corrupted. What changed? "*But God, being rich in mercy...made us alive together with Christ...and raised us up with him*"(Eph 2:4, 5, 6). *God acted.* From his great love and grace, he raised the dead, liberated the slaves, cleansed the impure. God saved me.

His wording is intentional because he has a misconception to clear up. "*For by grace you have been saved through faith. And this is not your own doing; it is the gift of God, not a result of works, so that no one may boast*"(Eph 2:8-9). God has *given* us salvation as a gift. He is responsible. "*And this is not your own doing.*" While I have things I must do to obey God, he is always the one who gets the credit. This means my relationship with him is "*not a result of works, so that no one may boast.*" I have not done anything to deserve it—and never could. I do not brag; I have only received a gift from a generous God.

Paul is addressing the problem of thinking that our right standing before God is something we have achieved on our own. Sometimes we mistakenly believe that we are pretty good people. After being Christians for many years, we can start to make revisionist history, believing that God has accepted us because we are just a little bit better than everyone else. At times our doctrinal debates about salvation lead us to be far too focused on what we do to comply with God's commands (baptism, obedience) and not nearly focused enough on what God does. If you are right with God, never forget: it is "*not your own doing.*"

One Thing to Think About: Why do we tend to want to take credit for our salvation?

One Thing to Pray For: The humility and gratitude that should accompany such wonderful gifts

WEEK 43—THURSDAY

Reading: Ephesians 2:11-16

Breaking Down the Wall

Because his audience is primarily non-Jewish, Paul reminds them of their distance from God before Jesus. "*Remember that you were at that time separated from Christ, alienated from the commonwealth of Israel and strangers to the covenants of promise, having no hope and without God in the world*"(Eph 2:12). The work God did with Israel was intensely exclusive, leaving the Gentiles out in the cold. Because they had no dependable, gracious God, they lived hopelessly. "*But now in Christ Jesus you who were once far off have been brought near by the blood of Christ*"(Eph 2:13). The blood of Jesus brings all believers—even those who have no claim on God—near to him. Now we belong.

But this movement also changes our relationship to others. "*For he himself is our peace, who has made us both one and has broken down in his flesh the dividing wall of hostility by abolishing the law of commandments expressed in ordinances, that he might create in himself one new man in place of the two, so making peace, and might reconcile us both to God in one body through the cross, thereby killing the hostility*"(Eph 2:14-16). The Law of Moses—Israel's founding document—divided Jews from all other people, creating hostility. This is best seen in the refusal of New Testament-era Jews to even be in the same *room* with Gentiles (John 18:28, Acts 10:28, Acts 11:3). Yet Jesus "*has broken down in his flesh the dividing wall of hostility.*" In his death, Jesus abolishes the law and its resultant division, condescension, and hatred. Now there can be unity and peace.

We are many centuries downwind of the Jew-Gentile hostility that permeates the NT, so it can be hard for us to relate to these words. Yet we certainly know the reality of racial hatred. We are also well-acquainted with the way groups can condescend to and separate themselves from those who are not a part of their group. Jesus gives us a great gift when he breaks down the wall of separation. He longs for people of all races and histories to join together as his people as they come to faith in him. Because we are at peace with God, we can truly be at peace with one another.

One Thing to Think About: Whom do I tend to condescend to?

One Thing to Pray For: Unity and peace with my fellow-Christians—despite our differences

WEEK 43—FRIDAY

Reading: Ephesians 2:17-22

A Holy Temple

After Jesus broke down the wall of separation between Jew and Gentile on the cross, the good news about Jesus began to spread throughout the world. "*And he came and preached peace to you who were far off and peace to those who were near. For through him we both have access in one Spirit to the Father*"(Eph 2:17-18). Interestingly, Paul declares that Jesus himself came and preached to the Ephesians, although it was actually Paul, Apollos, and other men who did so. But the message is "*peace*" between men, who can now together come to God through Jesus. This is particularly good news for non-Jews, who previously were without hope (Eph 2:12). "*So then you are no longer strangers and aliens, but you are fellow citizens with the saints and members of the household of God*"(Eph 2:19). Gentiles are welcomed instead of viewed as foreigners; Gentiles are not strangers, but members of God's family.

Yet even though Gentiles have already received this blessing, God is not done. He continues to build his people: "*built on the foundation of the apostles and prophets, Christ Jesus himself being the cornerstone, in whom the whole structure, being joined together, grows into a holy temple in the Lord. In him you also are being built together into a dwelling place for God by the Spirit*"(Eph 2:20-22). God has not just brought this widely divergent group of people together; he also is molding them together into a new entity. We are now his church, Christ's body, and a "*holy temple*" in which God can dwell. Just as each brick and board loses its individual identity as it becomes a part of a building, so our Jewishness and Gentileness fades away as we become something bigger together than what we are alone. We receive the exalted blessing of becoming the place where God lives.

When we choose to follow Jesus, we do not do so alone. We join other believers of all nations to work, worship, and grow together. When we struggle with frustration with other fellow Christians—when we feel discouraged and isolated—when we battle with selfishness—we will gain strength from remembering that we are "*being built together into a dwelling place for God by the Spirit.*"

One Thing to Think About: Why is unity so hard?

One Thing to Pray For: The tremendous honor of God living in me and my brethren

Reading: Ephesians 3:1-6

No Longer a Mystery

Motivated by the idea that God is building a temple for himself out of all peoples, Paul talks about his own role in the project. "*For this reason I, Paul, a prisoner for Christ Jesus on behalf of you Gentiles—assuming that you have heard of the stewardship of God's grace that was given to me for you*"(Eph 3:1-2). Paul feels that God has given him a special ministry in preaching to the Gentiles—a "*stewardship of God's grace.*" Stewardship means giving someone temporary charge over an area of responsibility. His stewardship is a gift from God *and* it is a stewardship of the gift of God's gospel.

Paul has also been given the gift of special revelation of God's will: "*how the mystery was made known to me by revelation, as I have written briefly. When you read this, you can perceive my insight into the mystery of Christ*"(Eph 3:3-4). God's will is a "mystery," but God has revealed it to Paul. One of the main purposes of this letter is to share what God has given him. The mystery "*was not made known to the sons of men in other generations as it has now been revealed to his holy apostles and prophets by the Spirit. This mystery is that the Gentiles are fellow heirs, members of the same body, and partakers of the promise in Christ Jesus through the gospel*"(Eph 3:5-6). God's will is a mystery because it has been hidden from man for centuries. No one could have guessed his plan. Yet now God has revealed himself to the apostles and prophets. The vital part of that revelation, for Paul's purposes here, is that God has accepted Jew and Gentile as one people in Christ, a shocking shift from the past.

God has a knack for planning and acting in ways that humans cannot anticipate. Like the final scene in a mystery novel, when he reveals himself, it all begins to make sense. We see all the prophecies and how they came to pass in unexpected ways. There are still some things that are mysteries to us, such as the exact nature of the age to come, God's purposes in the nations at the present moment. God's gift of revealing the mystery gives me hope that there will be a day when the full mystery is unraveled before us and it all begins to make even more sense.

One Thing to Think About: Why does man never seem to be able to anticipate God?

One Thing to Pray For: A deeper understanding of what God has revealed

WEEK 44—TUESDAY

Reading: Ephesians 3:7-13

The Very Least of All the Saints

Even though Paul is in prison as he writes this letter, his view of God's goodness sustains him. "*Of this gospel I was made a minister according to the gift of God's grace, which was given to me by the working of his power. To me, though I am the very least of all the saints, this grace was given, to preach to the Gentiles the unsearchable riches of Christ*"(Eph 3:7-8). He repeatedly refers to his ministry as a grace or gift. But the greatness of the gift is expanded as Paul sees how undeserving he is. "*To me, though I am the very least of all the saints, this grace was given.*" Paul knows his limitations and his shameful past and is certain that *any other Christian* would be more deserving of the blessing of preaching good news to the Gentiles. Yet God gave it to him anyway.

As a result, Paul finds himself swept up in God's cosmic mission: "*to bring to light for everyone what is the plan of the mystery hidden for ages in God who created all things, so that through the church the manifold wisdom of God might now be made known to the rulers and authorities in the heavenly places*"(Eph 3:9-10). Through Paul's preaching, the multiethnic church can demonstrate God's genius to the greatest powers of heaven and earth. He is on the front lines of unfolding God's perfect will, despite his unworthiness. "*So I ask you not to lose heart over what I am suffering for you, which is your glory*"(Eph 3:13). In the context of such an epic gift, Paul doesn't mind enduring his hard situation for a little while.

It is tempting to dismiss Paul's statement that he is "the very least of all the saints" (and his later statement that he is the "foremost" sinner, 1 Tim 1:15) as hyperbole. Yet he models for us a deep personal awareness of our own failings. We do not deserve God's good gifts. The fact that God continues to bless us anyway—forgiving us, maturing us, and involving us in his plans for today and the future—gives us courage, motivation, and hope.

One Thing to Think About: Could I call myself "the very least of all the saints"?

One Thing to Pray For: The humility to acknowledge my unworthiness

WEEK 44—WEDNESDAY

Reading: Ephesians 3:14-21

The Grace to Go Deeper

Having summed up the incredible gift God has given the Ephesian Christians—accepting them as his people and building them together with Jewish believers into his dwelling place—Paul prays for them: "*that according to the riches of his glory he may grant you to be strengthened with power through his Spirit in your inner being*"(Eph 3:16). He asks God for the gift of inner spiritual strength by the agency of the Holy Spirit. "*so that Christ may dwell in your hearts through faith*"(Eph 3:17). He asks for the continued indwelling of Jesus in the hearts of believers (even as he lives in the entire group, Eph 2:22).

He goes further: "*that you, being rooted and grounded in love, may have strength to comprehend with all the saints what is the breadth and length and height and depth, and to know the love of Christ that surpasses knowledge, that you may be filled with all the fullness of God*"(Eph 3:17-19). Paul asks God to enable them to fully grasp the extent of God's love. He wants them to know the love that surpasses knowledge. He wants them to be full of God's fullness. He wants them to have the strength to experience the things they know intellectually. He asks God for the grace to go deeper. "*Now to him who is able to do far more abundantly than all that we ask or think, according to the power at work within us, to him be glory in the church and in Christ Jesus throughout all generations, forever and ever. Amen*"(Eph 3:20-21). Paul prays confident that God is able to do this and far, far more than all we could ever ask.

Christians can plateau. We quickly grasp the essentials of the faith and the (rather simple) things Jesus asks us to do. Paul's prayer here is not that we go deeper in the sense that we start musing on heavy theology. He asks God for the favor of deeper understanding of—and connection to—him. Firmer strength, more intimate knowledge, better emotional understanding, further confidence—these are gifts from a good God.

One Thing to Think About: Do I have a desire to go deeper in my relationship with God? Do I want this for others?

One Thing to Pray For: The strength to comprehend the breadth, length, heigh, and depth of Christ's love for me

Reading: Ephesians 4:7-16

He Gave Gifts to Men

If God has made a new people from both Jews and Gentiles, how do we preserve its unity and help it grow? It involves the use of God's gifts. "*But grace was given to each one of us according to the measure of Christ's gift. Therefore it says, 'When he ascended on high he led a host of captives, and he gave gifts to men*'"(Eph 4:7-8). Paul's citation of Psalm 68 emphasizes that Jesus' enthronement proves his lordship and results in his showering of regal blessings on mankind. We benefit from them directly. "*And he gave the apostles, the prophets, the evangelists, the shepherds and teachers, to equip the saints for the work of ministry, for building up the body of Christ*"(Eph 4:11-12). These gifts are not merely offices so someone can be in charge; they are gifts Jesus gives to bless and build up his people. As Jesus' disciples teach one another, we all grow stronger and the gift-giver is glorified.

As we grow to individual maturity, the entire group is strengthened. The goal is that "*we all attain to the unity of the faith and of the knowledge of the Son of God, to mature manhood, to the measure of the stature of the fullness Christ, so that we may no longer be children, tossed to and fro by the waves and carried about by every wind of doctrine, by human cunning, by craftiness in deceitful schemes*"(Eph 4:13-14). Jesus does not exercise his power by eliminating false teaching and temptation; he instead guides us with his truth and his people who "*(speak) the truth in love*"(Eph 4:15). It is not that the church becomes essential as if we have any power in ourselves; it is that Jesus has given gifts of teaching and leadership to bless the whole group. In this way, the church becomes a body that "*builds itself up in love*"(Eph 4:16).

It is easy to see the church from a purely human standpoint: some men are more charismatic or power-hungry, so they naturally take charge. Paul corrects our misconception: Jesus has given gifts to all people with the goal of *helping others*. We share our gifts to strengthen one another and others in turn strengthen us. As Jesus' disciples teach one another, we all grow stronger and the gift-giver is glorified.

One Thing to Think About: In what ways do I see my brothers and sisters using their gifts?

One Thing to Pray For: Continued growth toward maturity

WEEK 44—FRIDAY

Reading: Ephesians 4:25-5:2

Talk that Gives Grace

Paul details the behavioral changes that Christians make when they begin to follow Jesus. There is a pattern to the verses: we put away a sinful or damaging practice and replace it with something spiritual or beneficial. "*Therefore, having put away falsehood, let each one of you speak the truth with his neighbor, for we are members of one another*"(Eph 4:25). It is not enough to stop lying; we must also be committed to telling one another the truth to bless and strengthen them. "*Let no corrupting talk come out of your mouths, but only such as is good for building up, as fits the occasion, that it may give grace to those who hear*"(Eph 4:29). Paul also urges us to stop using "*corrupting talk*"—language, topics, and content that discourages, pollutes, or harms—and replace it with talk that gives grace. Our verbal filter should be set to whether our words are "*good for building up.*"

Woven throughout this list are reminders of God's grace toward us. Instead of living in bitterness and malice, "*be kind to one another, tenderhearted, forgiving one another, as God in Christ forgave you*"(Eph 4:31-32). This forgiveness is a way we "*walk in love, as Christ loved us and gave himself up for us, a fragrant offering and sacrifice to God*"(Eph 5:2). God doesn't expect us to merely receive his gifts, but to duplicate them by loving and actively doing good for others—even those who have wronged us.

Our talk can "*give grace to those who hear.*" We can give gifts with our words. We can compliment others, encourage them to do good things, and share positivity. People can leave their interactions with us better than before. It will require conscious attention and selflessness, but we can transform our speech into a blessing.

One Thing to Think About: How does my talk affect others? Am I building others up?

One Thing to Pray For: Opportunities to spread positivity

WEEK 45—MONDAY

Reading: Ephesians 6:10-20

Armor for the Battle

Paul writes from prison (where it is possible that he is guarded by Roman soldiers) and likens the Christian life to a war. "*Put on the whole armor of God, that you may be able to stand against the schemes of the devil. For we do not wrestle against flesh and blood, but against the rulers, against the authorities, against the cosmic powers over this present darkness, against the spiritual forces of evil in the heavenly places*"(Eph 6:12-13). Our battle is not with other people—though people are often instrumental in it—but with the devil and the spiritual forces of evil. Since we are not naturally equipped to fight such intense spiritual battles with unseen powers, God has given us armor for the battle.

Our job is to use God's equipment. "*Therefore take up the whole armor of God, that you may be able to withstand in the evil day, and having done all, to stand firm*"(Eph 6:13). Paul then enumerates the tools God has given us: truth, righteousness, the gospel, faith, salvation, the word of God, prayer. Each of these is a battleground on which we will engage with Satan, yet God has prepared us. We need God's truth to combat Satan's lies, God's grace to make us (and keep us) righteous, God's gospel to prepare us for Satan's attacks, confidence in God to sustain us, God's salvation to preserve us (especially when we fail), and God's word to enable us to attack the evil we see within and around us.

Paul's language could not be more serious. We are engaged in a battle that is both personal and cosmic. We cannot win alone. Yet each of God's gifts arms us for a different aspect of our struggle with sin and Satan. He has graciously prepared us so that we can succeed.

One Thing to Think About: How will Satan attack me today?

One Thing to Pray For: God's strength to help me in the battle

WEEK 45—TUESDAY

Reading: Philippians 2:1-11

Jesus Emptied Himself

Paul wants the Philippians to grow in humility by putting a higher value on others. "*Do nothing from selfish ambition or conceit, but in humility count others more significant than yourselves. Let each of you look not only to his own interests, but also to the interests of others*"(Phil 2:3-4). We all naturally look to our own interests; this is a call for something higher. By actively considering others and their concerns, ideas, and needs, we give them a gift. We lower ourselves before them and act for their good.

Our model in this is Jesus. "*Have this mind among yourselves, which is yours in Christ Jesus, who, though he was in the form of God, did not count equality with God a thing to be grasped, but emptied himself, by taking the form of a servant, being born in the likeness of men. And being found in human form, he humbled himself by becoming obedient to the point of death, even death on a cross*"(Phil 2:5-8). Prior to Jesus' birth, he had a status in heaven ("*equality with God*") that he willingly forfeited to become a human. He "*emptied himself*"—setting aside his own will, status, and glory—to become a man. He humbled himself again and again, absorbing shame upon shame. Why? He did all of this in obedience to the Father *to bless us*. Giving this kind of gracious attention to others and their interests will require emptying ourselves.

We often press toward status, power, and respect. We seek these things in our work, in our relationships, and in the church. Jesus challenges us. He shows us that the truly worthwhile things in life come from sacrifice, giving, and forgetting self. Others are unworthy of our attention and focus, but that is what makes emptying ourselves for them an act of grace.

One Thing to Think About: In what ways am I tempted by "selfish ambition or conceit"?

One Thing to Pray For: The courage to empty myself to serve and bless others

WEEK 45—WEDNESDAY

Reading: Philippians 4:4-9

A Peace that Relieves Anxiety

Paul speaks to the inner life of the Philippians because our thoughts inevitably affect our behavior. "*Rejoice in the Lord always; again I will say, rejoice*"(Phil 4:4). Every situation holds many opportunities to complain and many to rejoice; every day we have the choice of which to accentuate. "*Do not be anxious about anything, but in everything by prayer and supplication with thanksgiving let your requests be made known to God. And the peace of God, which surpasses all understanding, will guard your hearts and minds in Christ Jesus*"(Phil 4:6-7). He acknowledges the human tendency toward anxiety and points us toward a God who is willing to hear and answer our requests. Taking our concerns to God in prayer helps us to let go of our worry and trust that he hears and sees our needs. This brings a peace "*which surpasses all understanding*"—one that we cannot fully describe or explain—that protects our hearts from the emotional roller-coaster each day brings.

In addition to airing our concerns and requests before God, we can also limit anxiety by controlling our thinking. "*Finally, brothers, whatever is true, whatever is honorable, whatever is just, whatever is pure, whatever is lovely, whatever is commendable, if there is any excellence, if there is anything worthy of praise, think about these things*"(Phil 4:8). Some things are simply unworthy of our attention and meditation. Fixating on all the imperfect, shameful, and disappointing things will have an impact on our spirits, words, and eventually, actions. What is good, positive, helpful, kind, or unexpectedly pleasant?

All people enjoy and seek inner peace. God promises to give us a peace beyond comprehension, but his gift is conditional. We must channel our anxiety into active requests that we give him, then trust that he will take care of them. This is a great gift waiting to be seized.

One Thing to Think About: What people, situations, or concerns are producing anxiety in me today? What can I ask God for?

One Thing to Pray For: The peace that passes understanding

Reading: Philippians 4:10-13

The Grace of Contentment

Paul has had his time in Roman custody brightened by the arrival of a gift from the Philippian church. *"I rejoiced in the Lord greatly that now at length you have revived your concern for me. You were indeed concerned for me, but you had no opportunity"*(Phil 4:10). Many years previously, the Philippians had regularly supported Paul (Phil 4:15-16), but that seems to have dried up for some time. Now Paul has received an unexpected gift from them. He is joyful and grateful.

But he wants to be clear that he was not simply hanging by a thread before the gift: *"Not that I am speaking of being in need, for I have learned in whatever situation I am to be content. I know how to be brought low, and I know how to abound. In any and every circumstance, I have learned the secret of facing plenty and hunger, abundance and need"*(Phil 4:11-12). This is not a natural gift for Paul; he has *learned* to be content. There are challenges in having much and in having little, especially in how it affects our attitude. Yet enduring times of poverty and abundance has taught Paul contentment in all situations. How? *"I can do all things through him who strengthens me"*(Phil 4:13). The strength of Jesus gives him confidence to face hardship.

Humans have a remarkable capacity to adapt to any circumstance, but we also can grow unhappy with even the best of situations. We struggle to be content. Paul sees contentment as an ongoing learning process by which he learns to trust the strength of Christ. Rather than merely seeing wealth as God's gift, he also sees *the ability to be content with or without wealth* as grace.

One Thing to Think About: Am I content with my circumstances at this moment?

One Thing to Pray For: The strength of Christ to sustain me in my current circumstance

WEEK 45—FRIDAY

Reading: 1 Timothy 1:12-17

Grace as an Example

In this more personal letter to Timothy, Paul lets down his guard and talks about his past. "*I thank him who has given me strength, Christ Jesus our Lord, because he judged me faithful, appointing me to his service, though formerly I was a blasphemer, persecutor, and insolent opponent*"(1 Tim 1:12-13). Paul has not forgotten who he was or what he did. He has sinned grievously against God and man, yet Jesus still "*judged me faithful*" and "*has given me strength.*" Instead of judgment, "*I received mercy because I had acted ignorantly in unbelief, and the grace of our Lord overflowed for me with the faith and love that are in Christ Jesus*"(1 Tim 1:13-14). Grace *overflows* for Paul—enough grace to cover and forgive and remove his sins forever. Now he is free and ready to serve the one he has blasphemed.

But as tempting as it is to think of Paul as exceptional, he insists that *this is what grace looks like for everyone.* "*The saying is trustworthy and deserving of full acceptance, that Christ Jesus came into the world to save sinners, of whom I am the foremost. But I received mercy for this reason, that in me, as the foremost, Jesus Christ might display his perfect patience as an example to those who were to believe in him for eternal life*"(1 Tim 1:15-16). Jesus came to save people just like Paul—and you and me. Yet since Paul sees himself as the "*foremost*" sinner, he also sees Jesus as showing patience to him "*as an example.*" This is what Jesus does for all people. Forgiving grievous, heinous, violent offenses—wiping the slate clean—employing the former enemies as servants—is what he does for us too.

There is a clue here as to how God intends us to view the entire New Testament. This is not simply a historical record of the beginning of the Jesus movement. These are people whose life-changes and obedient faith are examples for exactly what Jesus wants to do to and through us. Each time we see grace for unbelievers in Scripture—and each time we see undeserving people receiving forgiveness today—it is an example for us.

One Thing to Think About: What has Jesus forgiven me?

One Thing to Pray For: The humility to remember that I am a sinner who has been saved

WEEK 46—MONDAY

Reading: 1 Timothy 2:1-6

A Ransom for All

In this letter, Paul gives Timothy instruction and wisdom about how to effectively work with a group of Christians. "*First of all, then, I urge that supplications, prayers, intercessions, and thanksgivings be made for all people*"(1 Tim 2:1). Timothy should never restrict prayer to a certain group of people. The implication is that we are praying for the lost and those who are not like us. He even specifies "*kings and all who are in high positions*" in the government (1 Tim 2:2), asking that they will leave us alone to live in the way God desires.

The reason for this focus on "all people" is that this is God's focus. "*This is good, and it is pleasing in the sight of God our Savior, who desires all people to be saved and to come to the knowledge of the truth*"(1 Tim 2:3-4). God has his eye on all the people of the world and is constantly working in the world to draw them toward him. Prayers for them will be answered because we are on God's wavelength. "*For there is one God, and there is one mediator between God and men, the man Christ Jesus, who gave himself a ransom for all, which is the testimony given at the proper time*"(1 Tim 2:5-6). Jesus's sacrifice is a ransom (payment of debt) for *all people*. We pray for all people because saving all people is God's desire and the whole point of Jesus's mission.

The gift Jesus gives in this text is *himself*—he "*gave himself a ransom for all.*" No person is outside the scope of his love and salvation. He does not merely offer himself for who are good and deserving, for the basically moral, or for those of a certain class. He gives himself for *all.* As we enjoy the freedom his ransom gives, we are also enlisted in the cause. If God desires all people to be saved, I pray for that, work toward it, and grow to want it too.

One Thing to Think About: Do I desire that *all people* be saved?

One Thing to Pray For: Our leaders, that we may lead a peaceful and quiet life

WEEK 46—TUESDAY

Reading: 2 Timothy 1:3-12

I Know Whom I Have Believed

Paul writes from prison and he senses that the end is near. He also seems concerned that, as persecution and trouble increase, Timothy might lose his nerve. "*Therefore do not be ashamed of the testimony about our Lord, nor of me his prisoner, but share in suffering for the gospel by the power of God*"(2 Tim 1:8). He reminds Timothy of his long history in knowing about God, which began at the knee of his mother and grandmother (2 Tim 1:5). "*For this reason I remind you to fan into flame the gift of God, which is in you through the laying on of my hands, for God gave us a spirit not of fear but of power and love and self-control*"(2 Tim 1:6-7). Renewed fervor is needed, which Paul likens to fanning a dying flame back to life. God has given his people a spirit, but it is not a spirit of fearfulness and timidity. It is a spirit of strength, care, and discipline.

This courage also stems from a deep confidence in the character of God. He has "*saved us and called us to a holy calling, not because of our works but because of his own purpose and grace, which he gave us in Christ Jesus before the ages began*"(2 Tim 1:9). God has saved and called us of his own giving nature; we do not deserve it in any way. Yet before we existed, God gave us the gift of his Son. So Paul is bold: "*But I am not ashamed, for I know whom I have believed, and I am convinced that he is able to guard until that Day what has been entrusted to me*"(2 Tim 1:12). I know my God—his nature, his character, his faithfulness—and so I know that he can guard me, even if I die. The wording is odd because it can mean that he is able to guard what he entrusted to Paul (the ministry of the gospel) or what Paul entrusted to him (his faith and his life). Whichever rendering we choose, the point is clear: God can be depended on.

God is consistently gracious and faithful. He continues to be today. So when we take risks for him in faith—when we face opposition or reach the limits of our ability—we can live confidently. He has given us salvation and given us a spirit of power, love, and self-control. How can we be ashamed of him?

One Thing to Think About: How has God proven his reliability to me?

One Thing to Pray For: A spirit of power, love, and self-control—instead of fear

Reading: 2 Timothy 3:10-17

The Grace of Scripture

Paul is in dire straits and warns Timothy that such things will continue. Yet Timothy already knows this because he is well aware of the tortuous history of Paul's life and ministry. Timothy himself hails from Lystra, where Paul was stoned and left for dead. The lesson Paul wants him to learn is that "*all who desire to live a goldy life in Christ Jesus will be persecuted, while evil people and impostors will go on from bad to worse, deceiving and being deceived*"(2 Tim 3:12-13). Often circumstances occur in precisely the opposite way from what we would like or expect because of our connection to God.

So how should Timothy prepare himself for this distressing fact? "*But as for you, continue in what you have learned and have firmly believed, knowing from whom you learned it and how from childhood you have been acquainted with the sacred writings, which are able to make you wise for salvation through faith in Christ Jesus*"(2 Tim 3:14-15). He can focus on the very familiar words of the "*sacred writings,*" meaning the Hebrew Scriptures (what we call the Old Testament). He has learned these things "*from childhood,*" surrounded by a faithful mother and grandmother (2 Tim 1:5) who show the nature of true faith. "*All Scripture is breathed out by God and profitable for teaching, for reproof, for correction, and for training in righteousness, that the man of God may be complete, equipped for every good work*"(2 Tim 3:16-17). Scripture is the product of God's "breath" or "inspiration." Because it comes from God, it is eminently useful. It is "*profitable*" for many things, especially for teaching and guiding us so that we are "*equipped for every good work.*" Scripture is a thoroughly, eternally useful teacher.

Scripture is a gift from God—words that he has "*breathed out.*" Because they are God's words, they have an enduring value in every age. They do not need to be updated or improved on. We do not correct these words; they correct us. They are an anchor in turbulent times—as much today as in Timothy's time. Our duty is to use such useful words and to profit from these profitable things.

One Thing to Think About: Do I ever fail to appreciate the gift of Scripture?

One Thing to Pray For: Insight to know the best ways to apply Scripture so that I may be equipped for every good work

WEEK 46—THURSDAY

Reading: 2 Timothy 4:1-8

The Crown of Righteousness

2 Timothy contains some of Paul's last words. He is ready to pass the torch on to Timothy: "*Preach the word; be ready in season and out of season; reprove, rebuke, and exhort, with complete patience and teaching*"(2 Tim 4:2). Timothy will need a consistent dedication to helping people understand God's truth, whether it is in vogue or not. In fact, Paul foresees that things will soon get even more difficult. "*For the time is coming when people will not endure sound teaching, but having itching ears they will accumulate for themselves teachers to suit their own passions, and will turn away from listening to the truth and wander off into myths*"(2 Tim 4:3-4). Having been emotionally prepared for the difficulty, Timothy needs to keep preaching.

The reason for Paul's tone is that he knows the end is near for him. "*For I am already being poured out as a drink offering, and the time of my departure has come. I have fought the good fight, I have finished the race, I have kept the faith. Henceforth there is laid up for me the crown of righteousness, which the Lord, the righteous judge, will award to me on that day, and not only to me but also to all who have loved his appearing*"(2 Tim 4:6-8). As death approaches, he surveys his work. He lays down his arms confident that he has "*fought the good fight*" and walks off the track knowing that he has "*finished the race.*" Now what awaits him is "*the crown of righteousness,*" like the athlete's victory crown. He does not approach death with fear, but confidence that all his work and suffering has been worth it. This crown, he insists, is given "*not only to me but also to all who have loved his appearing.*" It is a gift God gives to all who put their faith in him.

Paul is not saying that he has *earned* this crown. It is a symbol of the righteousness that is Christ's, not ours (Phil 3:9). His point is that at death, he will transition from one of the overlooked and disdained on earth to a victor. Yet this is not just a gift for Paul, but "*all who have loved his appearing.*" There is a crown awaiting us.

One Thing to Think About: Do I think of death like Paul? Why or why not?

One Thing to Pray For: The courage to remain faithful to Jesus in difficult times

WEEK 46—FRIDAY

Reading: Titus 2:11-14

What Grace Teaches Us

As Paul tells Titus what needs to be taught among the Christians on Crete, he stresses that the goal is that "*in everything they may adorn the doctrine of God our Savior*"(Titus 2:10). This teaching motivates and educates. "*For the grace of God has appeared, bringing salvation for all people, training us to renounce ungodliness and worldly passions, and to live self-controlled, upright, and godly lives in the present age*"(Titus 2:11-12). God's goodness has been revealed, but it doesn't just give us salvation. It also "*(trains) us to renounce ungodliness and worldly passions.*" The word "*training*" here is a term for the full scope of children's education. God's grace teaches us to say no to the desires within us that corrupt us and take us away from him. It teaches us the great value of a self-controlled, disciplined life.

His grace also points us forward: "*waiting for our blessed hope, the appearing of the glory of our great God and Savior Jesus Christ*"(Titus 2:13). The one who has given us such rich gifts—the one who has taught us the best way to live "*in the present age*"—is coming back! And so his goodness teaches us to wait. How do we spend the meantime? We live for Jesus "*who gave himself for us to redeem us from all lawlessness and to purify for himself a people for his own possession who are zealous for good works*"(Titus 2:14). Grace teaches us to be "*zealous for good works,*" busying ourselves in things that will bless others. This makes us even more like our good God.

God's grace is not intended to be a "get out of jail free" card. He intends the coming of Jesus to teach us a new way of disciplining ourselves, looking upward and forward, and doing good to those around us.

One Thing to Think About: How has God's goodness changed my life?

One Thing to Pray For: God's help in living a self-controlled, upright, and godly life

WEEK 47—MONDAY

Reading: Titus 3:1-3

What We Once Were

The letter to Titus is full of practical instructions and important reminders for growing Christians. "*Remind them to be submissive to rulers and authorities, to be obedient, to be ready for every good work, to speak evil of no one, to avoid quarreling, to be gentle, and to show perfect courtesy toward all people*"(Titus 3:1-2). "*Remind them*" stresses that we tend to forget basic things and need to be refreshed in them. We need to be reminded "*to be submissive to rulers and authorities*" because we may let our emotions or opinions get the best of us and forget our submissive, obedient posture. We need reminding "*to be ready for every good work*" because most needs are unscheduled. When there are "*cases of urgent need*"(Titus 3:14), we should be mentally (and perhaps financially) prepared to do good.

But we also have a certain posture toward others—not speaking evil, not quarreling, and showing "*perfect courtesy toward all people.*" Why? "*For we ourselves were once foolish, disobedient, led astray, slaves to various passions and pleasures, passing our days in malice and envy, hated by others and hating one another*"(Titus 3:3). We treat people kindly because *we used to be like them.* We have been foolish and enslaved. We know how to hate; we have done it. There is a natural compassion as we look at others through the lenses of what we once were. Instead of taking their hatred, malice, and envy personally, we remember how in our confusion we lashed out at others. We remember the misdirected anger we held, the confusing despair we felt, and the shame we carried.

Paul's language—"*for we ourselves were once*"—emphasizes that this is *our* past. God has changed us from this and redeemed our lives. Yet if this is our past, keeping in touch with what we once were will help us relate to and show grace to those who are still there.

One Thing to Think About: What do I remember about my past? How can those memories be beneficial?

One Thing to Pray For: A heart to "*show perfect courtesy toward all people*"

WEEK 47—TUESDAY

Reading: Titus 3:4-7

According to His Own Mercy

Paul wants Titus to remind the Christians on Crete to show kindness to all people because they used to be just like them. What changed? "*But when the goodness and loving kindness of God our Savior appeared, he saved us, not because of works done by us in righteousness, but according to his own mercy*"(Titus 3:4-5). Jesus came as a manifestation of God's goodness and loving kindness, like a light in the darkness. "*He saved us*" reminds us that salvation is a rescue mission, not a joint project. This stresses how undeserving we are of such blessings because no amount of "*works done by us in righteousness*" could ever earn such a gift. Instead it is "*according to his own mercy,*" something God has chosen to do for us of his own free will. He saved us because he wanted to.

Our change in state happened "*by the washing of regeneration and renewal of the Holy Spirit, whom he poured out on us richly through Jesus Christ our Savior, so that being justified by his grace we might become heirs according to the hope of eternal life*"(Titus 3:5-7). "*Regeneration,*" the creation of new life, is given through a "*washing,*" which implies baptism. Yet even in baptism, the rebirth and renewal comes through the Holy Spirit, not our own action. That same Spirit, who is given to us in rich measure, ensures that we will inherit eternal life (a staple in Paul's teaching, Eph 1:13-14, Rom 8:16-17, Gal 4:6-7). God has chosen to create new life in us, renew us through his Spirit, and give us eternal life. He did it because he wanted to.

It matters what we decide about how we were saved. If God saved me because I was righteous—or mostly righteous—then I am partly responsible. That's why Paul stresses that it is "*not because of works done by us in righteousness.*" The truth is more humbling and more liberating. I, in my desperate sinfulness, was lost without hope. And God saved me because he wanted to.

One Thing to Think About: How am I different than when I began to follow Jesus? Who is responsible for that?

One Thing to Pray For: Thankfulness for God's remarkable mercy

Reading: Hebrews 2:1-4

The Danger of Neglect

The Hebrew writer has been emphasizing that Jesus the Son is far greater than angels. What difference does that make? "*Therefore we must pay much closer attention to what we have heard, lest we drift away from it. For since the message declared by angels proved to be reliable, and every transgression or disobedience received a just retribution, how shall we escape if we neglect such a great salvation?*"(Heb 2:1-3). If the Law of Moses, given by and through angels, was true and severe, how much more the message of Jesus? God has graciously given us further revelation through a far more exalted messenger. That grace prompts an eager, determined spirit: "*we must pay much closer attention to what we have heard.*" How tragic to not give the Son of God the focus he deserves! What recourse or excuse will we have? "*How shall we escape if we neglect such a great salvation?*"

He expands on the greatness of the gift of this revelation: "*It was declared at first by the Lord, and it was attested to us by those who heard, while God also bore witness by signs and wonders and various miracles and by gifts of the Holy Spirit distributed according to his will*"(Heb 2:3-4). The message is first taught by the Son himself, then confirmed by the apostolic witnesses. But God did not stop there, continuing to confirm its truth by giving all manner of miracles, healings, and spiritual gifts. God keeps giving and giving to ensure that we give this message its due importance.

Several of the terms here speak to the subtle danger of neglect. We "*must pay closer attention,*" resisting the idea that because we know the message we can focus elsewhere. He is concerned that we might "*drift away from it,*" stressing the possibility that by imperceptible movements we slowly move away from Jesus. We can "*neglect such a great salvation*"—not giving it the place in our hearts it deserves. God has given us so much; are we neglecting his gifts?

One Thing to Think About: Do I need to pay closer attention to Jesus?

One Thing to Pray For: Help to stay close to Jesus—and not drift away

WEEK 47—THURSDAY

Reading: Hebrews 2:14-18

A Merciful and Faithful High Priest

When Jesus died as a man, he defeated death (and Satan) from the inside out. "*Since therefore the children share in flesh and blood, he himself likewise partook of the same things, that through death he might destroy the one who has the power of death, that is, the devil, and deliver those who through fear of death were subject to lifelong slavery*"(Heb 2:14-15). Jesus shared in our humanity, including the problem of death that has plagued man since the Garden. Yet by his resurrection he has defeated death and given us the victory. This means hope for our own mortality, but it also liberates "*those who through fear of death were subject to lifelong slavery.*" We don't have to live in fear of the approach of the end of our days. We are free.

But this is just one aspect of how Jesus helps us. "*Therefore he had to be made like his brothers in every respect, so that he might become a merciful and faithful high priest in the service of God, to make propitiation for the sins of the people. For because he himself has suffered when tempted, he is able to help those who are being tempted*"(Heb 2:17-18). Not only has Jesus shared in our "*flesh and blood,*" but he became like us "*in every respect,*" including the temptations and troubles of everyday life. This is good news for us. Now he is "*a merciful and faithful high priest*" for us. He understands our difficulties and weaknesses; he is sympathetic to our situation. He has been tempted and so he is uniquely "*able to help those who are being tempted.*"

We seek desperately for others to understand us. We want them to see our point of view, appreciate our challenges, and accept our sincere efforts. Because Jesus has lived as a man now serves as our high priest before God, we can be confident that he understands. He is merciful and faithful. He helps us.

One Thing to Think About: Do I turn to Jesus for help when I am tempted? Why or why not?

One Thing to Pray For: Freedom from the slavery of the fear of death

WEEK 47—FRIDAY

Reading: Hebrews 4:11-16

Grace to Help in Time of Need

The Hebrew writer has been using Old Testament references to show that God still holds out a rest for his people. "*Let us therefore strive to enter that rest, so that no one may fall by the same sort of disobedience*"(Heb 4:11). The ancient Israelites were not allowed to enter Canaan because of their unbelief—and we face the same danger. "*For the word of God is living and active, sharper than any two-edged sword, piercing to the division of soul and of spirit, of joints and of marrow, and discerning the thoughts and intentions of the heart*"(Heb 4:12). God's words—even the ancient descriptions of God's dealings with his people—are not dead words on a page, but still powerful and applicable, convicting us today. If God's words are true—and they are—then he is still watching over and evaluating his people (Heb 4:13).

Yet Christians have an advantage over ancient Jews. We "*have a great high priest who has passed through the heavens*"(Heb 4:14) who can aid us in our frail state. "*For we do not have a high priest who is unable to sympathize with our weaknesses, but one who in every respect has been tempted as we are, yet without sin. Let us then with confidence draw near to the throne of grace, that we may receive mercy and find grace to help in time of need*"(Heb 4:15-16). Jesus has been tempted "*in every respect*" like we have, so he knows our situation intimately. This gives us a new confidence as we approach God to "*receive mercy*" for our sins and to "*find grace to help in time of need.*"

That last phrase—"*find grace to help in time of need*"—is pregnant with possibilities. God has special grace—new gifts to give—when we are in places of need. With regularity he sustained Israel through the desert—giving water, food, meat, guidance, law, and leadership. When they cried out, he heard them. We now approach through a superior representative—our merciful and faithful high priest. When we wrestle with physical illness, relationship breakdowns, wounds to forgive, financial setbacks, and personal insecurity, our God wants to hear from us and give us grace to help in time of need.

One Thing to Think About: How does God's word discern my thoughts and intentions?

One Thing to Pray For: God's help in my needs

WEEK 48—MONDAY

Reading: Hebrews 6:9-12

God Does Not Overlook Your Work

This passage follows a strong rebuke. The writer has criticized these Christians for failing to grow as they should ("*for though by this time you ought to be teachers,*" Heb 5:12) and warned them of the danger of reaching a state in which one cannot be renewed to repentance (Heb 6:4-8). Now he dials it back: "*Though we speak in this way, yet in your case, beloved, we feel sure of better things—things that belong to salvation. For God is not unjust so as to overlook your work and the love that you have shown for his name in serving the saints, as you still do*"(Heb 6:9-10). The Hebrew Christians are at a crossroads, and the writer is convinced that they will choose to refocus on Jesus. But he also assures them that God has not forgotten the work and love they have *already* done. They are still serving the saints and God sees that—even though there are other areas in which they desperately need to grow. God simultaneously approves and disapproves of different parts of their behavior.

But the writer wants them to rekindle that spirit they once had. "*And we desire each one of you to show the same earnestness to have the full assurance of hope until the end, so that you may not be sluggish, but imitators of those who through faith and patience inherit the promises*"(Heb 6:11-12). They know how to serve with great "*earnestness*" but are also in danger of growing "*sluggish.*" He encourages them to look toward the great heroes of faith who pleased God "*through faith and patience.*" Our service to God is a marathon, not a sprint. Sometimes we must renew our strength even as we continue to run.

Our lives, words, and actions appear to make little difference in our world. We are merely one of 7 billion. We speak thousands of words a day, yet they are rarely remembered (even by us). A small kindness done, an encouraging word spoken, a commitment to faithfulness—are scarcely noticed. Yet "*God is not unjust so as to overlook your work.*" He sees—he knows—he is pleased. God's constant eye on us and his long memory are extensions of his grace.

One Thing to Think About: Are there good things going on around me that I overlook? How might this affect how I feel about my own service?

One Thing to Pray For: A renewal of the earnestness of my spirit

WEEK 48—TUESDAY

Reading: Hebrews 6:13-20

An Anchor for the Soul

Can we trust promises God makes—even when we don't see immediate physical confirmation? The Hebrew writer takes us back to God's word to Abraham, stressing that God "*swore by himself, saying, 'Surely I will bless you and multiply you*'"(Heb 5:13-14, see Gen 22:16-18). The reason God has to swear by himself is that people often swear by something greater to confirm their word (Heb 6:16). But what is greater than God for him to swear by? Abraham, meanwhile, shows himself to be among "*those who through faith and patience inherit the promises*"(Heb 6:12) and perseveres. The writer concludes that he "*obtained the promise*"(Heb 6:15). God promised, sealed it with an oath, and then delivered by blessing Abraham with a (at least partial) fulfillment.

Yet we still hold out hope of being a part of this promise: "*in your offspring shall all the nations of the earth be blessed*"(Gen 22:18). So this double oath means something to us too. "*So when God desired to show more convincingly to the heirs of the promise the unchangeable character of his purpose, he guaranteed it with an oath, so that by two unchangeable things, in which it is impossible for God to lie, we who have fled for refuge might have strong encouragement to hold fast to the hope set before us*"(Heb 6:17-18). God—who cannot lie—has both promised and sealed it with an oath. This is all to *convince us to trust him*—to "*show more convincingly to the heirs of the promise the unchangeable character of his purpose*." God wants us to know that he *still intends to bless us*—he *swore* it. The hope of God's ultimate fulfillment of this is "*a sure and steadfast anchor of the soul, a hope that enters into the inner place behind the curtain*"(Heb 6:19).

An anchor is only as good as the ground or rock to which it is attached. Yet an anchor, when well-grounded, keeps a boat in its place in the most tumultuous conditions. God wants us to be this firmly attached to him—absolutely determined to hope in his goodness, no matter what circumstances confront us. He has given us an anchor.

One Thing to Think About: How firm is my hope that God will fulfill his promise?

One Thing to Pray For: A stronger hope in God's goodness for me

WEEK 48—WEDNESDAY

Reading: Hebrews 9:11-14

How Much More?

The Hebrew writer wants to convince his audience of the superiority of Jesus to the Levitical sacrificial system. Jesus is "*high priest of the good things that have come*" who has entered the "*greater and more perfect tent*" and gone all the way into "*the holy places*"(Heb 9:11-12). Just as the Aaronic priests would carry the atoning blood into the tabernacle (and later the temple), so Jesus has done. But there are significant differences: Jesus is a high priest of better things, ministering in the greater tabernacle (heaven itself), and has gone into the actual holy places. He also proceeds "*not by means of the blood of goats and calves but by means of his own blood, thus securing an eternal redemption*"(Heb 9:12). He carries his own blood into the presence of God, becoming both the priest and the sacrifice.

So to those who are familiar with the Levitical system, it raises an awestruck rhetorical question: "*For if the blood of goats and bulls, and the sprinkling of defiled persons with the ashes of a heifer, sanctify for the purification of the flesh, how much more will the blood of Christ, who through the eternal Spirit offered himself without blemish to God, purify our conscience from dead works to serve the living God*"(Heb 9:13-14). Knowing the power of the Law's regulations to purify defiled flesh, "*how much more*" will better blood in a better tabernacle cleanse the conscience? Jesus' sacrifice holds out hope for us to be truly, deeply, inwardly purified—and then newly empowered to serve God.

The priestly system allowed an imperfect people the opportunity to remove sin and impurity to come before God. God gave this great gift to achieve his burning desire for fellowship with his people. Yet now he has done far more—sending Jesus to offer a superior sacrifice to cleanse not only our bodies, but our hearts and consciences. We can be truly forgiven.

One Thing to Think About: Why is God so concerned with our cleanness?

One Thing to Pray For: A pure conscience

WEEK 48—THURSDAY

Reading: Hebrews 9:23-28

The Sacrifice of Himself

As the Hebrew writer contemplates the magnitude of Jesus' sacrifice, he reasons from the Law of Moses forward to Jesus. Under the Law, blood purifies and brings forgiveness (Heb 9:22). "*Thus it was necessary for the copies of the heavenly things to be purified with these rites, but the heavenly things themselves with better sacrifices than these. For Christ has entered, not into holy places made with hands, which are copies of the true things, but into heaven itself, now to appear in the presence of God on our behalf*"(Heb 9:23-24). While the tabernacle—which is only a copy of the throne room of heaven—could be purified with animal blood, heaven itself needed better blood. Jesus has gone into the very presence of God, atoning for us with his own blood, paving the way for us to come to God through him.

His sacrifice is so great that it does not ever need to be repeated (unlike the Levitical offerings). "*But as it is, he has appeared once for all at the end of the ages to put away sin by the sacrifice of himself*"(Heb 9:26). "Once for all" stresses that *this sacrifice fully accomplished its purpose*. He has put away sin by sacrificing himself. Now the only unfinished part of his work is his return. "*So Christ, having been offered once to bear the sins of many, will appear a second time, not to deal with sin but to save those who are eagerly waiting for him*"(Heb 9:28). When Jesus returns, it is not sin that he will deal with, but death and final justice.

It is hard to miss the grace in this passage. Jesus has gone into places we could never go, offered things we could never offer, and put away sins we could never atone for. He has accomplished all of this "*by the sacrifice of himself*." It is one thing to give gifts to others; it is something entirely different to *give ourselves*. He has given his life to us.

One Thing to Think About: What is challenging to me about sacrificing for others?

One Thing to Pray For: A consistent attitude of "*eagerly waiting for him*"

Reading: Hebrews 10:1-14

No Reminder of Sins

The very repetition of animal sacrifices under the Levitical priesthood shows their ineffectiveness to truly cleanse sin. The Hebrew writer insists that the law "*can never, by the same sacrifices that are continually offered year after year, make perfect those who draw near. Otherwise, would they not have ceased to be offered, since the worshipers, having once been cleansed, would no longer have any consciousness of sins?*"(Heb 10:1-2). If these rituals truly removed sin, then they would remove it once and for all. Yet the yearly practice only serves as a "*reminder of sins every year*"(Heb 10:3). The "*consciousness of sins*" persists no matter how many sacrifices are offered. This proves the dirty little secret of the Mosaic system: "*For it is impossible for the blood of bulls and goats to take away sins*"(Heb 10:4). Something better is needed.

This is why Jesus has not come to offer more sacrifices (Heb 10:5), but to offer his body in obedience to the point of death (Heb 10:5-10). This is a different kind of sacrifice. "*And every priest stands daily at his service, offering repeatedly the same sacrifices, which can never take away sins. But when Christ had offered for all time a single sacrifice for sins, he sat down at the right hand of God*"(Heb 10:11-12). Priests stand because their work is unfinished; Christ has sat down. Priests offer the same sacrifices over and over because their work is ineffective; Christ has offered a single sacrifice for all time.

The major problem in the background of this text is "*consciousness of sins*"(Heb 10:2). We are aware that we are sinful creatures and our consciences are violated by what we have done. Killing animals does not change this. What we have done is so grievous that a perfect, effective offering must be made. Jesus' sacrifice cleanses the *conscience*, assuring us of God's complete forgiveness. Knowing that God is willing to offer his own Son as a superior offering for us assures us of his goodwill. Now we do not have yearly reminders of sin, but daily reminders of forgiveness and hope.

One Thing to Think About: How have I experienced "*consciousness of sins*"? Do I still? How might this passage help me?

One Thing to Pray For: "Behold, I have come to do your will, O God"

WEEK 49—MONDAY

Reading: Hebrews 10:19-22

Grace Brings Confidence

Because of Jesus' sacrifice, Christians have an incredible new access to God. "*Therefore, brothers, since we have confidence to enter the holy places by the blood of Jesus, by the new and living way that he opened for us through the curtain, that is, through his flesh*"(Heb 10:19-20). This confidence springs from the fact that we *belong* where we are (in the presence of God) because Jesus has opened the way for us by offering his blood and flesh. The curtain that divided the rest of the tabernacle from the inner sanctum—that divided God from the people—has been torn down. When we approach God in prayer, worship, or for healing and forgiveness, we do so with confidence.

Knowing what great things God has done for us, the Hebrew writer exhorts us to take advantage of them. "*Since we have a great high priest over the house of God, let us draw near with a true heart in full assurance of faith, with our hearts sprinkled clean from an evil conscience and our bodies washed with pure water*"(Heb 10:21-22). Jesus, the superior, ever-living, Melchizedek-style priest is our mediator. So through him we "*draw near with a true heart in full assurance of faith*," knowing with certainty that God accepts us (because he accepts Jesus!). Just as the Israelites were sprinkled with blood to cleanse them—and the priests were washed before entering God's presence—so we have been cleansed and washed, inside and out. God has made all things ready. We belong here.

Grace brings confidence. It is not the confidence in our own capabilities. We do not look back in pride on "how far we've come" when we come to Jesus. Instead, we laud *his* goodness and kindness—that *he* has granted us access, *he* has torn down the curtain, *he* will wash us clean. Yet if God has gone to all this trouble to reconcile us to himself, we know with certainty that he wants us to come to him. So we approach with confidence, assurance, and clean consciences. We belong here.

One Thing to Think About: Why is it hard to balance confidence and humility? To which extreme do I tend to go?

One Thing to Pray For: A true heart with the full assurance of faith

WEEK 49—TUESDAY

Reading: Hebrews 11:1-7

He Rewards Those Who Seek Him

As the Hebrew writer encourages his audience, he wants them to identify as people of faith. "*But we are not of those who shrink back and are destroyed, but of those who have faith and preserve their souls*"(Heb 10:39). So what does it mean to have faith? "*Now faith is the assurance of things hoped for, the conviction of things not seen*"(Heb 11:1). Faith involves confidence about things that are uncertain. It has both an intellectual and emotional dimension—and frequently plays out in the life-choices we make.

So faith is like Abel offering a God he has never seen a sacrifice worthy of him—and gaining God's praise. Faith is like Enoch walking with God, then being taken up. Faith is like Noah, who has never seen rain, building a giant boat to survive a rainstorm. "*And without faith it is impossible to please him, for whoever would draw near to God must believe that he exists and that he rewards those who seek him*"(Heb 11:6). Drawing near to God requires, of course, believing that he exists. But it also involves *faith in his goodness*: that "*he rewards those who seek him.*" Faith hinges on the assumption that our efforts to find God are welcome, that our seeking doesn't upset him, and that he has the capability and desire to bless those who pursue him.

Hope in God's goodness, then, is fundamental to faith. God doesn't have to be this way. He could remain aloof. He could find fault with our bumbling attempts to obey him and do right. Of course these thoughts would be horribly demotivating to us. Instead, God is actively good, letting himself be known, guiding and encouraging us in our journey, and at the end, rewarding us.

One Thing to Think About: Am I seeking God?

One Thing to Pray For: A deeper confidence in the true things that I cannot (yet) see

WEEK 49—WEDNESDAY

Reading: Hebrews 11:8-12

As Good As Dead

In exhorting his readers to become a people of faith, the Hebrew writer naturally turns to Abraham. So many of his decisions illustrate the power and helplessness of faith. "*By faith Abraham obeyed when he was called to go out to a place that he was to receive as an inheritance. And he went out, not knowing where he was going*"(Heb 11:8). Instead of a careful decision made over a clear itinerary, Abraham shows an almost blind confidence that God will lead him where he needs to go. "*By faith he went to live in the land of promise, as in a foreign land, living in tents with Isaac and Jacob, heirs with him of the same promise. For he was looking forward to the city that has foundations, whose designer and builder is God*"(Heb 11:10). It must be shocking to hear such grand promises—lands, families, and blessings—while continuing to move from place to place in tents. Yet Abraham has his eyes fixed on the true city of God, believing that God has unimaginable blessings in store for his people.

And then God finds an unprecedented way to begin to fulfill his promises. "*By faith Sarah herself received power to conceive, even when she was past the age, since she considered him faithful who had promised. Therefore from one man, and him as good as dead, were born descendants as many as the stars of heaven and as many as the innumerable grains of sand by the seashore*"(Heb 11:11-12). Sarah is biologically unable to have children. This couple has been infertile for decades and now their window has closed. Abraham is 100 and "*as good as dead,*" winding down his days. Nothing here points toward the rich blessings God will bring. Yet God blesses and blesses and blesses: Sarah receives strength, Abraham becomes a father (several times over) in his old age, and the line grows into a great nation. Using his faith, God moves Abraham from "*as good as dead*" to the pinnacle of his life.

It is one thing to know that God is good and powerful. But if God is good, then he is willing to use his power to bless and help. Nothing is off limits. This does not mean that we can demand things of God—or blame him when his will differs from ours—but it does open us up to fantastic possibilities. Just what could God do?

One Thing to Think About: How have I seen God do seemingly impossible things?

One Thing to Pray For: The true city that God has built

Reading: Hebrews 11:13-16

Not Ashamed to Be Called Their God

The Hebrew writer is showing us what faith looks like by reviewing the lives of Abraham, Sarah, Isaac, and Jacob. "*These all died in faith, not having received the things promised, but having seen them and greeted them from afar, and having acknowledged that they were strangers and exiles on the earth*"(Heb 11:13). Abraham and his family did not see the fulfilment of all God had promised, but they are worthy of admiration because they trusted and obeyed God anyway. They embraced the promises only "*having seen them and greeted them from afar*" and came to terms with the fact that they would live as nomads while waiting on God.

Behind their acceptance is a quiet confidence. "*For people who speak thus make it clear that they are seeking a homeland. If they had been thinking of that land from which they had gone out, they would have had opportunity to return. But as it is, they desire a better country, that is, a heavenly one*"(Heb 11:14-16). It would have been easy for Abraham to go back home when he realized that God wasn't going to immediately give him land or descendants. But instead he stuck around in the land of Canaan, seeking something higher—a "*better country, that is a heavenly one.*" Being in God's favor and remaining in God's will meant more than living comfortably. "*Therefore God is not ashamed to be called their God, for he has prepared for them a city*"(Heb 11:16). These are the kind of people that God seeks and blesses.

I am intrigued by the phrase that "*God is not ashamed to be called their God.*" It implies that sometimes our behavior embarrasses and shames God. Yet when we walk by faith, God gives us a gift: he not only accepts us, but he is proud to have us as his people. Like Job, he brags about us. Rather than seeing this as an unattainable standard only great Bible people can achieve, we should see this as an expression of the great gracious heart of God. When we trust and obey him, he is proud to be connected with us.

One Thing to Think About: How do my actions reflect on God?

One Thing to Pray For: A place in the city of God

WEEK 49—FRIDAY

Reading: Hebrews 11:32-40

Made Perfect Together

As the Hebrew writer moves through the litany of faith-heroes, he realizes that he could go on and on. *"And what more shall I say? For time would fail me to tell of Gideon, Barak, Samson, Jephthah, of David and Samuel and the prophets—who through faith conquered kingdoms, enforced justice, obtained promises, stopped the mouths of lions, quenched the power of fire, escaped the edge of the sword, were made strong out of weakness, became mighty in war, put foreign armies to flight"*(Heb 11:32-34). The Bible student recognizes in each of these names and phrases a powerful story of God's deliverance and his people's confidence in him. God has done amazing things and very often has used faithful people to accomplish them. There are also "*others*" that we don't know—whose stories are not recorded, whose sacrifices are unappreciated, yet whose names God knows. They are mocked and flogged, stoned and sawn in two, homeless and helpless.

Yet this great chorus of faith persisted despite not seeing the realization of their faith. *"And all these, though commended through their faith, did not receive what was promised, since God had provided something better for us, that apart from us they should not be made perfect"*(Heb 11:39-40). He pulls no punches; they "*did not receive what was promised.*" Yet this is not the end of their story because "*God had provided something better for us.*" He wanted to bring his Son into the world to atone for the sins of the world and consummate the faith of all people. Those who have gone before are not perfected without us. Instead all of us will be made perfect together by "*the founder and perfecter of our faith*"(Heb 12:2), Jesus.

Many great men and women have gone before us, yet they are not made perfect "*apart from us.*" We hold a great commonality with them. The battle of faith may look different in each age—different for Noah, for Moses, for Samson than for us—yet all of us look forward to the time when God gives the final expression of his goodness and returns his world to order. We join the great chorus of faith and add our witness in our time—and await the time when we are made perfect together.

One Thing to Think About: What are the struggles of faith in my life and my times?

One Thing to Pray For: The courage to act out of my faith

WEEK 50—MONDAY

Reading: Hebrews 12:1-3

The Grace of Witnesses

The writer has detailed great men and women of faith and now pictures them as seated in a stadium, watching us run a race. "*Therefore, since we are surrounded by so great a cloud of witnesses, let us also lay aside every weight, and sin which clings so closely, and let us run with endurance the race that is set before us*"(Heb 12:1). These great heroes are now watching *us*. But the word "witness" signifies not only an observer, but also someone with testimony to give. As Abraham, Abel, and Rahab watch us, they encourage us to have faith. They know firsthand how hard it is when people oppose us, when we yearn for more certainty, and when we have to make tough decisions. They shout their encouragement. So we lay aside the weights that hinder our race and "*run with endurance*." We keep going as they urge us on.

Many ancient races in the Greek world would host past victors to watch the race in seats of honor. In the same way, we run the race while "*looking to Jesus, the founder and perfecter of our faith, who for the joy that was set before him endured the cross, despising the shame, and is seated at the right hand of the throne of God*"(Heb 12:2). Jesus has run our race—particularly, he has endured pain and shame. Now he is highly exalted at God's right hand. When our focus drifts, we can "*consider him who endured from sinners such hostility against himself, so that you may not grow weary or fainthearted*"(Heb 12:3). Jesus has shown us the path of focusing on the "*joy that was set before him*" to strengthen us.

Doing hard things is difficult; doing hard things *alone* is much more challenging. Yet God does not leave us alone; there is a great cloud of witnesses whose stories he has preserved for our encouragement. He gives us brothers and sisters who run alongside us. And our eyes turn toward Jesus, who has blazed the trial of seeking glory through suffering.

One Thing to Think About: How do other people help me to be stronger?

One Thing to Pray For: Help in laying aside every weight

WEEK 50—TUESDAY

Reading: Hebrews 12:18-29

A Kingdom that Cannot Be Shaken

To help us see how richly we have been blessed, the writer takes us back to God's appearance to Israel on Mount Sinai. That scene was terrifying, full of "*blazing fire and darkness and gloom and a tempest and the sound of a trumpet*"(Heb 12:18-19). The people begged not to hear from God and even Moses shook with fear. Yet we have not come to Sinai, but something greater: "*But you have come to Mount Zion and to the city of the living God, the heavenly Jerusalem, and to innumerable angels in festal gathering, and to the assembly of the firstborn who are enrolled in heaven, and to God, the judge of all, and to the spirits of the righteous made perfect, and to Jesus, the mediator of a new covenant*"(Heb 11:22-24). We belong at the mountain at the center of God's great city. We have assembled with all the great heroes of faith and angels in worship to our Savior and our God.

But Sinai still helps us. "*See that you do not refuse him who is speaking. For if they did not escape when they refused him who warned them on earth, much less will we escape if we reject him who warns from heaven*"(Heb 12:25). Sinai reminds us that Jehovah is not a God to be trifled with. If his presence and wrath terrified then, how much more will we who have received greater blessings deserve fearsome punishment if we ignore or rebel? "*Therefore let us be grateful for receiving a kingdom that cannot be shaken, and thus let us offer to God acceptable worship, with reverence and awe, for our God is a consuming fire*"(Heb 12:28-29). God has promised to judge the world (he calls it "shaking" the world), but he has given us a kingdom that *cannot* be shaken. Our connection to him will persist through judgment—if we do not refuse him.

Almost nothing in our lives is truly permanent. We get used to things tarnishing, spoiling, fading, going out of style, aging, and dying. Everything seems subject to circumstances and corruption. Yet God has *given* us something that will last forever: a part in his reign and a place at his table. The appropriate reaction is to be "*grateful*" and serve him "*with reverence and awe.*"

One Thing to Think About: Is it appropriate to be scared of God?

One Thing to Pray For: Reverence and awe

Reading: Hebrews 13:7-16

Grace Strengthens the Heart

As he closes his letter, the Hebrew writer stresses the need to cling to what they have learned and resist new teachings. "*Remember your leaders, those who spoke to you the word of God. Consider the outcome of their way of life, and imitate their faith. Jesus Christ is the same yesterday and today and forever. Do not let be led away by diverse and strange teachings, for it is good for the heart to be strengthened by grace, not by foods, which have not benefited those devoted to them*"(Heb 13:7-9). Their leaders have taught them God's word; this is where their focus should be. Jesus does not change, so some "*diverse and strange teachings*" that arise do not originate with him. It appears that some are promoting certain foods as "strengthening the heart," endowing meals with spiritual significance. He pushes back, insisting that *grace* strengthens the heart by calling our attention to God's good gifts and the hope they give us.

Part of that grace is a unique connection to God through Jesus: "*We have an altar from which those who serve the tent have no right to eat*"(Heb 13:10). Christians have a blessing that even the priests are denied—the heavenly sacrifice of Jesus crucified. Accepting this gift means that we embrace the rejection Jesus experienced (Heb 13:12-13). We also, like a new order of priests, offer our own sacrifices: "*Through him then let us continually offer up a sacrifice of praise to God, that is, the fruit of lips that acknowledge his name. Do not neglect to do good and to share what you have, for such sacrifices are pleasing to God*"(Heb 12:15-16). Praise, good works, sharing—these are gifts we offer back to God after he has given so much to us.

The good news of God's grace *makes our hearts stronger*. Knowing that we serve a good God who has offered himself for us gives us confidence and hope because our lives and futures are not solely dependent on us. We know that whatever we need to thrive spiritually, he will provide. This gives us peace. Rather than relying solely on some physical activity to strengthen us—eating, exercise, sleep—our time is best spent in contemplation of God's grace.

One Thing to Think About: What activities do I seek to "strengthen my heart"?

One Thing to Pray For: A stronger heart

WEEK 50—THURSDAY

Reading: James 1:2-8

He Gives Generously to All Without Reproach

James writes "*to the twelve tribes in the Dispersion*"(James 1:1), who evidently are undergoing some difficulty. His opening instruction is for them to "*count it all joy, my brothers, when you meet trials of various kinds*"(James 1:2). The reasoning is that hardships produce patience, forcing us to learn the skill of continuing to move forward through difficulty. There is no other way to learn patience than having to wait. Accepting (and even rejoicing in) trials leaves us "*perfect and complete, lacking in nothing*"(James 1:4).

But it is not just patience that we lack. "*If any of you lacks wisdom, let him ask God, who gives generously to all without reproach, and it will be given to him*"(James 1:5). James takes Jesus' well-known teaching ("*Ask, and it will be given to you,*" Matt 7:7) and applies it to wisdom. Sometimes our lack of wisdom is exposed—we realize we don't know what to do, we suffer by doing something stupid, or we encounter situations outside our experience. He urges us to ask God because he "*gives generously to all without reproach*" and will surely give us what we ask. However, he warns that we must "*ask in faith, with no doubting, for the one who doubts is like a wave of the sea that is driven and tossed by the wind*"(James 1:6). We ask confident that he hears and will respond in a way consistent with his gracious nature.

We ask God for the things we need because he "*gives generously to all without reproach.*" God is a giver. He does not "*reproach*" us for asking for the things we need. We don't need to be embarrassed to ask; he is the creator and we are the creatures; he is the Father and we are the children. Certainly we should use discernment to filter out of our prayers requests that violate God's will, but he is not going to reproach us as if we are asking too often or for too much. He is not looking for reasons to deny our requests; *he wants to give.* He gives generously to all without reproach.

One Thing to Think About: What kinds of spiritual qualities am I "lacking"?

One Thing to Pray For: The maturity to accept the good that comes with trials

WEEK 50—FRIDAY

Reading: James 1:12-18

Every Good and Perfect Gift is from Above

What we attribute to God matters. "*Let no one say when he is tempted, 'I am being tempted by God,' for God cannot be tempted with evil, and he himself tempts no one. But each person is tempted when he is lured and enticed by his own desire. Then desire when it has conceived gives birth to sin, and sin when it is fully grown brings forth death*"(James 1:13-15). He warns us that we are mistaken if we believe that God is tempting us to do evil. God's gifts are never intended to push us toward sin because he "*cannot be tempted by evil, and he himself tempts no one.*" There is also a dangerous refusal to take accountability in this attitude; we blame God when we give in to our own desires.

God's gifts are of a different type. "*Do not be deceived, my beloved brothers. Every good gift and every perfect gift is from above, coming down from the Father of lights with whom there is no variation or shadow due to change*"(James 1:16-17). There is a risk that we will be "*deceived,*" misunderstanding God's sovereignty as his approval of evil. God gives better gifts. "*Every good gift and every perfect gift is from above.*" The things that are true, pure, and kind come from above. When we receive something good, we know that God is behind it (even if we can't document how he gives it).

With regularity, we experience good things in our lives. We know the joy of healthy relationships, the satisfaction of a good day's work, and the simple pleasures of food, laughter, and peace. Where does such richness come from? "*Every good and perfect gift is from above.*" For all the good and perfect things we receive, we give thanks.

One Thing to Think About: Who do I tend to blame when I do wrong?

One Thing to Pray For: Eyes to see all the good and perfect gifts in my life

WEEK 51—MONDAY

Reading: James 4:1-4

You Don't Have Because You Don't Ask

James starts this section with an intriguing question: "*What causes quarrels and what causes fights among you?*"(James 4:1). Conflict has always been part of human existence and we cannot escape it. But where does it originate? "*Is it not this, that your passions are at war within you? You desire and do not have, so you murder. You covet and cannot obtain, so you fight and quarrel*"(James 4:1-2). Our fighting with others stems from our passions, which boil over into our relationships. We hurt others to try to get what we want, yet this doesn't usually work. We desire and still we *do not have*, we covet and still we *cannot obtain* what we want so desperately. What's missing from this mentality is that *it assumes we are all on our own and must get what we want for ourselves.*

James opens our minds to other possibilities: "*You do not have, because you do not ask*"(James 4:2). God wants us to reach out to *him* for the things we need. The God who "*gives generously to all without reproach*"(James 1:5) and is giver of "*every good gift and every perfect gift*"(James 1:17) stands ready to bless us with the things we want, but he wants us to ask him. Yet there is more: "*You ask and do not receive, because you ask wrongly, to spend it on your passions*"(James 4:3). Even when we do ask, if we are merely using God to satisfy sinful or selfish pleasures, he will not bless us. Such a heart makes us friends of the world and enemies of God (James 4:4); why would God empower his enemies?

This text identifies three interrelated problems: our conflict with others, our failure to pray, and how selfish desires corrupt our prayers. God wants us to rely on him to give us good things rather than grasping them for ourselves—or hurting others to get them. While we need to ensure that our requests are not merely for our own selfish pleasures, he still wants us to pray for what we need. When we are convinced that our desires are good, yet we don't have what we're seeking, we should remember James' words: "*You do not have, because you do not ask.*"

One Thing to Think About: Am I ever reluctant to pray? Why might that be?

One Thing to Pray For: God's help to treat others well—instead of just trying to get things out of them

WEEK 51—TUESDAY

Reading: James 5:13-20

Great Power in Prayer

James challenges us to seek spiritual outlets for our physical and emotional states. "*Is anyone among you suffering? Let him pray. Is anyone cheerful? Let him sing praise. Is anyone among you sick? Let him call for the elders of the church, and let them pray over him, anointing him with oil in the name of the Lord*"(James 5:13-14). We take our emotions and concerns to God and his people. When we are suffering, James urges *us* to pray; when we are sick, he tells us to *seek out the elders to pray*. Even though he mentions "*anointing him with oil in the name of the Lord*"—probably a reference to oil as a medical treatment or general hygiene—the power of the act is in prayer. Medicine may be a way God chooses to heal, but James reminds us that it is God who has the power. We connect to God through prayer.

He lists the benefits of this prayer. "*And the prayer of faith will save the one who is sick, and the Lord will raise him up. And if he has committed sins, he will be forgiven. Therefore, confess your sins to one another and pray for one another, that you may be healed. The prayer of a righteous person has great power as it is working*"(James 5:15-16). Faithful prayer saves sick people. Faithful prayer heals sinful people. We ask others for prayers because "*the prayer of a righteous person has great power as it is working*." Prayer is not powerful because it is a secret of the universe or because the people who offer it have power. The great power in prayer comes from the God who hears it. As if to stress this, James points us to Elijah, who has "*a nature like ours*," yet was able to prayer earnestly and change weather patterns for years (James 5:17-18). Faithful prayer holds great power.

Prayer is a gift from God. He doesn't have to hear us or answer us, yet he does. He notices our wounds—physical and spiritual—and is willing to heal. Prayer is an emphatic reminder of our limitations. We know that there is so little that we can accomplish on our own, but we also know that God has no limitations. Faithful prayer holds great power.

One Thing to Think About: Do I ask others to pray for me?

One Thing to Pray For: Confidence in God's power

WEEK 51—WEDNESDAY

Reading: 1 Peter 1:3-9

The Grace of Guarding

Peter opens his letter with this celebration of the great grace God has given. "*Blessed be the God and Father of our Lord Jesus Christ! According to his great mercy, he has caused us to be born again to a living hope through the resurrection of Jesus Christ from the dead, to an inheritance that is imperishable, undefiled, and unfading, kept in heaven for you, who by God's power are being guarded through faith for a salvation ready to be revealed in the last time*"(1 Pet 1:3-5). He has given us a new birth. He has given us an inheritance—glorification with Jesus—that is "*imperishable, undefiled, and unfading, kept in heaven for you.*" Nothing threatens, tarnishes, or ages this great promise, since it is reserved far away from this earth. In the meantime, we "*by God's power are being guarded through faith for a salvation ready to be revealed in the last time.*" God protects us by his power, preserving us until the time that our inheritance is realized and his plan completed.

Yet it is clear that this "guarding" does not mean that we are kept from all difficulty. "*In this you rejoice, though now for a little while, if necessary, you have been grieved by various trials, so that the tested genuineness of your faith—more precious than gold that perishes though it is tested by fire—may be found to result in praise and glory and honor at the revelation of Jesus Christ*"(1 Pet 1:6-7). His audience is experiencing "*trials*" which are testing the genuineness of their faith. Yet God continues to guard them, even through hardship, assuring them that such trials are only "*for a little while*" and will ultimately only purify their faith so that it glorifies him even more.

Jesus prays for God to keep or guard his disciples (John 17:11). "*I do not ask that you take them out of the world, but that you keep them from the evil one*"(John 17:15). In this way, even today, God does not save his people by removing them from the world, but by guarding them from the evil one. He preserves us through trials, assuring us that we still have an inheritance with him despite people's attacks. This does not mean that God will save us if we give up on him, but that when we place our faith in him, he gives even more gifts to give us confidence in him.

One Thing to Think About: What might this guarding look like?

One Thing to Pray For: My response to trials to bring praise, glory, and honor to my Savior

WEEK 51—THURSDAY

Reading: 1 Peter 1:10-12

More than Prophets and Angels Know

What God accomplished in Jesus had been a mystery for many centuries prior. "*Concerning this salvation, the prophets who prophesied about the grace that was to be yours searched and inquired carefully, inquiring what person or time the Spirit of Christ in them was indicating when he predicted the sufferings of Christ and the subsequent glories*"(1 Pet 1:10-11). The prophets, as they uttered these strange words, were intensely curious about their meaning. Who is the one who would suffer and then be glorified? When would this happen? They "*searched and inquired carefully*," wondering whether they would ever see the fulfilment of their own words.

God graciously answered them: "*It was revealed to them that they were serving not themselves but you, in the things that have now been announced to you through those who preached the good news to you by the Holy Spirit sent from heaven, things into which angels long to look*"(1 Pet 1:12). While the prophets did not have all their questions answered, they were told the most important part. Their words were not for their own time, but for a people to come at a later time—the era of the New Testament. Peter tells the Christians that the prophets "*were serving not themselves but you.*" He also adds that God's brilliant riches-to-rags-to-riches plan for his messiah and the conversion of the world are "*things into which angels long to look.*" Christians can know the full gospel—which is more than prophets and angels know.

Since we live 2000 years downwind of the life of Jesus, it is easy for us to lose the tremendous blessing of understanding God's will. The prophets were great men and women of God, yet they did not know what we know. The angels were curious, yet they did not know what we know. More, the subject of all their prophecy is "*the grace that was to be yours.*" God has blessed us in the extreme.

One Thing to Think About: Why is the idea of a suffering messiah so hard to grasp?

One Thing to Pray For: A hunger to know what God has revealed

WEEK 51—FRIDAY

Reading: 1 Peter 2:1-10

Called to Be a New Israel

Peter urges these Christians to "*long for the pure spiritual milk, that by it you may grow up into salvation—if indeed you have tasted that the Lord is good*"(1 Pet 2:2-3). Having experienced in some measure the *goodness* of Jesus, we are hooked. We want to know more, to grow deeper, to be stronger, and to fulfill his vision for us—because *he is good*. But that growth project is not merely personal. "*As you come to him, a living stone rejected by men but in the sight of God chosen and precious, you yourselves like living stones are being built up as a spiritual house, to be a holy priesthood, to offer spiritual sacrifices acceptable to God through Jesus Christ*"(1 Pet 2:4-5). We also grow *together* with other disciples as God builds us as a "*spiritual house*." The picture is of a new kind of temple in which God can live and sacrifices be offered.

So Peter refers to Christians in terms that were originally applied to Israel. "*But you are a chosen race, a royal priesthood, a holy nation, a people for his own possession, that you may proclaim the excellencies of him who called you out of darkness into his marvelous light. Once you were not a people, but now you are God's people; once you had not received mercy, but now you have received mercy*"(1 Pet 2:9-10). After saving Israel from Egypt, God brought them to Sinai and proclaimed them his own special people, a kingdom of priests, and a holy nation (Ex 19:5-6). Now those who put faith in Jesus are a new Israel—holy, priestly, and uniquely God's. Rather than identifying by our nationality, race, or family, God wants us to be identified by our connection to him.

God has given us an entirely new, unearned status. He has been good to us, which inspires our confidence to continue to seek to grow in his will. He has made us into his temple. He has created a new people and given us a place to belong. Now we "*offer spiritual sacrifices*"—our bodies, our money, our time, and our hearts.

One Thing to Think About: Have I tasted that the Lord is good? How?

One Thing to Pray For: Growth

WEEK 52—MONDAY

Reading: 1 Peter 4:7-11

Good Stewards of Varied Grace

Peter writes during a time when some kind of "*fiery trial*" is imminent (1 Pet 4:12) and he wants the Christians in his audience to band together. "*The end of all things is at hand; therefore be self-controlled and sober-minded for the sake of your prayers. Above all, keep loving one another earnestly, since love covers a multitude of sins. Show hospitality to one another without grumbling*"(1 Pet 4:7-9). Serious times call for serious people; Peter urges self-control and sobriety. It is not a time for Christians to turn on each other or find fault; Peter urges earnest love. It is not a time to turn inward or stop providing for each other; Peter urges hospitality. External opponents help us to remember that we have a common enemy and we can stop hurting each other with friendly fire.

Peter wants us to shift our perspective: "*As each has received a gift, use it to serve one another, as good stewards of God's varied grace: whoever speaks, as the one who speaks oracles of God; whoever serves, as the one who serves by the strength that God supplies—in order that in everything God may be glorified through Jesus Christ*"(1 Pet 4:10-11). The human tendency is to hoard our gifts and blessings for ourselves. Instead, Peter reminds us that we are recipients of God's gifts, "*stewards of God's varied grace.*" A steward is a temporary caretaker who will give account to the true owner of how he used his goods. *What have we done for others with all the gifts and talents God has given us?* This is the measure of our stewardship.

God's grace varies person by person. He gives each one of us different personalities, experiences, and talents. Yet he exhorts us to use them for others, not just ourselves. If I get along well with others, how can I use that to bless people? If I work diligently, how can I serve others with my gift? Someday we will give account for what we have done with God's gifts. What will he say?

One Thing to Think About: How do I tend to use my gifts?

One Thing to Pray For: A heart for unity, service, and love

WEEK 52—TUESDAY

Reading: 2 Peter 1:3-11

Partakers of the Divine Nature

Grace soaks through these verses. "*His divine power has granted to us all things that pertain to life and godliness, through the knowledge of him who called us to his own glory and excellence*"(2 Pet 1:3). He has given us everything necessary for life and godliness. He has given us great promises (2 Pet 1:4), one of which is that an entrance into the kingdom will be "*richly provided for you*"(2 Pet 1:11). Especially notable is that through the promises and gifts of God, "*you may become partakers of the divine nature, having escaped from the corruption that is in the world because of sinful desire*"(2 Pet 1:4). "Partakers of the divine nature" means that we share something in common with God. This does not mean that Christians become God, but that we share in his immortality and pure holiness. He has elevated us to share rich gifts that are not ours by right, but grace.

This should motivate us. "*For this very reason, make every effort to supplement your faith with virtue…*"(2 Pet 1:5). Peter lists traits that we can add to our faith with diligence because we know the wonderful gift that awaits us. Our growth in self-control, virtue, and love shows that we are heading in God's direction. "*For if these qualities are yours and are increasing, they keep you from being ineffective or unfruitful in the knowledge of our Lord Jesus Christ*"(2 Pet 1:8). He adds that "*if you practice these qualities you will never fall*"(2 Pet 1:10). Our effort in adding to our faith never earns our salvation for us, but it helps us to mature so that we are strong enough to withstand the assaults of Satan and bear fruit for God. If he gives us such gifts—and wants so desperately for us to grow—how can we not?

While God has ever reason to be aloof (or even angry), he invites us into his presence. He cleanses us and assures us and gives us a chance to share in his divine nature. His call is for us to grow in our faith and "*confirm your calling and election.*"

One Thing to Think About: What do I need to add to my faith?

One Thing to Pray For: Contentment with the fact that God has given me "*all things that pertain to life and godliness*"

WEEK 52—WEDNESDAY

Reading: 1 John 3:1-3

We Shall See Him as He Is

It's a big deal to add someone to our family. That's why it's so notable that—knowing what he knows about us—God has done it for us. "*See what kind of love the Father has given to us, that we should be called children of God; and so we are. The reason why the world does not know us is that it did not know him*"(1 John 3:1). The Father has called us his children—and that means that we *are* his children. This helps me understand myself (I am a child of *God*!) and the rejection I experience when I live for God (the world rejected Jesus, my brother).

But this is not simply a change in status; it portends greater things. "*Beloved, we are God's children now, and what we will be has not yet appeared; but we know that when he appears, we shall be like him, because we shall see him as he is*"(1 John 3:2). Despite his inspiration, there is still mystery for John about the way God's plan finishes ("*what we will be has not yet appeared*"). Yet there are a couple of things he is certain of: "*when he appears, we shall be like him*" and "*we shall see him as he is.*" At present we do not see Jesus—perhaps we *cannot* see him—yet when he returns, we shall see him truly and share in his immortality. This is a rich promise. The one whom we have long served by faith, not sight, *we will see.* We will look in his face and hear his voice and know him fully. We have an appointment with the King of kings.

John makes the application for us: "*And everyone who thus hopes in him purifies himself as he is pure*"(1 John 3:3). Given the lofty nature of this opportunity, I must prepare! I want nothing to jeopardize that meeting! So I live in a focused and disciplined way, purifying myself for that day when I see him as he is.

One Thing to Think About: What will it be like to see Jesus?

One Thing to Pray For: Purity in preparation for that day

WEEK 52—THURSDAY

Reading: Revelation 2:7, 10-11, 17, 26-28; 3:5, 12, 20-21

I Will Give

In these letters to the seven churches of Asia, Jesus promises gifts to his people if they persevere through the challenges before them. In each case the gift itself—white stones and hidden manna—is highly figurative and symbolic of the favor of God. The Ephesians must overcome the challenge of a faith that has grown stale as they have "*abandoned the love you had at first*"(Rev 2:4). Those in Smyrna are soon to face prison, suffering, and tribulation, yet if they are faithful to the point of death, they will receive the crown of true life. In Pergamum, there are obstacles within the church (false teaching) and without (Satan's throne is there and people are being martyred for their faith). If they overcome, Jesus promises to give hidden manna, a white stone, and a new name (Rev 2:17).

Thyatira is beset by a false prophetess. Sardis has a great reputation, but is spiritually dead. Philadelphia has remained faithful despite a "*synagogue of Satan*" in their midst (Rev 3:9). Laodicea has grown lukewarm because of their wealth (Rev 3:17). All of them are urged to "conquer" or "overcome" the problems of their unique situation. Jesus will reward them if they do. It is tempting to read these texts—especially with the translation "*the one who conquers*"—as if these people are earning their right standing with God. But Jesus insistently says "*I will give*." He holds out promises of grace, which means that we never deserve them.

Like these churches, each of us has our own unique set of challenges to "*overcome*." It may be church conflict or family turmoil. It may be personal weakness or the consequences of past poor choices. It may be outside opposition or physical suffering. It may be learning to live with wealth and prosperity without growing spiritually dull. One thing is certain: for those who overcome, Jesus offers rich gifts.

One Thing to Think About: What do I need to "overcome"?

One Thing to Pray For: Faithfulness to Jesus

WEEK 52—FRIDAY

Reading: Revelation 7:9-17

In the Presence of God

John sees a vision of a great crowd standing before God on his throne and the Lamb. The people are too many to number and come from all nations. They cry out in worship: "*Salvation belongs to our God who sits on the throne, and to the Lamb!*"(Rev 7:10). In chorus around them are the angels and the elders and four living creatures—a mighty throng praising God.

Who are all these people? "*These are the ones coming out of the great tribulation. They have washed their robe and made them white in the blood of the Lamb. Therefore they are before the throne of God, and serve him day and night in his temple; and he who sits on the throne will shelter them with his presence*"(Rev 7:14-15). If we were on earth, we would only see them suffering and dying for the cause of Christ. Yet John can see that they are in a much better place: before God's throne, washed clean, sheltered in the presence of God. Their trials have ended. "*They shall hunger no more, neither thirst anymore; the sun shall not strike them, nor any scorching heat. For the Lamb in the midst of the throne will be their shepherd, and he will guide them to springs of living water, and God will wipe away every tear from their eyes*"(Rev 7:16-17). It gets better: they no longer experience need or danger. The Lamb himself is their shepherd, providing for them. All the tears they have cried over the hardships of earthly life are wiped away by God himself.

While some of this passage is cloaked in figurative language, the sense is clear: *the presence of God is where we want to be!* God wants to comfort our grieving, damaged hearts. He wants to protect us. He wants to wipe away our tears.

One Thing to Think About: What is most appealing to me about being the presence of God?

One Thing to Pray For: A stronger hope in the time when I can be with God

WEEK 53—MONDAY

Reading: Revelation 21:1-8

He Will Dwell with Them

After watching the final defeat of Satan and the destruction of Death and Hades, John sees something even more spectacular. "*Then I saw a new heaven and a new earth, for the first heaven and the first earth had passed away, and the sea was no more. And I saw the holy city, new Jerusalem, coming down out of heaven from God, prepared as a bride adorned for her husband*"(Rev 21:1-2). John is later able to inspect this amazing city and is awed by its beauty and perfection. Yet most significant about the new Jerusalem is not its appearance, but its most important inhabitant. God will be there.

In case John has missed this, someone lets him know. "*And I heard a loud voice from the throne saying, 'Behold, the dwelling place of God is with man. He will dwell with them, and they will be his people, and God himself will be with them as their God. He will wipe away every tear from their eyes, and death shall be no more, neither shall there be mourning, nor crying, nor pain anymore, for the former things have passed away*"(Rev 21:3-4). God will live with people. Throughout the Old Testament, God sought to live in the midst of Israel—in the tabernacle and in the temple—yet often the people were so rebellious that God could not. Now he will dwell with them. This existence will be far superior to any we have ever known because sadness and pain and death are over. "*The one who conquers will have this heritage, and I will be his God and he will be my son*"(Rev 21:7). Now, instead of just being his people (as Israel was promised), we will be his *children.*

God has given us life. He has had patience with us despite our stubbornness and rebellion. He has sent his Son to remove our sins. He has indwelled us with his Spirit. He has revealed his heart. He has worked in us to help us grow and fulfill his purpose for us. Now he promises new grace—eternal life in his presence, free from all pain and sorrow. It is grace upon grace.

One Thing to Think About: What will life be like when there is no death?

One Thing to Pray For: Gratitude for all God's grace to me

A Note from the Author

Thanks for reading *Exploring God's Grace*! I would greatly appreciate your feedback on the book. Would you take a moment to review the book on Amazon? Amazon reviews ensure that more people find *Exploring God's Grace* and also help me know what readers find helpful or problematic about the book. You can review by searching for the book on Amazon's site and scrolling down to the "Write a review" button.

For more information about other titles, visit my website at jacobhudgins.com.

Thanks!

Jacob Hudgins

Made in the USA
Coppell, TX
28 May 2026

78361907R00156